Winner of the Jules and Frances Landry Award for 1993

The Fable
of the
Southern Writer

Lewis P. Simpson

The Fable
of the
Southern Writer

Louisiana State University Press
Baton Rouge and London

03 02 01 00 99 98 97 96 95 94   5 4 3 2 1

Designer: Glynnis Phoebe
Typeface: Bembo
Typesetter: G & S Typesetters, Inc.
Printer and binder: Thomson-Shore, Inc.

Library of Congress Cataloging-in-Publication Data

Simpson, Lewis P.
    The fable of the Southern writer / Lewis P. Simpson.
        p.   cm.
    Includes index.
    ISBN 0-8071-1871-0 (alk. paper)
        1. American literature—Southern States—History and criticism.
    2. American literature—20th century—History and criticism.
    3. Authorship—Social aspects—Southern States.   4. Southern States—
Intellectual life.   5. Southern States in literature.   I. Title.
    PS261.S468   1993
    810.9′975—dc20   93-8699
                                                      CIP

For Mimi

For now hath time made me his numbering clock;
My thoughts are minutes; and with sighs they jar.
—King Richard II in Shakespeare,
Richard II, Act V, Scene 5

Faith is not a form of knowledge, for all knowledge is
either knowledge of the eternal, excluding the temporal
and the historical as indifferent, or it is pure historical
knowledge. No knowledge can have for its object the
absurdity that the eternal is the historical.
—Kierkegaard

Contents

Preface

For a number of years, something like forty to be more precise, I have attempted to be a historian of American letters. It may be that in moments when the going has been good, I have succeeded in being, more broadly, what it is nowadays so fashionable to be, a cultural historian. If I have learned anything at all in my prolonged inquiry into the significance of our country's literature, I think it may be summed up only in a nonspecific principle governing historical inquiry in general: Although the search for meaning illuminates the historical context of the seeking, it can in no wise transcend it, being in itself an inextricable part of whatever meaning may be disclosed.

This pretentious Nietzschean platitude occurs to me as I find myself adding a volume to several others that in one way or another explore aspects of the literary vocation in America. Two of these, *The Man of Letters in New England and the South* and *The Brazen Face of History,* are of rather broad scope. The present book brings together a series of essays written during the past decade and a half. Most of them focus on writers of the twentieth-century American South who fall within the aura of the period now usually referred to as the Southern Renascence. There are two exceptions. One is a brief speculation by way of prologue about the significance of John Randolph, the eccentric and unhappy Virginian of the early decades of the Republic whose shadowy presence still haunts our history. The other exception, offered by way of an overlong epilogue, is a personal memoir. The reason for its inclusion in the book is, I trust, more than vanity. At least it has, I think, a relevance to what I dis-

covered to be the centering theme of the essays herein brought together when I made a retrospective reading of them, namely, the
attention they pay to the autobiographical element in southern fiction and criticism. The center is obviously loosely defined. Even the
pieces in which the search for the autobiographical motive is overtly
visible were not purposefully written to set forth the characteristics
of autobiography as a southern form. The primary concern in all the
studies is with the larger question I have struggled with in print a
good many times. I did not ask it first. It is a question asked, either
explicitly or by implication, by all the writers of the South from
Thomas Jefferson to Walker Percy: What does it mean to be a writer
of the American South in the modern world? No more than in prior
studies is this a problem that I expect to resolve or, for that matter,
seek to resolve. Even the seeking would demand that I answer the
larger question that is the context of the search: What is the South?

As uncertain as ever about the answer to this question, we may
be becoming weary of asking it, even in its most daring formulation:
Is the South definable as an empirical reality, or a poetic entity? Or,
more bluntly, Is the South a historical or a fictional entity?

This is the complex question that lies at the center of William
Faulkner's imaginative involvement in the history of his own "little
postage stamp" of a world—the question that, indirectly, but all the
more compellingly for that, the Canadian Shreve McCannon put to
the desperate Quentin Compson that winter night in the dormitory
room at Harvard when he and the nineteen-year-old Mississippi
youth struggled to fathom the meaning of the improbable lives of
Thomas Sutpen and his children, and of Quentin's own improbable
life: "Jesus, the South is fine, isn't it? It's better than the theatre, isn't
it? It's better than Ben Hur, isn't it?" Quentin didn't answer. In his
way he knew the answer, or part of it, knew that the South of Sutpen, Bon, and Judith, of Caddy and Jason and himself, was at once a
grotesque and tortured fiction and a "true story." But he could not
formulate a reply to Shreve. It was too soon. In the inescapable doom
of his involvement in the history of the House of Sutpen and the
House of Compson, he was living the answer, and he had not quite
lived all of it yet. In some dark, enigmatic way he finally signified his
response when he drowned himself in the Charles River at Cambridge, Massachusetts, on the night of June 2, 1910. In bringing

Quentin—the character with whom Faulkner identified himself most closely, who may indeed be called his persona—to this climactic moment in his first great novel, *The Sound and the Fury* (1929), Faulkner transformed the history of the Sutpens and the Compsons into a fable of the South. Expanding this fable in *Absalom, Absalom!*, he implied the extent to which all his greater work may be read as the complex autobiographical fable of the modern literary artist in the South.

Later, although he convinced himself that it was his greatest work, Faulkner overreached himself when he attempted to make his art all-encompassing and project the history of the whole of modern Western civilization in terms of the Christian fable. His tortured absorption for a period of several years in the novel he called *A Fable* indicated not the energy of artistic innovation but a falling off from the autobiographical motive that had gripped Faulkner from *The Sound and the Fury* through *Go Down, Moses*. But the autobiographical definition of the South was not a singular impulse among southern writers. It was compellingly present, as I suggest, in Elizabeth Madox Roberts, Allen Tate, and Robert Penn Warren, exerted itself perversely but at times powerfully in the massive diary of Arthur Crew Inman, and, in spite of his effort to remove himself from the context of the Southern Renascence, operated strongly in the work of Walker Percy. Pursuing the autobiographical motive in Faulkner and the other writers named, I emphasize in the following studies the relation to be discovered in the southern literary imagination between history and self-biography. All of the essays—I hope not to the point of tiresome reiteration—offer variations on this emphasis.

A depletion of the source of motivation that sustained their forerunners in the earlier part of the century has become obvious in the later twentieth-century southern novelists and poets. The intricate drama of the southern striving for identity in Faulkner, Warren, Tate, and others has distinctly fallen off. This is not, it seems to me, because writers born in the recent South do not constitute another definable generation of skillful literary craftsmen who use the southern setting effectively. My own experience as an editor of the *Southern Review* testifies that they do. What is missing, one senses, is the literary power generated by the encounter between the imagination of a Faulkner, a Tate, a Warren, a Lytle, an Elizabeth Madox Roberts, or a Caroline Gordon and the historical society of the

South. The tension produced by this encounter—the quarrel within the self of the artist and between the artist and society that Yeats saw as the essential condition of great poetry and drama—had charged the notable writers of New England in the nineteenth century, but it had been largely absent in writers living in the semiclosed society of the nineteenth-century South. When the literary imagination of the South at last became openly responsive to the tensions of the southern historical situation, it was capable of creating the famous scene in *Absalom, Absalom!* in which Quentin Compson protests to Shreve that he does not hate the South; or, another classic scene in Faulkner, the moment near the end of *Intruder in the Dust* when Chick Mallison recalls his uncle Gavin Stevens' eloquent homily on the South, in which he says that every southern boy has at his memory's instant command the moment at Gettysburg before Pickett began his charge. The literary imagination cannot remedy the fact that the southern writer born in the mid-twentieth-century South had to find out about Gettysburg from a textbook rather than from the memory of an uncle, though of course he might have found out from an uncle who remembered what an uncle had told him. By the 1960s personal links with the memory of the Civil War had become insubstantial. So had personal links with the memory of slavery and its overthrow by the Civil War.

One of the delusions scholars and critics seem to subscribe to in our present historical moment is the notion that we understand the motives of literary artists because critics are themselves literary artists. But historians and critics simply talk about poets and novelists, and if there has been a diminution of literary power in the South, critics cannot do anything but talk about it.

Yet literary historians and critics do participate in the southern self-interpretation. At this point perhaps their recognition of a continuing connection between the autobiographical impulse and the self-interpretation of the South may be of particular value. Almost a century and a half after Appomattox—in a world that may seem to resemble antebellum America not at all, although the one is as much a part of modern history as the other—the definition of the South continues to be a need vital not only to southerners but to all Americans. The Civil War is still fully with us, the crisis it represented far from being resolved. When asked during the Chinese Revolution what he thought the influence of the French Revolution had been on history, Mao Tse-tung, adhering to the "long view" that used to be a part of Marxism before it became nationalized, replied that it was too soon to say. Although he did not derive the idea from Marx, Faulkner took the long view also. Pondering the complexities of the history of the rise and fall of the modern world the southern slave-holders had made in its relation to national and world history, to be sure, Faulkner and the other serious southern writers of his generation were joined in a vision that discovered the source of the Civil War as an unending, tragic quarrel within individual Americans and within American society as a whole. As they described this quarrel it has no resolution save in its own essential source, the "heart's driving complexity," which is to say it has no resolution. But this impossibility is the hope in the vision. The poetry of it suggests that the Civil War was fought in an effort to resolve the quarrel that in the most fundamental sense had prompted the American Revolution but had been left unresolved in the institution of the new nation: a quarrel about nothing less than the nature of man, in which one of the most basic issues is the question, Does the nature of man demand that men have property in other men?

In a way *The Fable of the Southern Writer* is the most personal book I have written. It is about my own small participation in the southern self-interpretation. I am very conscious of the fact that I am dealing with the white writers of the South. But at the same time I am conscious of the possibility that even at this late date in the history of the southern self-interpretation there may be a further fulfillment of the literary promise of the South. This will occur when the African-American quest for identity turns from the self-conscious rejection of the South toward participation in the southern self-interpretation.

The possibility of not only the development of a southern African-American authorship but the attendant development of a coherent southern African-American critical movement suggests more than I can discuss here. Let me draw on the perceptive analysis of Fred Hobson in his recent *The Southern Writer and the Postmodern World* (1991), in which, referring to C. Vann Woodward's comment that the black southerner is the "quintessential Southerner," he makes the point that black southerners may also be regarded as the "quintessential agrarians." Because they have worked it for four centuries, they have a closer acquaintance with the soil, a deeper intimacy with it "than most of the upper-case Agrarians ever had." The black southerner who is a writer, Hobson adds, is fully aware—may have an enhanced awareness—of "the well-known qualities of the southern experience": the emphasis on "family and community," on "essentially concrete vision," on a "feeling for place," on the sense of a "*legacy* of poverty, [and] defeat," on the sense of an "*immersion* in history and what it has produced." Is there a possibility that the southern African American is "the truest contemporary heir to the southern literary tradition"? That, in fact, the black southern writer may "be seen as the quintessential southern writer"? Will the discovery of a *southern* African-American identity lead to another Southern Renascence, a renascence that will in the next century do for black writing in America what the Harlem Renaissance did in the present century?

In posing such questions I am assuming with Hobson that the deepest truth about southern literary history may finally be discovered in the "intertextuality" of white and black writing.

The Fable
of the
Southern Writer

Prologue
John Randolph and the Inwardness of History

In his study of John Randolph, Robert Dawidoff suggests that the biography of Randolph by Henry Adams (American Statesmen Series, 1882) displays the author's "unacknowledged yet unmistakable if muted and as yet incomplete aura of identification" with his subject. This became complete, Dawidoff says, in *The Education of Henry Adams* (privately printed, 1907), in which Adams implies that he has himself suffered the fate he had ascribed to the eccentric Virginian: the discrepancy between his education and his actual experience of life being too great, he had become a historical derelict.[1]

Although his approach to Randolph through Adams is fundamentally revealing, affording us not only the most stimulating study we have yet had of Randolph but a provocative look at Adams as well, Dawidoff's argument is not altogether convincing, particularly in its insistence that Randolph's career provided the model for Adams' conception of his own career as one shaped by "miseducation, helplessness, and eccentricity." For one thing, it is doubtful if Adams' description of himself as "miseducated" and "helpless" may be taken literally. R. P. Blackmur, Ernest Samuels, J. C. Levenson, James M. Cox, and other students of Adams have demonstrated that his celebrated report in the *Education* on the failure of his education masks a highly self-conscious, deeply ironic autobiographical drama, the subtleties and complexities of which are carefully controlled by an author possessed not only of formidable intellectual powers but of the unusual psychic resources of a gifted literary artist. Able to

1. Robert Dawidoff, *The Education of John Randolph* (New York, 1979), 13, 229–300.

distance himself from himself, Adams made a book out of his observation of the complex drama of his own mind that, even in the current misguided game of canon making and canon bashing among American literary scholars, is consistently recognized as one of the most distinguished ever written by an American.

But a more fundamental reason why the thesis that Adams identified himself with a miseducated Randolph seems doubtful is simply that Adams thought of Randolph as insufficiently educated rather than as miseducated. In a "small, struggling, exhausted country, without a government, a nationality, a capital, or even a town of thirty thousand inhabitants," he says, Randolph did not have "the means of supplying such an education as a young man wanted, however earnestly he tried for it." At the same time, Adams recognized that a youth of Randolph's preciosity and sensibility might well in a way have been overeducated in the tensions and anxieties of an age of unprecedented historical change.

The boy was born at the moment . . . the country had plunged into a war which in a single moment cut that connection with England on which the old Virginian society depended for its tastes, fashions, theories, and above all for its aristocratic status in politics and law. The Declaration of Independence proclaimed that America was no longer to be English, but American; that is to say, democratic and popular in all its parts—a fact equivalent to a sentence of death upon old Virginian society, and foreboding dissolution to the Randolphs and their pride, until they should learn to master the new conditions of American life. For passing through such a maelstrom a century was not too short an allowance of time, yet this small Randolph boy, not a strong creature at best, was born just as the downward plunge began, and every moment made the outlook drearier and more awful.[2]

A prime value of Dawidoff's elucidation of Randolph's career is that it exhibits a feel for his life transcending Dawidoff's specific analytical penetration of it. Thus he suggests that the true affinity

2. Henry Adams, *John Randolph* (New York, 1882), 4.

Adams felt with Randolph lay in Randolph's dramatization of the modern self's response to history. "Having formed his views in his young manhood, according to the teachings of a world" that he "increasingly understood to be disappearing," Randolph, Dawidoff observes, "developed a habit of declension, of seeing in every change a disintegration." Acutely alert to the nuances of Randolph's personality, to shades of feeling experienced by a fragile self at once appalled and fascinated by its historical role, Dawidoff suggests that Randolph's fundamental significance is his representation, during the initial stage of the democratic experiment in America, of the novel experience of the personal entering the political and the political entering the personal. In effect, regarding himself as inflexibly formed in the image of "the last of the old school, a militant Cassandra of a noble and embattled tradition," Randolph became a fateful personification of the union of the personal and the political. More cogently than Jefferson and Madison and the liberal, cosmopolitan founders of the Republic, he exemplified the inner motivation of his age.[3]

A quarter of a century before he described it in the *Education* Adams had suggested that young Randolph's situation mirrored the modern self's discovery of history as an all-enveloping force. Contemplating the relation between Randolph's temperament and his historical situation, he had drawn a graphic analogy between the image of the Virginian in his time and place and the fabled knight of Cervantes in his time and place: "As the character of Don Quixote was to Cervantes clearly a natural and possible product of Spanish character, so to the people of Virginia John Randolph was a representative man, with qualities exaggerated but genuine; and even exaggerations struck a cord of popular sympathy; his very weaknesses were caricatures of Virginia genius; and thus the boy grew up to manhood, as pure a Virginia Quixote as ever an American Cervantes could have conceived." Randolph's mind, Adams said,

> was always controlled by his feelings; its antipathies were stronger than its sympathy; it was restless and weary, prone to contradiction and attached to paradox. In such a character there is nothing very new, for at least nine out of ten, whose

3. Dawidoff, *Randolph,* 278, 30.

intelligence is above the average, have felt the same instincts: the impulse to contradict is as familiar as dyspepsia or nervous excitability; the passion for referring every comparison to one's self is a primitive quality of mind by no means confined to women and children; but what was to be expected when such a temperament, exaggerated and unrestrained, full of self-contradictions and stimulated by acute reasoning powers, remarkable audacity and quickness, violent and vindictive temper, and a morbid constitution, was planted in a Virginian, a slave-owner, a Randolph, just when the world was bursting into fire and flame?[4]

Adams somewhat neglects the connection between the cultivation of the intelligence and temperament and Randolph's self-education in reading, especially during his early years. Something of its variety and extent is indicated in the letters he wrote to his nephew, Dr. Theodore B. Dudley, in which the young relative is specifically advised to read what amounts to an eighteenth-century library. Randolph's reading was such a major aspect of his education that it would seem to suggest that, as Claude G. Bowers said, had Randolph "been born in England, he probably would have aspired to a literary career," but "in America he turned to politics." His political presence, however, was as well a literary presence, his total presence being expressed in his matchless performance as an extemporaneous orator. For years, as a matter of fact, Randolph drew more spectators to the gallery of the House of Representatives than any other congressional orator. A striking description of a Randolph performance is found in Francis W. Gilmer's *Sketches of American Orators* (1816):

The first time that I ever felt the spell of his eloquence was when a boy, standing in the gallery of the capitol in the year 1808. I saw rise a gentlemen, who in every quality of his person, his voice, his mind, his character, is a phenomenon among men. His figure is tall, spare, and somewhat emaciated: his limbs long, delicate, slow and graceful in all their

4. Adams, *Randolph*, 13–15.

motions, his countenance with the lineaments of boyhood, but the wrinkles, the faded complexion, the occasional sadness of old age and even of decrepitude: possessing, however, vast compass and force of expression. His voice is small, but of the clearest tone and most flexible modulation I have ever heard. . . . His manner of thinking is as peculiar as his person and voice. He has so long spoken parables, that he now thinks in them. Antitheses, jests, beautiful conceits, with a striking turn of expression and point of expression, flow from his lips with the same natural ease, and often with singular felicity of application, as regular series of arguments follow each other in the deductions of logical thinkers. His invective, which is always *piquant,* is frequently adorned with the beautiful metaphors of Burke, and animated by bursts of passion worthy of Chatham.[5]

However much the world in which Randolph was reared turned on outward action—on planting and harvesting, on hunting, fishing, and horse racing, on social ritual and family ceremony—it was, as Henry Adams put it, a world given not only to "audacity and vigor" but to letters and "mind." Owing in part at least to the early lapse in Virginia of a coherent ecclesiastical motive, even as it persisted in the Massachusetts colony, the remarkable world of Thomas Jefferson and his peers, Richard Beale Davis has effectively shown, was the culmination of two centuries of secular literacy and "cerebration."[6] It was no historical accident that out of Virginia came such world-historical acts of thought as the Declaration of Independence and, ten years later, after a hard-fought struggle, a legislative decree formally divorcing church and state. Based on the assumption that the model of society and history is no longer a transcendent society shining in eternity but is the free mind as expressed by the rational individual, these actions of mind symbolized a permanent reversal of the basis of order. They made Virginia an expression of the radical and decisive

---

5. *Letters of John Randolph to a Young Relative* (Philadelphia, 1834); Claude G. Bowers, quoted in Jay B. Hubbell, *The South in American Literature, 1607–1900* (Durham, N.C., 1954), 225; Francis W. Gilmer, quoted *ibid.,* 226.

6. See Richard Beale Davis, *Intellectual Life in the Colonial South, 1585–1763* (3 vols.; Knoxville, Tenn., 1978), especially I, xxi–xxxi, III, 1635–53.

secularity of the seventeenth and eighteenth centuries—the scene of a climactic moment in the progress of the encompassing, modern, secular critique of man and society, nature and God, conducted by Bacon, Newton, Locke, and a host of others, including Shakespeare, Milton, and Pope, all of whom in the old sense of the term were men of letters. In the Virginia microcosm of modernity, secular, rational mind, through a series of remarkable men of letters, clearly manifested its desire to become a polity of its own. More than this, mind made plain in the Virginia microcosm its determinative motive in modern history, this being nothing less than its assumption of all dominion and power through the subjectification of man and society, nature, and God to its processes. The Virginia microcosm was also a place where the psychic expense of this all-embracing transaction to the man of letters—the sense of history as a grievous personal burden—became plainly evident. For all his confidence that mind is a beneficent power, Jefferson knew doubts and anxieties that had not arisen before the identification of history and mind. But a man of letters with a weaker temperament, like Randolph, experienced more acutely than Jefferson the cost of mind's looking to itself as the model of history: agonizing tensions between the personal and the political, between self and history, resulting in despair bordering on or, as in Randolph's case, crossing into, madness. In Randolph, to be sure, who sometimes drugged himself with opium and alcohol, who at times gave the appearance of being in a hallucinatory state, who may at times have been truly psychotic, we find—as later in another Virginia man of letters, Edgar Allan Poe—a focus for a study in an American political and literary psychopathology.

Imaging the disturbed condition of the sensitive, educated self in America, and particularly in patrician Virginia, Randolph mirrors the tension between history and the thought and emotion implicit in the writings Dawidoff describes as the major source of the literary and political education of the early Republic: the Augustan satirists and the Old Whig or Commonwealth or, as they were often called, the "country" philosophers and pamphleteers (John Trenchard, Thomas Gordon, and others). "At the core of country thinking, as in Augustan literature, one senses the assertion of a particular kind of individual man claiming for himself the virtues he believes are lost to public life in this time," Dawidoff says. "Surely this belief haunted the cult of independence: principle was understood as individual honor, integrity, *character*. The character of a people and its rulers is what country politics comes down to. And it is character as virtue under attack that typically triggered the country response."[7]

Resisting the corruption of political and social values by power and greed, the Augustan writers and country thinkers vested the source of public virtue, once envisioned as a transcendent, immutable order decreed by God, in the personal character of the man of letters. The burden on the individual could become overpowering. Even an Emerson, who accepted the optative mood of modernity and proclaimed ecstatically that the self is the world, came to doubt his ecstasy, and to fear to some extent (as Thoreau more obviously) that, having become identical with self-consciousness, the world had become an inescapable prison. This intimation, graphically imaged in Emerson's Virginia contemporary, Poe, was related to the insurgence of the democratic element in America, foreboding the displacement of the educated mind as the image of order by that of raw, contentious, essentially anarchic public opinion. Randolph anticipates Poe in taking cognizance of this probability and its result. "I am more and more satiated with the world," he complained in a letter to Francis Scott Key in 1819. "It is to me a fearful prison house of guilt and misery. . . . I have lost all hope of public service, and whithersoever I direct my eyes a dark cloud seems to impend."[8] Although responsible, rational mind as exemplified by the Old Whig school had maintained respect for politics as a realm of expression reserved for the open forum—a space in which the private self may be truly transformed into a public self—respect for the ideal of the forum, the space in which the patrician leaders of the Revolution had performed, had sadly degenerated in Randolph's eyes.

> In fact, the old gentry are gone and the *nouveaux riche,* where they have the inclination, do not know how to live. *Biscuit not half cuit,* everything animal and vegetable, smeared with melted butter or lard. Poverty stalking through the land, while we are engaged in political metaphysics, and, amidst

7. Dawidoff, *Randolph,* 150.
8. Hugh A. Garland, *The Life of John Randolph of Roanoke* (2 vols.; New York, 1856), II, 345, 346.

our filth and vermin . . . look down with contempt on other nations, England and France especially. We hug our lousy cloaks around us, take another *chaw* of *tubbacker,* float the room with nastiness, or ruin the grate and fire-irons, where they happen not to be rusty, and try conclusions upon constitutional points.

Presiding at such a convocation, Randolph might well have added, was that degenerate Virginia patrician who had become for him a prime symbol of despair, the author of the Declaration of Independence. "I cannot live in this miserable undone country," Randolph lamented in 1829, "where as the Turks follow their sacred standard, which is a pair of Mahomet's green breeches, we are governed by the old red breeches of that prince of Projectors, St. Thomas of *Cantingbury;* and surely Beckett himself never had more pilgrims at his shrine than the saint of Monticello." [9]

Randolph's career is an archetypal version of the politics of self in America, in which the self has lost any way to discriminate between its being a private entity on the one hand and a public entity on the other. In his efforts to recover a nostalgically idealized social structure, Randolph—like John Taylor of Caroline, though in a more frenzied way—adopted the role of the old-fashioned Virginia gentleman as prophet. In manners, dress, and general demeanor, he sought to incarnate a lost ideal of public order. "The country is ruined past redemption," Randolph said in 1829, "it is ruined in the character and spirit of the people. . . . Where now could we find leaders of a revolution? The whole Society will precipitate itself upon Louisiana and the adjoining deserts. Hares will hurdle the Capitol. . . . Congress will liberate our slaves in less than twenty years." [10]

In a displaced public self like Randolph, do we not glimpse a centering of order in the self as desperate as that we see in Thoreau, who altogether denied the efficacy of public order? Like Thoreau, Randolph symbolized the injunctive need to represent the politics of self implicit in the Declaration of Independence, which, endorsing the political sovereignty of the individual, implies the self-evident

9. *Ibid.,* II, 345, 317.
10. *Ibid.*

right of the self to determine what kind of order, or nonorder, it wants to be in.

Yet, sensitized by his historical awareness of the complex interactions of self, slavery, and liberty in America, Randolph, in certain moments of shrewd political insight, transcended self-dramatization, as in his grasp of the fateful connection between states' rights and slavery. In 1824, in his most cogent argument about the character of the nation invented by reason, Randolph said in an address to the United States House of Representatives that the power of the House to control commerce through the funding of internal improvements could be construed as the power to emancipate the slaves.

On the whole . . . this speech . . . may be fairly taken as Randolph's masterpiece [Adams says], and warrants placing him in very high rank as a political leader. Grant that it is mischievous beyond all precedent even in his own mischievous career; that its effect must be to create the dangers which it foretold, and to bring the slave power into the peril which it helped to create; grant that it was in flagrant contradiction to his speeches on the Louisiana Purchase, his St. Domingo vote, and his outcry for an embargo; that it was inspired by hatred of Clay, that it was related to a scheme of internal improvements which Mr. Jefferson himself had invented, and upon which he had looked upon as the flower, the crown, the hope, and aspiration of his whole political system; that it was a deliberate, cold-blooded attempt to pervert the old and honorable principle of states' rights into a mere tool for the protection of negro slavery, which Randolph professed to think the worst of earthly misfortunes; that it assumed, with an arrogance beyond belief, the settled purpose of the slave power to strain the Constitution in its own interests, and to block the government at its own will,— grant all of this and whatever more may be required, still the speech is wonderfully striking. It startles, not merely by its own brightness, although this is intense, but by the very darkness it makes visible.[11]

11. Adams, *Randolph*, 277–79.

The Fable of the Southern Writer

In his mischievous but brilliant insight (as Adams characterizes it), Randolph comprehended that the liberty and independence of the slaveholders in the existing American Republic would depend on their successful insistence that slavery is an integral part of the Constitutional—the textual—structure of freedom. Although he believed all of his life that the right of human beings to buy and sell other human beings as chattel property is the antithesis of the sacred right of the individual to be free (and that slavery victimizes the slaveholder as much as or more than the slave and enslaves him along with his slave), Randolph finally had no illusions about the shaping force of slavery on the future of history. He discerned that a government modeled, as Alexander Hamilton said, on "reflection and choice"—modeled on mind and formulated in a printed and published text—becomes a government based on the latitude of interpretation. And Randolph saw that interpretation, if not controlled by careful discrimination, whether exercised by the individual or the state, tends to be wholly subjective. As he understood the political situation in the American Republic, the power to overturn slavery by incorporating abolitionist thought in national legislative action was the power to overturn the independence the Revolutionary War had been fought to obtain.

Intrigued by Randolph's insights, Adams attributed to the Virginian a solitary but awesome influence on the course of history, declaring that if we look beneath Randolph's almost incredible capacity for attitudinizing, we can see that "he discovered and mapped out from beginning to end a chart of the whole course on which the slave power was to sail to its destruction." Although the eccentric congressman "did no legislative work, sat on no committees, and was not remotely connected with any useful measure or idea," he "organized the slave power on strong and well-chosen ground; he taught it discipline, gave it popular cohesion, pointed out to it the fact that before it could hope for power it must break down Henry Clay, and, having taught his followers what to do, helped them to do it."[12]

Granting that Adams' fascination with Randolph led him to overstate his political significance, we must yet wonder at the considerable power wielded by this strange man, who, as a consequence of

12. *Ibid.,* 301.

illness in early manhood, was impotent and of feminine voice; and who often acted as though he were bereft of his senses, and more than once was in fact quite irrational in his behavior. Adams, and Randolph's other biographers, are of less help in explaining the enigma that was Randolph than Dawidoff, who sums up the secret of Randolph's power when he says that "Randolph himself, not any abstracted opinions, constituted his politics." Unlike Adams, Dawidoff does not separate attitudinizing Randolph from the Randolph who was capable of establishing the logical ground of the slave states. They were one and the same, integrated in the knowledge, even if unspoken and unspeakable, that the self has no existence in the eternal, only in history.

In interpreting himself as the solitary relic of an age of superior virtue—an age that had instituted a successful revolution—Randolph (who was born in 1773 at the beginning of the Revolution and died in 1833 as the full democratic tide began to sweep the new nation) fulfilled the classic role of the civil prophet: to warn the citizenry of the dangers of postrevolutionary ambition and lust for power. But in his struggle to play the prophetic role, Randolph responded to a new, more profound, yet less definable danger than the traditional peril of the unweening desire for power: the emergence of the historical self. In Randolph's story we witness the apprehension of the self's awareness of its identity with mind, and its discovery of its interiorization, its inward embodiment, of history. Aware, if not articulately, that mind, self, and liberty had become integral in his world, the world the southern slaveholders were engaged in making (and *would* have made perhaps had they had more leeway than history finally permitted them), Randolph discerned that the southern states must, utilizing the ideology of states' rights, make mind the support of slavery. The power to overturn slavery by incorporating abolitionist thought in the text governing the nation by means of national legislative action was the power to overturn independence. The idea of the right of self-determination made slavery the condition of freedom.

This interpretation of the meaning of the new Republic was the contribution of one who in the name of a government and a society modeled on rational mind opposed the forces, whether they came from the president or the Congress, that would have reestablished the centralization of power denounced by the Declaration of Independence and prohibited by the Constitution. His advocacy of the "strict construction" of the Constitution was the end product of an education in the novel inwardness of power in a nation conceived through deliberate acts of self-will, brought into historical existence by the incarnation of these acts in armed rebellion, and sustained in existence by an unceasing action of thought, the continuous self-interpretation of its meaning in history. The prophetic Randolph to whom Adams was strongly attracted was, like Adams, though less deeply and less intelligibly, haunted by the education in self-failure that inescapably accompanies the peculiarly intense identification of self and history in America. In the South of the first American Republic—the South that existed from the ratification of the Constitution to the outbreak of the War for Southern Independence—Randolph received an education in failure so profound that Adams says he, like the Miltonic Satan, was capable of a vision of history that "startles" us "by the very darkness it makes visible."

Randolph died while on a visit to Philadelphia in 1833. According to a popular report, the scene of his death was the anonymous ambience of a hotel room. If so, possibly it was the scene he desired. He had been overwhelmed by the history of his country. Noted for his allegiance to Virginia, he came to regard his ancestral acres as a "savage solitude." He was in danger of willing himself to be homeless. One account states that on his deathbed Randolph was heard to cry out, "Remorse! Remorse!"[13] The story is apocryphal but appropriate to the history of a man who by a self-conscious act of his imagination transformed his role in life from that of an actor in a story of early political success and brilliant promise into that of a player in a darkly nostalgic legend of despair and failure. While we cannot characterize the nature of the transforming imagination in Randolph with precision, it would hardly be wrong to regard his imagination as essentially literary, nor would it be wrong to say that it is a tendency of the literary imagination as it has been exhibited in writers from Randolph to Simms to Mark Twain to Faulkner to Walker Percy to invent characters who are involved in what may be called a southern culture of failure.

13. Russell Kirk, *John Randolph of Roanoke: A Study in Conservative Thought* (Chicago, 1954), 12.

I

The Fable of the Agrarians and the Failure
of the American Republic

Around 1850, Roland Barthes says in *Writing Degree Zero,* classical literature simply "disintegrated," having yielded to the pressure of a cultural situation in which literary order, like social order, had ceased to be hierarchical and had become democratic and pluralistic. In the vacuum left by the loss of the classical mode, what had seemed to be the very basis of literature, a closely disciplined use of words, became increasingly uncertain, with the result that—Barthes makes the usual French equation between the French aspect and the total aspect—"the whole of literature, from Flaubert to the present day, became the problematics of language."

Sixty or seventy years earlier Nietzsche had anticipated the Barthean vision of literary disorder in his projection of a general disintegration of European culture, declaring in *Beyond Good and Evil: Prelude to a Philosophy of the Future* (1886) that the governing attitude, and chief virtue, of "modern men" (meaning men of letters and, more specifically, philosophers and poets) is no longer the classical but the *historical* sense. A "sixth sense," unknown until it was discovered "in the wake of that enchanting and mad *semibarbarism* into which Europe . . . [has been] plunged by the democratic mingling of classes and races," the historical sense, Nietzsche declared, prevents us from truly experiencing "that which is really noble in a work or [in a] human being"—that is to say, the classical moment, the "halcyon" moment of "self-sufficiency," the magical moment, graced by the "golden and cold aspect of all things that have consummated themselves."[1]

---

1. Friedrich Nietzsche, *Beyond Good and Evil: Prelude to a Philosophy of the Future,* trans. Walter Kaufmann (New York, 1966), 151–52.

But modern men, Nietzsche observes, have a potentially power-ful compensation for the loss of the classical sense. No longer con-strained by the sense of "measure" that has preserved order in West-ern culture—this through the maintenance of the classical sense against the constantly threatened reemergence of the barbaric or in-stinctual sense—they "can drop the reins before the infinite," and as semibarbarians themselves experience the "bliss" of exposure to the maximum of "danger." Having come into possession of the histori-cal sense, modern men know the truth of history: it is a "carnival," in which "moralities, articles of faith, tastes in the arts, and religion" are merely the "costumes" of a given age. Although Nietzsche in-cludes language among the "costumes" in the modern "carnival" of historical interpretation only by implication, he in effect anticipates Ferdinand de Saussure's theory of structural linguistics and may in general be regarded as a major precursor of the emphasis Barthes and other critics assign to the problem of language: since the problem of language and the problem of culture are identical, a theory of lan-guage is a theory of culture and vice versa.[2] Thus it is presently taken for granted that a theory of the particular element of culture we call literature is fundamentally a theory of language.

Nietzsche himself resisted the nihilistic vision that rose before him as he contemplated the loss of the classical mode. Have more recent poets and philosophers easily submitted to the doctrine of his-torical relativity? On the whole, they have not, as Nietzsche pre-dicted, lost all faith in meaning in history and so become mere "par-odists of world history and God's buffoons."

Yet, although prolonged by the massive effort at cultural resto-ration that produced Thomas Mann, Proust, Joyce, Pound, T. S. Eliot, Hemingway, Faulkner, and other giants of literary modernism during the period between the two world wars of the twentieth cen-tury, the saving tension between classicism and barbarism has, one must say, finally altogether disintegrated. Barthes' declaration that the nature and content of literature consist in the problematics of language—or, to put this another way, his announcement that the work of literature is wholly a historical artifact—places another de-cisive seal on the classical reverence for the permanence of the work of literature. In the Barthean world, the classical concept of literature has

2. *Ibid.*

become a relic of an outmoded ideology. Meanwhile, attendant upon twentieth-century efforts to devise comprehensive theories of history—as in Henry Adams, Spengler, Toynbee, and Eric Voegelin—we have seen the emergence of numerous efforts to respond to Jean-Paul Sartre's fundamental question, "What is literature?" In fact, the diverse multiplicity of attempts to set forth all-embracing theories of literature during the past fifty years is unprecedented.

Because of the pluralistic character of American culture—and the American acceptance of pragmatic British attitudes toward history and literature, so markedly different from the Continental attitudes—American critics (save for a limited exposure to literary theorizing based on Marx and Freud) did not effectively encounter twentieth-century literary theorists until recent years. Faculty offices on American university campuses (since the death of Edmund Wilson, all serious American critics have been associated with the academic hothouse) that not long ago echoed with the names of Eliot, Leavis, Trilling, Wilson, Tate, Brooks, and Warren now resound with other names in the "carnival" of critics: Heidegger and de Man, Adorno, Benjamin, Derrida, Foucault, and Barthes. In the last twenty years, to be sure, theory in its many guises has become so well established in the literary departments of American universities that one may ask a member of any department that sponsors graduate instruction, "Who is your Derridain or your Foucaultian or your Barthean or your Paul de Mannian?" with as much, if not more, assurance than one may ask, "Who is your Shakespearean?" No language department of any size is without several members who are pursuing the theoretical aspects of literature as disciples of such figures. As a matter of fact, no university department devoted to a foreign language is at this moment not doing the same thing. Universities might save money by consolidating all departments concerned with language and literature into departments of theory.

Involving a literature that has developed into a national literature in such a short span of time that it was scarcely yet identified as American at the moment in the mid-nineteenth century when Barthes says literature became the problematics of language, the relationship between literary theory and American literature hardly conforms to the Barthean model of the history of modern criticism. Although its manner—outwardly shaped by the eighteenth-century movement to restore a classical sensibility—tends to belie its true character, this relationship was in the Barthean sense entirely post-classical. If we date the self-conscious development of an American national literature from the time of the American Revolution, we recognize that both the makers of the Revolution and the post-Revolutionary makers of the new nation were deeply engaged with the problems of language. Adapting their devoted knowledge of classical rhetoric to the manipulation and accommodation of language to their eminently self-conscious historical purposes, they not only set forth a novel, provocative theory of revolution but transformed the text elucidating this theory into a bloody action entailing massive historical consequences. Subsequently they invented a nation and made its future dependent on the endless interpretation of the words in the compact text of a Constitution—a text that even with its series of amendments is no more than six thousand words in length, yet, together with the carefully worded texts of countless judicial decisions interpreting the intention of the original text, becomes a text of millions of words. No nation in history, in actual historical practice, has put such a stress on the word: on the spoken and the written word, yes, but, more significantly, on the *printed* word—the origin of the American Republic being the first world-historical revolution based on the power of the printing press.

At the one moment in our history so far when the authority of the Supreme Court, the final interpreter of the intention of the text, failed to be accorded sufficient acceptance—failed in the critical interpretation of the text to reconcile the "strict constructionists" and the "loose constructionists"—Americans entered into a civil conflict of unprecedented ferocity. Having decided at the expense of this massive bloodletting that the founding text of the Union does not allow the right of an individual state to secede from the compact entered into in 1790, Americans emerged from the Civil War as citizens not of the Republic of 1790 but in effect of a Second American Republic, which we somehow regard as being at one and the same time the constitutionally mandated, rational order established in 1790 and a mystical, "indivisible" nation-state born out of the bloody defeat of the southern states in their bid for independence.[3] As citizens

3. I wrote these words two or three years before the appearance of Garry Wills' *Lincoln at Gettysburg: The Words That Remade America* (New York, 1992), a study that graphically

of the Second Republic we have committed ourselves for the past hundred years not only to the imperialistic extension of constitutional democracy to all the nations of the world but to the sacrifices in blood and treasure necessary to the fulfillment of the commitment; and we have continued to pursue this commitment down to the present moment, even though it has involved us in a series of undeclared wars that pose critical and as yet unresolved questions regarding their constitutionality. Such questions are fraught with historical irony for the southern states of the Second Republic, which—although aware that in doing so they support a nation ratified as an indissoluble entity by their defeat in the War for Southern Independence—have endorsed American imperialistic politics more fully than the rest of the nation.

I mention the problems of constitutionality and the South not to the purpose of pursuing the issue further but simply as a way of suggesting that the issues concerning the historical and theoretical interpretation of the literature of the American South reflect a phenomenon that has always been germane to interpretations of southern literature: a devotion to textuality that, while it is fundamental to the American existence, is more intensely and complexly so to the southern existence. If, in addition to the American centering in political textuality, we consider the relatively stronger centering of the nation's Bible Belt in Protestant biblical textuality, we may well conclude that southerners, more than the generality of American citizens, have been a people who live and die by the text. We may perhaps further conclude that the sense of textuality has been relatively greater among southern intellectuals—novelists, poets, historians, literary critics—than among their counterparts in other parts of the nation. It would seem hardly to have been by chance that the theory and practice of a major critical school in twentieth-century America, the New Criticism, had a primary association with three southern men of letters, John Crowe Ransom, Robert Penn Warren, and Cleanth Brooks. Nor would it seem to have been by chance that Ransom and Warren, together with Donald Davidson and Allen Tate, were associated with the inception of the Southern Agrarian

---

reveals how in effect Lincoln created the American nation-state by subordinating the text of the Constitution to the mystique of the Declaration of Independence.

movement and the writing of its primary text, *I'll Take My Stand;* or that Brooks, a few years younger, became an Agrarian disciple.

Ironically, although it has always been called the manifesto of the Agrarian movement and is universally looked upon as its primary historical document, the collection of twelve markedly individualistic and diverse approaches to "the South and the agrarian tradition" that make up the body of *I'll Take My Stand* was not intended to be an authoritative but a provisional statement. The volume resembles a manifesto only in the introductory "Statement of Principles"; and this statement, written by Ransom in the name of all the contributors, simply reflects the desire of the Agrarians to give the volume the character of a prophetic southern reaction to the industrialization of the nation. A generalized articulation of opposition to so powerful a force hardly served as an authoritative, programmatic assertion of an Agrarian movement. Such a statement was never published. Interestingly enough, only one clear-cut assertion about a systematic Agrarian program was devised. It is found in the correspondence of Allen Tate, who in 1929, while *I'll Take My Stand* was in uncertain progress, wrote letters to Warren and Donald Davidson in which he set forth in prescriptive detail an elaborate scheme for an organized "Southern Movement." To be led by "an academy of positive Southern reactionaries," the movement Tate envisioned would be far-reaching yet rigorously disciplined. But the academy—to consist of "fifteen active members (poets, critics, historians, economists) and ten inactive members (lawyers, politicians, private citizens who might be active enough without being committed to direct agitation)"—would not be secretive, save in the tactics it would employ in implementing a program mandated by "a philosophical constitution." To be "issued and signed by the academy, as the groundwork of the movement," the constitution would "be ambitious to the last degree." It would set forth "under our leading idea [*i.e.,* radical reaction to all forms of 'progressivism'] a complete philosophical, literary, economic, and religious system" based on "our heritage." This system would be supported by a full literary apparatus: "a newspaper, to argue our principles on the lower plane . . . a weekly, to press philosophy upon the passing show; and . . . a quarterly devoted wholly to principles." The completeness of the commitment Tate urged upon his colleagues is indicated in his cautionary note that the southern heritage "should be valued, not in what it actually performed, but in its possible perfection." To achieve the perfection of the southern heritage meant, Tate said, that "philosophically we must go the whole hog of reaction, and base our movement less upon the actual old South than upon its prototype—the historical social and religious scheme of Europe. We must be the last Europeans—there being no Europeans in Europe at present."[4]

This fabulous depiction of the Agrarian poets and critics as the last Europeans clearly was an attempt by Tate to identify and authorize the vocational role he had conceived for himself and his colleagues as twentieth-century white southern men of letters. In fulfilling his responsibilities, the southern man of letters must function not only as poet, novelist, and literary critic but as cultural theorist and social prophet—as an eminently self-conscious interpreter and moral guardian of values of social order to be secured through the restoration and perpetuation of the traditional Western amalgam of classical-Hebraic-Christian values. In depicting the idealized role of the southern poet and critic Tate assigned him a still more particular, more imperative role: that of being the creator of "an intellectual situation interior to the South."[5] He was charged with the retrogressive perfecting in the twentieth-century South of the old European social scheme. This was the order that the antebellum South should have emulated but that, Tate said, save in a superficial and futile imitation of manners, failed to do.

Tate's proposal to establish an intellectual situation interior to the twentieth-century South through codifying the Agrarian subscription to the traditional European society in the prescriptive text of a written constitution was in any literal sense absurd. Yet it was a logical poetic strategy. Tate would have rectified the antebellum failure by following what Henry James in *The American Scene* (1907) saw had been demanded by the intellectual situation of the Old South—namely, a radically reactionary critique of the nineteenth-century progressive concept of history. But in implying that the Old South intellectual had failed in his duty to support a traditionalist order, Tate misread historical reality. The actual antebellum South was an

4. John Tyree Fain and Thomas Daniel Young, eds., *The Literary Correspondence of Donald Davidson and Allen Tate* (Athens, Ga., 1974), 229–31. Cf. below, 201–207.

5. *Ibid.*, 230.

aspiring modern slave society that with tragic irony thought of itself as a dynamic, novel exemplar of the nineteenth-century doctrine of moral and material progress.

Reflecting on his impressions of Richmond, Henry James, never in the South but once, acutely discerned that the former capital city of the defeated Confederacy imaged the fact that the exponents of the antebellum slave society had less regard for the past than they had for a vision of the progressive fulfillment of the American Revolution in a modern slave society. Directed by a "budding" mind to make itself the embodiment of a "new criticism of history," the antebellum South in its ideal of itself was dedicated to the welfare of all mankind.[6]

In the light of what James says, it would seem that in seeking the prototypical southern scheme in the Old South image of feudal Europe, Tate, more or less deliberately, misread the primary shaping force of the intellectual situation interior to the South. But James's vision of the meaning of the Confederate South resembles the Agrarian vision of the South in that both belong to a poetics of interpretation animated—no less in *I'll Take My Stand* (although expressed in different terms) than in George Fitzhugh's 1854 treatise *Sociology for the South; or, The Failure of a Free Society*—by the prophetic theory that the destiny of the South is to lead a revolt against modern history.

What the prophets of the Old South may be said to have had strikingly in common with the Agrarian prophets of a later day was not a disposition to define their society as a traditionalist order but a radical desire to transform the actual South into the symbol of vital opposition to the whole modern movement toward a worldwide industrial capitalism. The theory, and to a degree the fact, of the slave society of the Old South, as Eugene Genovese and Elizabeth Fox-Genovese point out in *The Fruits of Merchant Capital,* held that the "patriarchal plantation" of the slave South "recapitulated" an earlier world founded in experience and feeling. The Old South society thus contrasted markedly with the society of the world outside its bounds, which, in violation of the truth of human nature, was seeking to model itself on the illusion that when the social relation in

6. Henry James, *The American Scene,* ed. Leon Edel (Bloomington, Ind., 1968), 373–74.

all nations is properly based on the connection of bourgeois entre-
preneur, wage earner, and consumer, a free society for all will result—including the hewers of wood and the drawers of water, who,
in all ages past, have been deemed to have their proper sphere of
freedom in the blessed relief from poverty that slavery affords.[7]

In impossible defiance of the irrevocable American commitment
to science, technology, and industrialism, the "theory of agrarian-
ism," according to the "Statement of Principles" in *I'll Take My
Stand,* advocated a society rooted in "experience and feeling," pro-
posing that "the culture of the soil is the best and most sensitive of
vocations, and that therefore it should have economic preference and
enlist the maximum number of workers."[8] In the case either of the
slaveholders' idea of the "true" historical character of their world, or
of the twentieth-century Agrarians' idea of the "true" historical character of the South, the limits of historical actuality and possibility
appear to be so far exceeded that neither concept can be properly
categorized as theory, or even as hypothesis, but may more accu-
rately be described as fantasy. Yet to assign either idea wholly to the
realm of the fantastic would be to deny the dynamic tension between
possibility and fantasy in historical interpretation. All compelling
interpretations of history are verbal or rhetorical artifices resulting
from an imaginative critique—a literary criticism—of the possibilities, mundane and fantastic, of history. Whether the criticism of history that has shaped the fate of man in modern times has been good
or evil has depended on the moral or immoral use of language. The
union of literary and social theory is integral. In its broadest sense
literary criticism is involved in the morality of society and culture—
in the entire problem of the moral relation between language, literature, society, and culture, and the power of the state; in other words,
in what in modern times must be seen as the ultimate literary problematics: the moral relationship between literary theory and the
power of the nation-state.

In the final analysis, the historical context of literary theory and
southern writing in Allen Tate and the Agrarians is the complex con-

7. Elizabeth Fox-Genovese and Eugene D. Genovese, *The Fruits of Merchant Capital:
Slavery and Bourgeois Property in the Rise and Expansion of Capitalism* (New York, 1983).

8. Twelve Southerners, *I'll Take My Stand: The South and the Agrarian Tradition* (Baton
Rouge, 1977), xvii.

nection between literary criticism and the state. The creation of an "intellectual situation interior to the South" that Tate saw as the prime goal of the Agrarians was not of course his, or theirs, to "create." In idealizing the relation of one independent farmer to another as the social relation in the South, and in seeking to develop a critical discourse that would provide a text to support this ideal, the Agrarians largely ignored the historical fact that the contextual background of their discourse was an antebellum discourse in which the idealization of the yeoman farmer (as in Jefferson) had been supplanted by the idealization of the master-slave relation. Set forth in antebellum proslavery novels, poems, sermons, and orations—as well as in more formal treatises, such as those presented in the two notable collections *The Pro-Slavery Argument as Maintained by the Most Distinguished Writers of the Southern States* (1852) and *Cotton Is King and Pro-Slavery Arguments* (1860)—the southern proslavery argument in the thirty years leading up to the War for Southern Independence constitutes the theoretical and prophetic text of a modern slave society in search of its authorization in history.

It is today a little startling to realize that although the actual slave society of the South ended almost a century and a half ago, the quest for the meaning of the society of the antebellum South has not ended—at least not for those possessed of genuine historical acumen—but has become more expansive, complex, and significant. Indeed, the quest has had a momentous augmentation with the fuller emergence in the past generation of the literature that once was referred to by the term *Negro American literature*. Although Ralph Ellison was still using this term in the late 1960s, *black American literature* had by then become the predominant expression. Later, though it was by no means a new term, *Afro-American literature* was most frequently used. Presently we most often employ the designation *African-American literature*. This conforms more pointedly, one supposes, to the present imperative to rewrite the history of American literature as an expression of multiculturalism.

Although the varying attempts to name it reflect a marked uncertainty about the identity of an African-American literature and suggest that it is still in the process of definition, there is certainty about a highly significant result of this process: the importance of the recovery of the suppressed text in the master-slave relation, as, for instance, in a work now considered to be a major American text, *Narrative of the Life of Frederick Douglass* (1845; rev. 1892). With respect to the South, the increasing presence of the African-American voice in American literature is but a part of a much larger consequence of the enlargement and complication of the intellectual and literary situation interior to the South. This must now be seen in the light of the increasing awareness of the ambiguous yet vital conjunction of a theory of white southern literary historiography and criticism and the assertions of an emergent African-American historiography and criticism—a historiography and criticism that at once significantly is and is not an "African-Southern" criticism.

We would appear to need a southern historiography and criticism—a theory of southern literature—adequate to the demands of the widening dimensions of southern history and its increased significance to our understanding of the historical destiny of the Second American Republic. The urgency of our need is enhanced when we reflect that the failure of the Republic of 1790 to preserve itself was a literary failure. A republic, founded as no other had been before, on the responsible use of words was by 1860 completely frustrated by the inability of its citizens to solve by self-interpretation the most crucial moral question raised by the text on which it was founded: do men have a right to own property in other men? Until the nineteenth century this right had been almost universally assumed. Insofar as the Civil War resolved the moral problem of slavery, it did so only through the association that was made between the moral issue of slavery and the political and economic issue of whether the Republic of the United States is a union of sovereign states or a unitary nation-state. In resolving but not essentially solving the moral problem of slavery by armed conflict, the Americans who fought the Civil War anticipated a world in which the problem of forced servitude would, as a consequence of the effort to fulfill the destiny of the nation-state, assume aspects more intricate and terrible than had heretofore been known. It is a world in which a responsive and responsible academic literary criticism, if it counts for anything at all, is more important than it has ever been before.

II

A Fable of White and Black
Jefferson, Madison, Tate

James M. Cox has said that since the "very idea of auto-biography" grew "out of the political necessities and discoveries of the American and French revolutions," it is "no mere accident that an astonishingly large proportion of the slender shelf of so-called American classics" is claimed by autobiographies: Franklin's *Autobiography,* Thoreau's *Walden,* Whitman's *Leaves of Grass,* Adams' *The Education of Henry Adams,* and Gertrude Stein's *The Making of Americans.*[1]

In spite of his brilliant insight into the origin of self-biography as a mode of American writing, Cox must give us pause. My own immediate response to his list of classic American autobiographies is to ask: Not one by a southerner, past or present, white or black? Not even Thomas Jefferson's *Autobiography?* Has not the judgment of a leading student of American autobiography—who is, incidentally, a committed Jeffersonian and deep-dyed Virginian—somehow gone seriously awry when he excludes from his list of classic American autobiographies a work that is not only the authorial account of the writing and ratification of the American doctrine of the self but the singular source of the original text of the Declaration of Independence?

Yet in terms of his own argument, Cox bears no culpability for his failure to recognize the document that uniquely describes the

---

1. James M. Cox, *Recovering Literature's Lost Ground: Essays in American Autobiography* (Baton Rouge, 1989), 11–12, 31. For significant suggestions concerning southern autobiography that differ somewhat from those advanced either in Cox's essay or in the present one, see James Olney, "Autobiographical Tradition Black and White," in *Located Lives: Place and Idea in Southern Autobiography,* ed. J. Bill Berry (Athens, Ga., 1990), 66–77.

composition of the Declaration. Begun in 1821 but never finished, what has come to be called Jefferson's autobiography, he explains, was referred to by its author simply as "memoranda." When the fragmentary narrative was first published in 1830, Jefferson's grandson and literary executor upgraded the Jeffersonian label to *Memoir.* Twentieth-century editors would seem simply to have taken the final step in recognizing its singular importance by giving it a magisterial title: *The Autobiography of Thomas Jefferson.* "But hold!," Cox exclaims, "Jefferson's text is neither history nor revelation of personality. It is memoir. As students of literature we might want to reveal Jefferson's ego; as students of history, we might want it to provide a myth of the American self. But it is autobiography as memoir, which means that it will relate itself to the external world of the author in history, not to the inner world of self-reflection."[2] If we accept Cox's distinction between "memoir"—a personal narrative "that relates itself to the external world of the author"—and "autobiography"—a personal narrative that relates itself to the "inner world of self-reflection"—the rationale of his list of classic autobiographies becomes clear, and the omission of Jefferson's *Autobiography* plausible. It was excluded from consideration by definition.

But again, hold! In the subsequent course of his essay on Jefferson, Cox reveals that his definition of *autobiography* is less than absolute. If he seems at first to say that Jefferson's grandson made the right editorial judgment about the title for his grandfather's personal narrative, Cox seems finally in his essay to allow, even to approve of, the transformation by editorial fiat of Jefferson's casual designation *memoranda* into the full-blown designation *autobiography.* Indeed, citing this change as one example of the present-day "imperial" interpretation of the term *autobiography,* Cox indicates his fascination with the possibility of reading novels, poems, essays—indeed almost any kind of text, as, for example, Henry James's prefaces to the New York Edition of his work and Freud's *Interpretation of Dreams*—as autobiographical expression.

Taken in its full range, Cox's provocative discussion of the distinction between memoir and autobiography offers us alternate perspectives on the subject of autobiography in the South. On the one

---

2. Cox, *Recovering Literature's Lost Ground,* 52.

hand, accepting Jefferson as a representative southerner, we may take the distinction between memoir and autobiography quite literally; and in doing so accept what the distinction implies, namely, that the memoiristic mode of self-narrative is inherent in the culture of a people who are incapable of self-reflection. On the other hand, we may be led by Cox's tantalizing qualification of the difference between autobiography and other forms of writing to pursue the possible insights offered by an imperial application of the term *autobiography* to southern writing.

My intention in what follows is to engage in the limited pursuit of such a possibility by examining the drama of the autobiographical impulse in southern white self-biography as it is revealed in Jefferson, James Madison, and Allen Tate. If this apparently arbitrary conjunction of southern men of letters seems odd, it has a certain logic that will, I trust, emerge in due course. Taking the most direct approach to my subject that occurs to me, I shall leave further discussion of Jefferson to later, and turn, as I do elsewhere in the present studies, to Allen Tate, who, as one explores the cultural history of the South, emerges more and more as a central figure. Eventually I will come to Madison.

Of wide-ranging intellectual capacities and acute cultural sensitivity, always both defender and antagonist of the South, always at war with himself whether defending or attacking the South, always withal, in the generic sense, a poet, Tate was, save perhaps for John Crowe Ransom, the only writer the South has produced who might conceivably have written an autobiographical work comparable to *The Education of Henry Adams.* Yet his attempt in 1966 to write what he thought of as no more than a simple "book of memories" was abandoned after he had written two chapters. The reason why is implied, I believe, in the sketch entitled "A Lost Traveller's Dream." Intended to have been the first chapter of his memoirs, this sketch begins with a discrimination between the roles of memoirist and autobiographer as precise as that by Cox. He will tell an external story, Tate says, adding that he is incapable of the inward mode: "Autobiography would demand more of myself than I know; it is easier to know other people than oneself because one may observe them; for one can but observe oneself, like Andre Gide, gazing daily into a looking glass, a way to self-knowledge from which I should recoil."[3]

But in his explicit denial of the autobiographical impulse Tate was offering inverse testimony to the fact that there was no southern writer of his generation in whom the autobiographical motive was stronger. From the writings that climax the first part of his career, the famous "Ode to the Confederate Dead" and the scarcely less well known essay commenting on it, "Narcissus as Narcissus," to the sophisticated meditation of his last years on the limitations of memory, "A Lost Traveller's Dream," Tate was engaged in recording the inward drama of a perpetual quarrel in his thought and emotion between self-repression and self-revelation. If he did not find a way to resolve the quarrel, it was because he did not seek, or desire, a resolution. "A Lost Traveller's Dream," it might be said, represents the final irresolution of the quarrel. "To conceive the past in an intelligible pattern," Tate says in that sketch, "is a labor of the imagination." But the imagination operates under constraints not only of forgetfulness and misremembrance but of "vanity, pride, and fear." Since to be "immodest enough" in his memoirs "to try to tell all would be shameful," Tate declares that he must, "as Henry James might have said," allow "the authenticity of fact [to] remain shadowy, for however truthful the memorialist may try to be, his anecdotal recollections will be closer to fiction than to history." Or, taking a more severe attitude toward the possibility of accurate remembrance, he suggests that recollections may represent neither history nor fiction but "the treacherous interplay of both." Confronting the dilemma created by the effort to write about one's life, one realizes one is in the modern *selva obscura*.

In the Dark Wood modern man may scarcely hope to find Virgil—merely Horatio, one's *alter ego* who is "not passion's slave" and who survives along with oneself "to tell my story." Horatio, at any rate, is the best narrator I have been able to find to allay the incredulity of the reader, if not my own. If I cannot wholly accept the order of what I think I

3. Allen Tate, *Memoirs and Opinions, 1926–1974* (Chicago, 1975), 3. *Cf.* below, 114–15.

remember, can I expect anybody else to accept it? I am therefore asking the reader of this book, if it shall have a reader, to think of what I shall tell him not as simple truth, but as "signatures" pointing to persons and events once as real as Johnson's cane tapping the pavement, but now faded into another kind of reality that will be perhaps in sight, but always a little beyond my reach.[4]

We are struck with the pathos of a certain immodest grandeur in Tate's tendency always—quite precisely like Adams—to conceive of himself as a symbol of the survival of the high culture of the West. Invoking the figures of Dante and Virgil and Hamlet and Horatio, and Dr. Johnson, he establishes the drama of his own personal act of remembrance in a grand context: the crisis of consciousness in a post-Christian world. Anticipated when Dante found himself in the dark wood, the tortuous character of the modern act of remembering was clearly revealed when Shakespeare imagined Hamlet's dying charge to Horatio. Being "more an antique Roman than a Dane," Horatio may think he can actually "report" his friend's "cause aright." He does not grasp, nor perhaps does Hamlet, the irony of trying to fulfill the charge in a world in which the old structure of memory as the heroic affirmation of the past has collapsed. Envisioning persons and events as dim "signatures"—each once registered on his consciousness as reality, but now only a fading registration on the faculty of consciousness called memory—Tate formulates a despairing aesthetics of memory: it resolves the elusive relationship between history and fiction by investing it in the cloak of a haunting, shadowy authenticity. Although Tate may not have had quite the "prodigious memory" the friends who urged him to write his memoirs attributed to him, his throwing over of his "book of memories" was not owing to any marked depletion of his recollective capacity. Nor was it owing to a lack of the energy required to do the hard work of memory. Nor surely was it owing to a lack of talent for memoiristic writing. Reading Tate's memoiristic fragments, one sees that he had the imaginative capacity to effect something like a Proustian coalescence of memory and history.

4. *Ibid.,* 4.

A Fable of White and Black

When he published a collection of miscellaneous pieces called
Memoirs and Opinions, 1926–1974 in 1975, Tate not only included the
two chapters he had written nine years earlier for his book of memories but in the preface offered a retrospective comment on his failure
as a memoirist. For one thing, he said, in trying to write his recollections he had discovered that his memory of persons and events in the
past was not always accurate; but more importantly, he had discovered that unlike Ernest Hemingway in *A Moveable Feast,* he was unable to bring himself "to tell what was wrong" with his friends—or
even mere acquaintances—"without trying to tell what was wrong
with myself." Remarking dryly that "on this slippery matter" he was
"unwilling to give the reader the chance to make up his own mind,"
Tate added a final comment about his failure as a memoirist: "Then,
too, I fell back on authority: I couldn't let myself indulge in the terrible fluidity of self-revelation." Although obviously intended to be
a decisive statement, this is enigmatic. Maybe intentionally so. What
authority did he fall back on? Did he regard self-revelation to be a
matter only for the authoritative secrecy of the confessional? Or did
he fear the possible discovery that under sufficient scrutiny the self
might reveal that far from being an autonomous entity, its existence
is fluid and inconstant, even mutable, even illusory? Or did he believe
with Henry Adams that autobiography is a form of suicide?[5] All of
these motives may have been present in Tate's decision to give up his
memoiristic effort. But the basic motive, I would suggest, is to be
discovered in his struggle to come to terms with the fate of the self
in the history, or the inner history, of the rise and fall and subsequent
historical situation of the last great modern slave society.

The most poignant "signature" in "A Lost Traveller's Dream" is an
account, as arresting as it is curious, of an incident that took place in
1912 or 1913, when he would have been about thirteen years old, of
Tate's being taken by his mother to visit Aunt Martha Jackson. Now
nearly one hundred years old, Aunt Martha had once been a slave in
the household of his maternal great-grandfather.

5. I am indebted to a brilliant study of this question by Martha Regalis, "Murderous
Historian: Henry Adams and the Forms of Autobiographical History" (Ph.D. dissertation,
Louisiana State University, 1993).

The visit had been arranged a few days before by Aunt Martha's granddaughter, a tall dignified mulatto who seemed to have time for sewing and other little tasks for my mother. I was ordered to address her as Aunt Atha. She came to our "residence hotel"—a designation which in those days meant a respectable boardinghouse for reduced gentility—in Logan Circle, and escorted us to her grandmother's house, a long street-car ride to northeast Washington.

Small, battened, and unpainted, the house stood back a few steps from a white-washed picket fence along which grew hollyhocks, castor beans, and sunflowers. The old woman, dressed in black, sat in a low rocking chair. The white-washed walls were spotless, like the immaculate old woman. She had a fixed gaze into space: I knew that she was blind. "Is that Nellie Varnell? she said—not "Miss Nellie." My mother said, "Yes, ma'am." She went to the old woman, bent over and kissed the high, pale yellow forehead. The next thing I remember I was being pushed forward and made to sit in a split-bottom chair, facing the old lady. Her sagging skin, too large for her shrunken flesh, had the dull patina of dried mullein; her hair was straight and snow-white. She ran her bird-like claws over my forehead, my ears, my nose, my chin. I was more embarrassed than frightened, and I wanted to get up, but I sat until my mother touched my shoulder; I rose and backed away. Aunt Martha said, "He favors his grandpa." I can still hear her voice, high and weak. It was Tidewater, not Negro. My recollection ends with the resemblance to my grandfather, which the old lady could see through the bony ends of her talons.

Later, Tate says, he learned that family legend had it that Aunt Martha, his great-grandmother's maid, was his great-grandfather's half sister, "the daughter of Dr. John Armistead Bogan (1766–1814) by a slave woman he had bought in the West Indies." "If the sense of a past comes less from family Bibles, old letters, country records, and tombstones, than from the laying on of hands from one generation to another," Tate continues, "then what sense of a living past I may have goes back though the bird-claws of an ancient female slave, my blood-cousin who, ironically enough, in family authority seemed to take precedence over my mother."[6]

For the time being, allow me to hold in suspension, along with further consideration of Jefferson, comment on the significance of Tate's recollection of his boyhood visit to Aunt Martha Jackson, this in order to suggest its context. This I take to have been Tate's lifelong struggle to come to terms with the self-reflective, the autobiographical, impulse. Although his correspondence, poetry, and criticism are obviously important in the record of this struggle, conformance to the necessities of space and time indicates that the focus here be on its most direct expression, which occurs in Tate the biographer and Tate the novelist.[7]

Tate's own acute sensitivity to the relation of autobiography to his three major biographical writings—*Stonewall Jackson: The Good Soldier* (1928), *Jefferson Davis: His Rise and Fall* (1929), and an unfin-

6. Tate, *Memoirs and Opinions*, 13–14. I am indebted to Thomas A. Underwood, the biographer of Tate, for his generous and detailed assistance in the preparation of this essay. With respect to the problem of the authenticity of Tate's connection with Aunt Martha Jackson, the help of Underwood has been indispensable. He has shared with me his knowledge of a nineteenth-century photograph of two black women standing in front of a log cabin with four children, two boys and two girls. An item in the Tate Papers in the Princeton University Library, the photograph bears on the back an annotation in Tate's hand locating the cabin as at either Chestnut Grove or Pleasant Hill, Fairfax County, Virginia, and describing the figures in the picture as Aunt Martha Jackson's daughters and her grandchildren. Born in 1814 or 1815 according to the annotation, Aunt Martha was about 105 years old when she died in 1920 (Thomas A. Underwood to Lewis P. Simpson, December 15, 1991, in author's possession).

7. Thomas D. Young and John J. Hindle remark that in the letters between Tate and his close friend and confidante John Peale Bishop, "One can follow clearly Tate's search for an authoritative source to give order, direction, and meaning to his personal life, from his early hope for the traditional society of the antebellum South to the dogma, doctrine, and discipline of the Roman Catholic Church" (*The Republic of Letters in America: The Correspondence of John Peale Bishop & Allen Tate* [Lexington, Ky., 1981], 7). But although a consideration of Tate's voluminous correspondence as autobiography would be entirely appropriate—he was perhaps the last great American literary correspondent—it would demand a book in itself. Something of the importance of Tate's letters emerges, I think, even in their limited employment in the present discussion. I also touch lightly here on another significant topic, autobiography as criticism in Tate. This is remarked upon in the essay on Tate and the "poetry of criticism" elsewhere in this volume. In the same place I mention the question of poetry as autobiography in Tate but deal only with his critical essays. A consideration of the autobiographical significance of Tate's poetry with respect to his racial attitudes must primarily emphasize his childhood memory of a lynching as set forth in "The Swimmers." For a provocative discussion of this poem, see Lem Colley, "Memoirs and Opinions of Allen Tate," *Southern Review*, n.s., XXVIII (1992), 948–64. *Cf.* below, 114–31.

ished (and unpublished) life of Robert E. Lee—has been illuminated by various students of Tate, including Michael Kreyling in *Figures of the Hero in Southern Narrative* (1987). Exploring the autobiographical inclination as deriving from a quest for exemplary images of heroic character in southern culture, Kreyling sees Tate as having established the proper distance between the biographer and his subject in his assessments of Jackson and Davis but as having had a hard time doing so in his study of Lee. Kreyling's analysis takes on additional meaning, I think, if it is seen in the light of a lengthy letter Tate wrote to John Peale Bishop after he had published his biographies of Jackson and Davis and had begun work on the Lee project. Bishop had just published *Many Thousands Gone,* which Tate characterized as a book of stories about "decayed" southern "ladies and gentlemen."

> I agree with you fully about the character of literature; it is best when it deals with the character of failure. But I think that Southerners are apt to identify the great political and social failure with their characters, or if they are poets and concerned with themselves, with their own failure. The older I get the more I realize that I set out about ten years ago to live a life of failure, to imitate, in my own life, the history of my people. For it was only in this fashion, considering the circumstances, that I could completely identify myself with them. We have an instinct—if we are artists particularly—to live at the center of some way of life and to be borne up by its innermost significance. The significance of the Southern way of life, in my time, is failure; those Southerners who leave their culture—and it is abandoned most fully by those who stay at home—and succeed in some not too critical meaning of success, sacrifice some great part of their deepest heritage. What else is there for me but a complete acceptance of the idea of failure? There is no other "culture" that I can enter into, even if I had the desire—and of course I assume that one needs the whole pattern of life: I can't keep half of it and live on another style the other half of the time. And it seems to me that only in this fashion can a Southerner achieve in his writing what you call the "impersonal judgement"; for otherwise his standards will be drawn for some other equally

temporary way of life, rather than a perception that the old Southerners did not reach perfection in the style that they developed or the style that they lived up to.[8]

The underlying rationale of Tate's biographical ventures, the above letter suggests, was the establishment of the three great leaders of the Confederacy—Jackson, Davis, and Lee—as exemplary figures of a culture he had conceived in his search to find his own identity. Shaped by the "great political and social failure" of the South, this culture, Tate suggested, conferred identity on all southerners whether they wanted to identify with it or not. Establishing the exemplary figures of this culture was a way of establishing his own identity. But Tate ran into trouble in the case of Lee. Over a year later, in October, 1932, Tate announced to Bishop that he had made a signal discovery: "Lee did not love power; my thesis about him, stated in these terms, is that he didn't love it because he was profoundly cynical of all action for the public good. He could not see beyond the needs of his own salvation, and he was not generous enough to risk soiling his military cloak for the doubtful salvation of others." Yet even though he had come to feel this way about Lee, Tate said, he was "kept awake at night" because he "couldn't prove a word of it."[9]

Tate's dilemma was that he could not accommodate Lee to the southern culture of failure. He had viewed Jackson as an example of the survival of the southerner as the "integral" man of action, a social type rendered obsolete by the failure of a traditional society in the South. He had seen Davis as an anticipation of the separation of intellect and feeling that accompanies the breakdown of tradition. But he was completely vexed by the problem of presenting "the marble man"—the southern leader who had become a deity—as a figure of southern culture. Tate's vexation was increased by the fact that for his biography of Lee he had an expectant audience of self-conscious southern intellectuals, including his fellow Agrarians, waiting for

8. Michael Kreyling, *Figures of the Hero in Southern Narrative* (Baton Rouge, 1987), 112–21; Allen Tate to John Peale Bishop, early June, 1931, in *The Republic of Letters in America,* ed. Young and Hindle, 34.

9. Tate to Bishop, October 19, 1932, in *The Republic of Letters in America,* ed. Young and Hindle, 64–65.

him to give them a Lee complex enough to personify the "innermost significance" of the defeated South—a Lee who could be mounted on the pedestal formerly occupied by George Washington as a southern father figure. Symbolizing the truth of the union of states achieved by the American Revolution, Washington had served as the emblem of the truth the Confederate States of America believed they represented and had appropriately enough been the figure chosen for the Great Seal of the Confederacy. The spiritual confederacy that arose after the military defeat of the South required another symbolic father, a hero of victory in defeat.

Seeing his friend's agony about the Lee biography, Bishop suggested that the key to Tate's difficulty was the suppression of his desire to identify Lee with himself. Allow Lee to take on your own character, Bishop advised Tate: "Proceed with your Lee: If it is not true to the facts of Lee's life, it will be true to you. And that is more important. You are, alas, a poet." Bishop asked Tate to remember "a work you may despise, Renan's *Life of Jesus,* which "is not a life of Jesus but of Renan." Yet "strangely that does not detract from its value. Many people could write us lives of Jesus. . . . But only Renan could write the life of Jesus as Renan." Thus, Bishop concluded, if Tate should "write the life of the Southerner (yourself, myself, all of us) in terms of Lee, so much more will it be than a life of Lee."[10]

But Tate was overwhelmed by his sensitivity to the problem of writing a life of Lee that would be at the same time his own self-biography and, so to speak, an autobiography of the South. His complex awareness of the moral burden his self-conscious quest for his cultural identity as a southerner had placed on him was too much. He had to find a way of alleviating it.

Actually, well before Bishop had written in 1932 urging him to go forward with the Lee biography, Tate had been thinking about finding a more direct way to come to terms with the autobiographical impulse. He now turned to this way, which would involve autobiography as genealogy or, less narrowly put, as family history.

I'm taking my own ancestry [he wrote to Bishop in February, 1932], beginning with Robert Reade in Va. about 1638 and

10. Bishop to Tate, October 19–26, 1932, *ibid.,* 65.

bringing it down to my brother and myself, who are fairly good types of modern America, absolutely different but motivated by the same blood traits. The mechanical, or external form, will be that of the regular genealogy, much epitomized and foreshortened; there will be two chief figures to a generation, who will be dealt with simultaneously for contrast, and each generation will get a chapter, about eight in all. Although each new chapter will introduce two new figures, each of them will continue what his father stood for, and I think the continuity will be preserved. The fundamental contrast will be between the Va. tidewater idea—stability, land, the establishment—and the pioneer, who frequently of course took on the Va. idea, even in Tenn., but who usually had some energy left over, which has made modern America. My brother and I will show these two types fairly well. Most of the names will have to be fictitious, especially those near me in time, and I will have to make some imaginative leaps in the dark where there are only records of birth, death, and marriage to go on. But that, I think, is legitimate. I believe the idea is almost wholly new, outside pure fiction.[11]

In his scheme to write autobiography as family history, Tate projects himself and his brother (Ben Tate, a successful businessman) as types less specifically of the South than of "modern America" and envisions a story essentially centered, not in the making of the modern South, but in the making of modern America. Yet he indicates he is at the same time thinking of a story emphasizing the intimate history of his own family, which he will to some degree disguise and, to some extent, when the historical record is inadequate, invent. Planning what would now be called a "nonfiction novel," Tate, had he fulfilled his plan, might conceivably have written an autobiography of a thoroughly self-conscious southern American who is at once fictional and real. It would have been a work comparable to Henry Adams' autobiography of an eminently self-conscious New Englander, but Tate could not do what Adams did in his *Education*. He could not devise a way to handle the self-referential element.

11. Tate to Bishop, February 11, 1932, *ibid.,* 52.

His inability to do so is implied in the revised scheme for his book Tate had developed by May 31, 1933, when he described it in a letter to Ellen Glasgow as involving "the growth of a family in Virginia, and its fall in the war," and "the wanderings and final settlement in Kentucky" of another family, "a typical Scotch-Irish family." The second part of the story would deal "with these two strains in the chaos of the Reconstruction," when "the Virginians go west to St. Louis, and the Kentuckians go there [too]; so that we get a typically modern combination, no longer based upon the land, but committed to the disorder and competitive struggles of modern capitalist society." The final chapter, to be called "Anonymous Confession," would consist of "the chaotic protest of a woman produced by the union of the Tidewater and Scotch-Irish strains—her protest against the aimless life to which she is committed without quite understanding why it is aimless." Through this character, Tate said, he would offer his "judgement upon the modern mind." [12]

By the time he had come up with the revised plan he sent to Glasgow, Tate had decided on a title for his book. He would call it "Ancestors of Exile," thus providing a specific and provocative focus on the idea that the sense of exile the modern southerner experiences is inherent in the failure of the exiles who were his forebears to establish a stable culture. As Tate summarized it for Glasgow, the plan of "Ancestors of Exile" would transform the Tennesseans in the original plan into Kentuckians. The reason for this may have had something to do with a perceived need to mask the identity of family members appearing in the story. It probably had more to do with the need Tate felt to increase the distance between himself and his projected work. This becomes clear in his scheme to turn over the whole story finally to the "anonymous" and "chaotic" confession of a family descendant, a woman who is living her aimless, rootless existence in the "modern capitalist society" of St. Louis. Her confession will reveal that her life is the product not of the simple merging of the "Va. tidewater idea" of landed stability and the pioneer compulsion to movement and acquisitiveness, but of "the union of the Tidewater and Scotch-Irish strains." Tate meant the blood union of

---

12. Allen Tate to Ellen Glasgow, May 31, 1933, quoted in Radcliffe Squires, *Allen Tate: A Literary Biography* (New York, 1971), 128–29.

the English strain represented by the manorial class of County Kent—
the aristocratic Kentish "cousinage" it has been called—and the Irish
strain represented by the small farmers and shopkeepers who made
up the bulk of the Protestant dissenters who took refuge in northern
Ireland. Tate's is the aristocratic presumption: Tradition is more than
a matter of class, it is a matter of blood. It has been destroyed, Tate
seems to mean, by the ominous, democratic union of bloodlines.
The anonymous woman in St. Louis will be the ultimate symbol of
the progressive exile of southerners from the original European
homeland. Whatever he was attempting to do in his effort to imagine
"Ancestors of Exile," Tate had arrived at the point of making an
equation between blood, self, and mind that he had not made in the
earlier scheme, and in doing so of implying that the Virginia culture—the culture of the Virginia cousinage, an integral culture of
land, mind, and blood—had been corrupted by the mixing of the
Virginia bloodline with that of the Scotch-Irish pioneers. Once he
allowed the mixing of bloodlines to become a theme in his projected
story of the "ancestors" of the exile of the modern southerner—and
thus of the experience of exile Tate was seeking to define as his own
fate—he had opened his story up to the most sensitive issue in southern culture, that of the blood relation between black and white.

There seems no direct evidence of any influence that Tate's awareness of the graphic symbol of this relation in his own family, that is,
the relationship between Major Bogan and Aunt Martha, may have
had on his imagination as he strove to devise a feasible plan for "Ancestors of Exile." He did not seem to consider injecting any racial
theme other than that of the difference between the Virginians (or
the English) and the Scotch-Irish. But one wonders whether the explanation Tate gave to Bishop when he finally abandoned "Ancestors
of Exile" may not hide as much as it reveals about his motives. He
had, he told Bishop, resolved "a crisis in his lengthening attempt to
get on with 'Ancestors of Exile'" by making a drastic decision: "I
have out of heroism or cowardice (take your choice) thrown over the
ancestry book forever." Saying that the "agony" of the decision was
"great but the peace of mind is greater," Tate observed that he had
"a simple problem" but could not solve it: "The discrepancy between the outward significance and the private was so enormous that
I decided I could not handle the material in that form at all without

faking either the significance or the material." He had wasted two years, Tate added, but had "learned a lesson." How valuable this lesson would be depended on whether he "made the same mistake again." [13]

Tate did not repeat the mistake. His rectification of it five years later in *The Fathers* makes this work, his only novel, one of his signal achievements—and perhaps, though it has not usually been thought of in quite this way, the most distinguished fulfillment of the impulse to autobiography on the part of any southern novelist. In *The Fathers,* which represents not an adaptation but a transformation of the two abortive schemes for "Ancestors of Exile," Tate and his brother become brothers-in-law: Lacy Buchan, scion of the landed Virginia aristocracy, who tells the story as one who had lived through it many years ago, and George Posey, son of a family that had given up its attachment to the land. But conceiving of the Poseys as being, like the Buchans, descendants of the Virginia bloodline, Tate eliminated from the scheme of "the ancestry book" the idea of a corrupt mingling of the Virginia and Scotch-Irish bloodlines. Instead he brought into *The Fathers* the far more crucial and powerful element of miscegenation. In doing so he resolved the "discrepancy between the outward significance and the private" that had earlier seemed so great that he could not write "Ancestors of Exile" except by "faking either the significance or the material." The key to the resolution was Tate's perception that the quintessential relation in a slave society is the social and personal connection between master and slave. Although the majority of the citizens of the southern states were not slaveholders, this relation, greatly complicated by the racial difference between master and slave, dominated all other relations in the Old South, thereby reducing the significance of the relation between the descendants of a European manorial class and a European rural class. Even though the American South still retained the characteristics of a frontier society, the social relation was not, as Tate had first attempted to see it, between traditionalists and frontiersmen. What happened to the myth of tradition in such a society?

Let us return to Tate's poignant record of his visit with Aunt

13. Tate to Bishop, October 30, 1933, in *The Republic of Letters in America,* ed. Young and Hindle, 84–85.

Martha Jackson in 1912 or 1913, an incident that, as he began later to "fit it into a pattern," afforded, he says, "a glimpse of the past that reversed my stance at the time it happened." He was no longer "looking back" but "had been shifted to the past" and from that vantage point was looking "into a future that nobody but myself at the end of the eighteenth century could have seen." At an early age a precocious mind had been brought into a special intimacy with memory and history.

Immediately before he begins the account of Aunt Martha, Tate falls into a provocative meditation on the meaning of memory that may be regarded as a preparation for the account of his visit with her:

> Poets, perhaps even more than novelists, are not unlike hunters who stand in tall weeds, waiting for the dove to fly from the field of millet to the water in the creek which will renew her life; and then we blaze away and the dove drops in the weeds on our side of the field. One September day in the valley below Sewanee, twenty-five years ago, I shot a dove that fell into the weeds, and when I found her she was lying head up with a gout of blood in each eye. I shot her again. Her life had been given to my memory; and I have never hunted from that day.

This account of Tate's last hunt is followed by a remarkable depiction of the progress of memory:

> Memory arrests the flow of inner time, but what we remember is not at the command of our wills; it has its own life and purposes; it gives what it wills. St. Augustine tells us that memory is like a woman. The Latin *memoria* is properly a feminine noun, for women never forget; and likewise the soul is the *anima*, even in man, his vital principle and the custodian of memory, the image of woman that all men both pursue and flee. The feminine memory says: Here is that dying dove; you must really kill it this time or you will not remember it from all the other birds you have killed; take it or leave it; I have given it to you. The imaginative writer is the archeologist of memory, dedicated to the minute parti-

culars of the past, definite things—*prima sacrimenti memoria.*
If his "city" is to come alive again from a handful of shards,
he will try to fit them together in an elusive jigsaw puzzle,
most of the pieces of which are forever lost.[14]

Juxtaposing the story of the visit to Aunt Martha Jackson, in
which Tate reveals not only that the ancient slave seems to have an
authority greater than his mother's but that she is his blood cousin,
and the story of the frustration of his autobiographical impulse, we
have—do we not?—the key to this frustration. And in *The Fathers,*
published five years after Tate gave up on "Ancestors of Exile," we
have the key at last placed in the lock and turned and the door
opened, though opened reluctantly, on the failed society of which
Tate considered himself to be an exemplary expression. The corruption of the bloodline of the Virginia cousinage was Tate's "dying
dove," and, if he was to be a true biographer of himself and his culture—a true archaeologist of memory—was that particular thing
that his memory must acknowledge in order to put the shards of the
past into a meaningful order. Thereby he would be enabled to write
the autobiography that would fulfill his quest for the paternity of the
South and of himself. Tate did not explicitly articulate this self-
knowledge until late in his life, and then only in one vivid moment
in "A Lost Traveller's Dream" the recollection of his visit with the
blind Aunt Martha, who confers on him his identity through her
voice—"Tidewater, not Negro"—and "through the bony ends of
her talons" on his face. But in *The Fathers,* through endowing the
memory of a surrogate, Lacy Buchan, with the "feminine memory,"
Tate had found a way to symbolize in the story of the mulatto Jim's
death at the hands of Semmes Buchan, Lacy's brother, and George
Posey, Jim's half-brother, a hidden yet major motive of the suppressed autobiography of the southerner and of the South.

Involving the whole configuration of southern history—a
tragedy, or tragicomedy, of land, mind, slavery, family, blood, race,
and memory—this motive seldom emerges in an overt way in antebellum records. One of the most dramatic instances of its doing so is
in a letter James Henry Hammond of South Carolina wrote to his

---

14. Tate, *Memoirs and Opinions,* 12.

son Henry in 1856. A complex, driven man, at one time governor of his state, at another a member of the United States Senate, and the author of a major defense of the institution of slavery, Hammond had in 1839 purchased a seamstress named Sally and her one-year-old daughter named Louisa. He had made Sally his mistress and, when Louisa was twelve, had taken her as a mistress as well. The tortured result of this relationship is set forth by the ailing Hammond in a letter about his will.

> In the last will I made and left to you, over and above my other children Sally Johnson the mother of Louisa and all the children of both, Sally says Henderson is my child. It is possible, but I do not believe it. Yet act on her's rather than my opinion. Louisa's first child may be mine. Take care of her and her children who are both of *your* blood if not of mine and of Henderson. The services of the rest will I think compensate for an indulgence to these. I cannot free these people and send them North. It would be cruelty to them. Nor would I like that any but my own blood should own as Slaves my own blood or Louisa. I leave them to your charge, believing that you will best appreciate and most independently carry out my wishes in regard to them. Do not let Louisa or any of my children or possible children be slaves of Strangers. Slavery in the *family* will be their happiest earthly condition.[15]

When *The Fathers* was republished in 1977 in the Library of Southern Civilization Series of the Louisiana State University Press, almost forty years after it had first appeared and seventeen years after its republication in the often-reprinted Swallow Press edition, readers discovered that Tate had not only revised the conclusion of his novel but added both a preface and an afterword in which he explains the purpose of the revision. In the original version of the ending, Lacy Buchan, an elderly bachelor physician recalling the

---

15. James Henry Hammond to James Henry "Harry" Hammond, February 19, 1856, in *Secret and Sacred: The Diaries of James Henry Hammond, a Southern Slaveholder*, ed. Carol K. Bleser (New York, 1988), 19.

story of his family and the Poseys of Virginia in the years right before the Civil War, tells about how he and his brother-in-law, George Posey, after having participated in the first battle of Manassas, go their separate ways. As George, taking leave of the Confederate forces for good, rides away into the dark, Lacy, in the first version of the ending of the novel, remembers thinking:

> I'll go back and finish it. I'll have to finish it. It won't make any difference if I am killed. If I am killed it will be because I love him more than any other man.[16]

In the second version Lacy says:

> I went back and stayed until Appomattox four years later. George could not finish it; he had important things to do that I knew nothing about. As I stood by his grave in Holyrood cemetery fifty years later I remembered how he restored his wife and small daughter and what he did for me. What he became in himself I shall never forget. Because of this I venerate his memory more than the memory of any other man.[17]

According to Tate, the revised ending of the story suggests to the reader more clearly than the original version Lacy's sense of a contrast between his father, Major Buchan, "a classical hero, whose *hubris* destroys him," and George Posey, "a modern romantic hero," who is capable of taking his family into the world of the New South. But the reader may well find, as does Cleanth Brooks, that Lacy's regard for George is even more difficult to understand in the revised ending than in the original one.[18] Even if Lacy mutes his declaration that he "loves" George "more than any other man" by saying that he "venerates" the memory of George "more than the memory of any other man," it is difficult to accept his regard for a man who, ignor-

16. Allen Tate, *"The Fathers" and Other Fiction* (Rev. ed.; Baton Rouge, 1977), 314.

17. *Ibid.*, 306–307.

18. Thomas Daniel Young, Introduction to Tate, *"The Fathers" and Other Fiction,* xxi; Cleanth Brooks, "The Past Alive in the Present," in *American Literature and the Historical Consciousness: Essays in Honor of Lewis P. Simpson,* ed. J. Gerald Kennedy and Daniel Mark Fogel (Baton Rouge, 1987), 222–25.

ing the ideals of proper conduct and good manners, not to speak of the principles of honor represented by Major Buchan, has shot Lacy's brother and driven his sister mad.

In the "Note" appended to the new edition of *The Fathers,* Tate says, "George shot Semmes not in rational revenge but in instantaneous reflex action," this being an "instinctive response" to an "all-but-forgotten scandal" in the Posey family, the result of which is that Jim is George's half-brother. "It is," Tate says, "almost as if Semmes had tried to shoot . . . George himself." Given that George, in need of ready cash, has somewhat earlier callously sold Jim and that Jim has come back to Pleasant Hill as a runaway, it is plausible to read George's act of killing Semmes as a spontaneous self-redemptive response to the violation of a generally suppressed yet at times, as in the case of James Henry Hammond, poignantly acknowledged historical reality. The historical credibility of George's motive in killing Semmes provides a credible basis for Lacy's seemingly unwarranted regard for George at the end of *The Fathers,* especially in the version of the ending when, standing by his grave, Lacy remembers how "George restored his wife and small daughter and what he did for me" and adds significantly, "What he became in himself I shall never forget." What George became in himself is of course what Lacy Buchan had become in himself, namely, a survivor. In order to survive in a new age Lacy has subtly but powerfully identified George with the sense of family and history that had been implanted in him at the Buchan plantation, Pleasant Hill. He has, in other words, paradoxically made George an emblem of the survival of the virtue of the past in the present. Necessary to Lacy's survival, this transformation of George's character is also necessary to Tate's survival, as Tate recognized when he said George Posey bore a resemblance to his own businessman brother, Ben, on whom Tate at certain times depended heavily for economic assistance.[19] If, as Tate observes, Lacy is George's surrogate in the sense that he attributes his own words to George, Lacy is in a deeper sense not merely Tate's surrogate but the author of Tate's autobiography. Through Lacy's imagination of the South as embodied in the relationship of George, Semmes, Jim, and himself, Tate symbolizes what he had largely suppressed: his aware-

19. Tate, *Memoirs and Opinions,* 6.

ness of the most essential aspect of the inner history of the South, its suppressed image of its existence—this in contrast to its official image of itself as a harmonious community of benevolent masters and happy servants—as a tortured and unwilling community of white masters and black slaves.

I said at the beginning of these remarks that I would be engaged with speculations, and it will be clear by now that no more than Tate could prove his intuitions about Robert E. Lee's character can I prove my speculation, or intuition, that in the character of Tate as a reluctant autobiographer lies the answer to the absence in southern writing of a deeply self-reflective narrative like *Walden*. I refer specifically to Tate's perception of the inhibition of the biographical impulse by the difference between the public and the private, or the inner, significance of his personal and family history. The answer becomes more plausible when we discover that long before Tate such a discrepancy is manifest in the expression of the autobiographical impulse in the antebellum South, not only in Hammond in the heyday of the Cotton Kingdom but earlier, in the time of the fathers of the Republic.

I would attach a primary importance to two texts that I believe may with some poetic license be thought of as autobiographies not only of the nation created by the Revolution and the Constitution but of that nation, the Confederate States of America, that was already standing in the wings of the historical stage when the Missouri crisis occurred in 1819 and 1820. By the time of the writing of the texts I have in mind—the time of the immediate aftermath of the Missouri crisis—this nation had moved perceptibly closer to the moment of its entrance on the stage.

One of these, as I indicated at the beginning of these remarks, is Jefferson's *Autobiography*.[20] Under the license granted by the imperial extension of the meaning of the term, we may include in the realm of autobiography both the Declaration of Independence and *Notes on the State of Virginia* and, for that matter, all of the letters Jefferson wrote in carrying on his monumental personal correspondence. And we may easily include surely the second text I have in mind at this point, a singular writing by Jefferson's fellow Virginian and his suc-

20. See Cox, *Recovering Literature's Lost Ground*, 33–34.

cessor in the presidency, James Madison. Entitled "Jonathan and Mary Bull," it is an allegorical fantasy concerning slavery and the American vis-à-vis the southern identity.

If one accepts as truth the notorious story of Jefferson's long liaison with Sally Hemings and his fathering of children by her, one must say that unlike a James Henry Hammond might have done, Jefferson absolutely suppressed the autobiographical imperative to reveal that liaison. To believe the story about Jefferson and his female slave on the basis of the psychohistorical evidence offered, most prominently by the late Fawn Brodie, is to accept unfounded hypotheses as empirical facts. We find a more certain guide to Jefferson's attitude toward the inward significance of slavery in his life in the insightful study of Jefferson by James Cox I have referred to above. I have in mind primarily his discerning analysis of the relationship of the original text of the Declaration to the *Autobiography*. Jefferson's recovery of his original text, Cox argues, is Jefferson's *Autobiography,* for forty-five years earlier in the Declaration he had "translated himself into a text that began the history and life of his people."[21] A major aspect of this history, as the Missouri crisis made apparent, was the question of slavery in a republic dedicated, according to the clear implication of the Declaration, to its origination in the fundamental sovereignty of the individual. Yet, taking a slightly different tack from Cox, we may observe that if Jefferson translated himself into the text of the version of the Declaration passed by the Continental Congress in 1775, he translated himself fully into the text of the original version. As set forth in the *Autobiography* this version included, in the enumeration of specific complaints against the king, Jefferson's strenuous condemnation of the sovereign for waging "war against human nature itself, violating its most sacred rights of life and liberty in the persons of a distant people, who never offended him, captivating & carrying them into slavery into another hemisphere, or to incur miserable death in their transportation thither."[22] Implying the necessity of maintaining a distinction between the history of a "distant people," who had been forcibly carried into the midst of those he knew as "his own people," Jefferson at the same

21. *Ibid.*
22. Thomas Jefferson, *Autobiography,* ed. Merrill D. Peterson (New York, 1984), 22.

time acknowledges the alien captives as being a part of the human community and thus entitled to the sacred rights of individual human beings. Jefferson in truth could not translate himself into the text that began the history and life of his people—that is, in the closest sense, the Anglo-Saxon Virginians—without, whether he wanted to or not, translating himself into a text that had also begun a new history of the life of the African slaves who had been imported into the new nation. Jefferson, to be sure, believed or tried to believe that the enslaved Africans belonged to another history and sought all of his life to reattach them to this other history by advocating their deportation to the world they had come from. Living this delusion, he could remain both the author of the Declaration and the slave master who, seated at Monticello, ruled a slave dominion consisting of several plantations and several hundred slaves; who advised his overseers not to overwork pregnant females in the fields, for their offspring would bring more in the slave market than fruit of their labor would in the commodity market; who as the slave question began to agitate the nation tended to become a southern nationalist, and would inevitably have become one, had he lived another ten years.[23]

In an overall sense Jefferson suppressed the knowledge he had intimated in the famous and singular eighteenth chapter of *Notes on the State of Virginia:* the knowledge that he was living with slaves who were becoming African Americans as surely as the British were becoming Anglo-Americans; the knowledge that the alien black self as it became less alien and more "Americanized" would emancipate itself from the self of the white master, while at the same time the self of the master—ironically trapped by the idea that its very freedom depended on its perpetuation of a benevolent but complete and permanent dominion over the black slaves—would realize more and more the impossibility of emancipating itself from its bondage to slavery.

Something like the ultimate irony in all of this is the way in which the Declaration of Independence in Jefferson's original version may be viewed as at once a fable involving three elements: the freeing

23. See John Chester Miller, *The Wolf by the Ears: Thomas Jefferson and Slavery* (New York, 1977), 264–72.

of the enslaved selfhood of the white colonists from a cruel parent, the British king; the king's inhuman enslavement of the inferior self-hood of the Africans; and (by implication) the ultimate freeing of the Africans through their return to their homeland after the Revolution. But the African slave, having been placed in the context of a society that had been invented in written texts energized by the dynamic idea of the sovereignty of the white (Anglo-Saxon) democratic self, needed only to attain literacy in the language of his master (sufficient reading and writing skills in English) in order to become a Frederick Douglass and assert the presence of a black selfhood in American history. Was it not this underlying possibility, the anxious fear of the awakened selfhood of the African slave, that caused Jefferson—divided, even contradictory, in some of his attitudes toward slavery—to remain so constant in his desire to see the slaves free only on condition of their transportation? And was this fear—one that becomes at least semiarticulate in Jefferson—accompanied by a more profound fear, namely, that the Anglo-Saxon selfhood had already been hopelessly corrupted by a mingling of the Anglo-Saxon and African bloodlines?

Whereas this deeper fear does not become articulate in Jefferson—was not even utterable to him—its existence in the patrician mind of Virginia is evident in the satirical fable Madison wrote at the same time that Jefferson was writing his *Autobiography,* a time when both the founders of the Republic, having grown old, saw the prospect of some catastrophic culmination of the "Great Experiment" they had helped to inaugurate.

Madison's little story is about Jonathan Bull and Mary Bull, "who were the descendants of old John Bull, the head of the family," and the inheritors of "contiguous estates in large tracts of land." The degree of the relationship of Jonathan and Mary is not made clear. Perhaps they can be thought of as first cousins; Old Bull, their "guardian," has a strong degree of control over them. Becoming "well acquainted" as they grew up, John and Mary advance toward a "matrimonial connexion" that will "put their two estates under a common superintendence"; but Old Bull, wanting "as guardian of both" to "get all the property into his own hands," tries to prevent their marriage. Eventually, nonetheless, "giving effect to the feelings long entertained for each other, an intermarriage was determined and solemnized, with a deed of settlement . . . duly executed." The marriage bore fruit, and as each new child was born the parent allotted a portion of land "to be put under the authority of the child on its attaining the age of manhood." But with "the tenth or eleventh fruit of the marriage," Jonathan raised "difficulties" about "the rules and conditions declaring the young party of age, and of giving him . . . the management of his patrimony." Declaring that "an arrangement ought to be made that would prevent the new farm from being settled and cultivated . . . indiscriminately," as had been the case before, by tenants from "his and Mary's estates," Jonathan wanted to restrict the migration to people from his own estate. He was also perturbed by the "selection of the head stewards," who seemed to come more often from Mary's estate than his.

A more important reason for Jonathan's difficulties with Mary, however, was his sudden revulsion against a "peculiarity" in her "person." In her childhood, it seems, she had been allowed to bathe in a river on her estate that had been contaminated by the spill of a "noxious cargo" of black dye. As a result, Mary's left arm was permanently stained black. Although Jonathan had known about this deformity and had never seemed concerned about it, he now began not only to point to the fact that he himself "was white all over" but to insist that if Mary could not have the color removed from her arm—even though this meant tearing "off the skin from the flesh," or even cutting off the offending limb—he would sue for divorce and make "an end to all connexion between them and their states." At first Mary was so taken aback by Jonathan's behavior that she made a violently emotional response to him, but in a calmer state thereafter considered the good qualities he had heretofore shown and "changed her tone to that of sober reasoning and affectionate expostulation." She reminded Jonathan that at the time of their marriage he too "had spots and specks scattered" over his body "as black as the skin on my arm." The "fatal African dye" had found "its way into your abode as well as mine," Mary observed to Jonathan. Although he had been able "in some measure" to remove the stain, it still visibly remained and should serve to remind him to have "forbearance and sympathy" with her condition, one much more difficult to alter.

Instead of that [Mary protested] you abuse me as if I had brought the misfortune on myself, and could remove it at will; or as if you had pointed out a ready way to do it, and I had slighted your advice. Yet so far is this from being the case, that you know as well as I do that I am not to be blamed for the origin of the sad mishap; as I am as anxious as you to be rid of it. . . . When you talk of tearing off the skin, or cutting off the unfortunate limb, must I remind you, of what you cannot be ignorant, that the most skillful surgeons have given their opinions that if such an operation were to be tried, it could hardly fail to be followed by mortification, or a bleeding to death? Let me ask, too, should neither of the fatal effects ensue, would you like me better in my mangled or mutilated condition than you do now?

Mary thereupon launches into a discussion of the mutual economic and political benefits presently derived from the connection of the two estates. The upshot is that Jonathan, "who had a good heart as well as a sound head and steady temper, was touched with this tender and considerate language of Mary, and the bickering which had sprung up ended, as the quarrels of lovers *always* do, and of married folks *sometimes* do, in an increased affection and confidence between the parties."[24]

In his impressive biography of Madison's later years, *The Last of the Fathers,* Drew R. McCoy describes "Jonathan and Mary Bull" as a "playful contribution to what was then a familiar genre of 'John Bull' satire." Only "a private source of personal amusement" to Madison, McCoy says, it remained unpublished until the 1850s, when "the collector in whose hands it had fallen published it in the midst of an even more serious sectional crisis." Cautioning that "drawing serious inferences about Madison's views on slavery from this whimsical flight" requires prudence, McCoy sees Madison's allegory of the Missouri crisis as a plea for moderation and reason in the treatment of the slave question and, in an indirect way, a plea for

24. James Madison, "Jonathan and Mary Bull," in *Letters and Other Writings of James Madison,* ed. William C. Rives and Philip Fendall (4 vols.; Philadelphia, 1865), III, 249–56.

its solution by the abolition of slavery and the removal of Africans from the United States.[25]

But Madison's singular attempt in the realm of literary fantasy tempts us to search his satire for more subtle meanings. One indirect suggestion Madison makes—one not so subtle in that it is common to all the satirical fantasies about John Bull and the American Revolution and its aftermath—is that the relationship between the American colonists and the Empire is rather different from that set forth in the Declaration of Independence. For rhetorical reasons Jefferson and his fellow rebels chose quite deliberately to portray their rebellion as one against monarchical tyranny and thus to charge all their grievances to George III. John Bull was no monarch. Invented—at least first given tangible embodiment by John Arbuthnot—he appeared initially in a series of satirical political pamphlets in 1712, which in collected form were entitled *The History of John Bull*. A substitute for the decline of the image of the king or the queen as the symbol of the energizing source of the nation, John Bull is described as an "honest, plain-dealing fellow, choleric, bold . . . very apt to quarrel with his best friends, especially if they pretended to govern him" yet, in spite of his mercurial temperament, also "a boon companion, loving his bottle and his diversion." In specific terms, John Bull is Scotland and his wife is Parliament, and she bears her husband three daughters: Polemia, Discordia, and Usuria. In a general sense, John Bull is the symbolic figure of an imperial Britain, the true image of which was not the royal but the bourgeois family. Becoming a widely known ichnography in the popular press, the John Bull satires took on an American dimension as the Revolutionary struggle developed. When an American preacher said in 1778, "Let this war be considered a family quarrel, disgraceful, shameful, into which we are innocently plunged," he no doubt was aware that ten years or so earlier the aspect of the family quarrel had been introduced into the pre-Revolutionary agitation in a satire in the Newport *Mercury* entitled, in imitation of Arbuthnot's original John Bull pamphlets, "The History of John Bull's Children." The children are the thirteen colonies, all bastards born of John Bull's liaison with a serving girl. Describing

25. Drew R. McCoy, *The Last of the Fathers: James Madison and the Republican Legacy* (New York, 1989), 275–76.

the cruel treatment of Bull's unwanted illegitimate offspring, the satire in the *Mercury* deplores—the time is that of the Stamp Act crisis—the way in which after his "early abandonment" of them, John Bull now demands their return.[26]

In the period after the Revolution, the best-known development in the John Bull mode was James Kirke Paulding's account of the history of the colonies and their revolt against England in *The Diverting History of John Bull and Brother Jonathan,* published in 1813 during the second war with England. But Madison's application of the John Bull convention seems to have no precise precedent in American political humor. In spite of the qualified hope it expresses for the achievement of unity and tranquility in the American Republic following the Missouri Compromise, Madison's curious allegory impresses one as being basically a dark autobiographical fable by an author-father of the new Republic—a nation that he, though not so dramatically as Jefferson, had indispensably helped to author, or to write into existence, or, in the popular metaphor, to father; a nation that had originated in bright promise but, like a character in a Hawthorne story, was doomed by a fatal defect. Presumably Madison's awareness of the more drastic implications of the metaphorical structure of his fable was limited. Yet to what extent, one wonders, did Madison consciously repress his awareness of the implications of his fable? Was he aware that in his portrayal of the origin of the American Republic in the merging of the estates of Jonathan Bull (the North) and Mary Bull (the South) he was suggesting a bizarre mingling of innocence, incest, and miscegenation in the national history? Did he fail to publish "Jonathan and Mary Bull" because he wanted to keep its significance private?

Like Jefferson, Madison had publicly pursued the policy of abolishing slavery through colonization. One way to read his fable—which, it will be noted, completely suppresses the threat of the self-hood or self-identity of the slaves—is as an implied plea for the removal from the nation, and not simply from the South, of an alien race of inferior selves. Indeed, Madison's allegory emphasizes that the unremediable stain of the "noxious spill" from the African cargo

26. John Arbuthnot, *The History of John Bull,* ed. Alan W. Bower and Robert A. Erickson (New York, 1976), 9; see Jay Fliegelman, *Prodigals and Pilgrims: The American Revolution Against Patriarchal Authority, 1750–1800* (New York, 1982).

is borne not only by the South but by the self-righteous North. To say that Mary Bull, the matriarchal symbol of the South, and the dominant voice in the fable, is stained by the African dye is virtually to say that the bloodstream of the South is fatally mixed with African blood; to say that the North has also been speckled with the same stain is virtually to say that the whole nation is tainted by African blood. In Madison's vision, if we take it literally, the progeny of an original incestuous or semi-incestuous Anglo-Saxon cousinage—Massachusetts, one must remember, was as vividly conscious of the Saxon bloodline as was Virginia—has been further corrupted by miscegenation. The American people are anything but a new people emancipated from the history of Old World imperialism and poised to begin a new history that will redeem the world.

Obviously Madison did not mean to say this. Maybe he is made to say it here only through a perverse flight of historical fancy on my part; we can hardly fail to see, nonetheless, that in his metaphorical structuring of history, Madison trafficked with a darkness in his quest for the meaning of the Republic and its legacy to the future. Following an impulse to reveal his intuition of the tragic pathos of the unfolding, intricately ironic story of himself and the nation he has fathered (written)—and yet unwilling to abandon hope for the outcome of the story—he hides it in the artifice of a satirical fable with a mock happy ending. Madison anticipates Tate over a century later, who, not being able to reconcile the private and public significance of the complex and appalling story of himself and of his family—a story of slavery, race, and America—hides it in the artifice of *The Fathers,* a dark tale that in a puzzling way toward the end of his life he revised to have a romantic and happy ending.

Tate's sense of identity depended on his will to imagine himself engaged in a final effort to redeem the South as a traditionalist community—perhaps the last surviving old European community in the West—from the forces of modern history, when in fact, descended from a great slave society, a modern chattel slave society that had been forcibly destroyed only in the generation before Tate was born, the South could not effectively serve as a symbol of the survival of the older culture.

Tate of course knew this. He had a gift of historical insight that he once described as having been bestowed on him when, reflecting on his childhood visit to Aunt Martha Jackson, he began to fit the incident "into a pattern," with the unexpected result that instead of the experiences of "looking back" he had the experience of being "shifted into the past," so that he was looking into a future that "nobody but myself at the end of the eighteenth century could have seen." But Madison, and Jefferson, too, had certain gifts of insight and would have understood the moment a century after their time when, according to his recollection as an old man, the thirteen-year-old Tate came into the presence of his great-grandfather's half sister, a slave freed by the Civil War. By the old southern convention, like any aging black woman she was called "aunt" (as an older black man was called "uncle"), but Aunt Martha Jackson had a blood claim on Tate's family and was, in ironic fact, Tate says, the dominant matriarchal presence in the Tate connection and its high priestess of memory. But as Jefferson and Madison did, in his struggles against history Tate at times repressed his insights.

The scene of Tate's childhood encounter with Aunt Martha is so exquisitely invested with the aura of the memory of a sacred moment that the implication of the portrayal of the laying of black hands on a white child's forehead may be unquestioned, or if questioned accepted as a sentimental endorsement of the standard notion southern whites have about the underlying community they share with blacks. But insofar as Tate's recollected moment implies the hidden truth of an actual generational unity of white and black blood in the South, it implies a bold bardic irresponsibility on the part of a white southern writer. Yet recording the moment of his meeting with Aunt Martha many years after it occurred, hearing her voice again and feeling again her ancient hands moving on his face—the fingers rejecting their reading of the outward physiognomy, writing the truth of the inward physiognomy—Tate recognized in the ancient slave, his blood cousin, the central symbolic figure in the fable of the white writer of the South, a fable he himself was living in its final formulation, even as Jefferson and Madison had lived it in its initial unfolding. And in living it had lived in the shadowy authenticity of truth.

III

History and the Will of the Artist
Elizabeth Madox Roberts

I feel myself to be a Kentuckian," Elizabeth Madox Roberts said, "and all my work . . . centers around Kentucky objects."[1] Just as her younger contemporary William Faulkner took as his subject the history of the Deep South state of Mississippi, Roberts took as her subject the history of the border state of Kentucky. As with Faulkner, this choice was dictated by the discovery that her imaginative reaction to life in her native state defined the encompassing experience of the modern literary artist: the experience of a constant tension between the self and history.

Roberts' historical sensibility was formed by a singular circumstance of her education: her early acquaintance with an eighteenth-century philosophical treatise, Bishop Berkeley's *The Principles of Human Knowledge*. She was introduced to this book by her father, Simpson Roberts, a Confederate veteran who had a penchant for philosophical speculation. Having early in his education developed an obsessive devotion to Berkeley, he made a strong effort to mold his sensitive, precocious daughter in the image of his discipleship. How seriously the child took her father is indicated by the way her entire career as a novelist suggests a struggle to repudiate Berkeley and, one supposes, not less her father. The major motive of Elizabeth Madox Roberts' fiction, to be sure, may be taken as her sense, seldom overt but constantly implied, of the pathos of the effort to tran-

---

1. In commenting on the motives that propel the work of Elizabeth Madox Roberts I have made a limited use of certain working notes and observations on her own work in the author's papers on deposit at the Library of Congress. For a careful, authoritative description of the Roberts papers, see William H. Slavick, "Taken with a Long-Handled Spoon: The Roberts Papers and Letters," *Southern Review*, n.s., XX (1984), 752–73.

scend the constraint the modern subjectivity of history imposes on the imagination of the literary artist.

I do not mean to imply that as she developed the matter of Kentucky the novelist Elizabeth Madox Roberts came to question a formal commitment to Berkeleian idealism. Her struggle against Berkeley arose from her realization of what the Berkeleian idealism her father had attempted to indoctrinate her with fundamentally represents: the registration—more directly so in Berkeley than in any other post-Baconian philosopher—of a profound internalization of being. Bacon, advising that nature be referred to mind, said mind must put nature on the torture rack and extract all her secrets. Locke, referring mind to mind, said mind must look "into mind and see how it works." Berkeley said mind must "consult" itself; then, conceiving a stronger imperative than either Bacon or Locke, added that mind must "ransack" itself. It is interesting that Berkeley tried his hand at poetry only once, when—under pressure of the strongest desire that ever gripped him, to establish a university in the New World—he set down his vision in the famous poem "On the Prospect of Planting Arts and Learning in America." Originally called "America, or the Muse's Refuge: A Prophecy," Berkeley's poem is conventional in its treatment of the paired themes of the transfer of empire and the transfer of letters and learning from East to West.

> There shall be sung another Golden Age,
> The rise of Empire and of Arts,
> The good and great inspiring epic rage,
> The wisest heads and noblest hearts.
>
> Not such as Europe breeds in her decay;
> Such as she bred when fresh and young,
> When heavenly flames did animate her clay,
> By future poets shall be sung.
>
> Westward the course of empire takes its way;
> The four first acts already past,
> A fifth shall close the drama with the day;
> Time's noblest offspring is the last.[2]

2. George Berkeley, "On the Prospect of Planting Arts and Learning in America," in *Works of George Berkeley,* ed. Alexander Campbell Fraser (Oxford, 1901), IV, 366.

What moves Berkeley's poem is not its treatment of an ancient commonplace, as compelling as this may be. The force of Berkeley's idea derives from the vision Bacon had a century earlier of the direct equation in the new age between knowledge and power. When he said knowledge is power, Bacon implicitly recognized that the old notion of a transfer of arts and learning from East to West had been replaced by the concept of a momentous, progressive transference of God, man, nature, and mind itself into mind; that, in short, mind had become the key to history, the source and model of historical order. In Berkeley's vision of the Baconian implication, the progress of letters, learning, and the various arts, or the succession of knowledge, will no longer be conceived to be an aspect of the succession of empire. Empire, mind, power, and history will be indivisibly related. The succession of knowledge *is* the succession of empire. Symbolized by Berkeley's dream of founding a university in the New World, the American destiny will be the fulfillment of the last act in the drama of history: the succession of knowledge to America and the subsequent American incarnation of the imperial power of mind.

The awareness of mind as the creating source and model of American history has been inescapably the major aspect of the literary imagination in America from the age of the American Enlightenment to the present. The evolvement of the literary imagination in America has been altogether a part of the movement of all things into mind. I am thinking at this point not simply of the literary perception of the rational mind as the model of our history but also about the unhappy imposition mind makes on the individual imagination and on the self of the writer when, as Berkeley suggested, it follows its imperative to ransack itself. Probably implying more than he intended to about the character of mind, Berkeley suggested what was later to become clear: in its seemingly infinite manifestations of itself, both conscious and unconscious, mind had begun by the seventeenth century, as is evident in Marlowe and Shakespeare, to experience the uncertainty of its own motives, to become burdensome to itself. The uncertainty was especially vexing and distressing to the poetic and artistic faculties of mind, which had always located mind's creative sources in transcendent, supermental, suprahistorical models of order. Through their embodiment in the particular poets and artists of a particular time and place, the transcendent, universal models of order controlled the visible society. The ancient and medieval bards, together with the sculptors, architects, and painters, all these inspired by the muses, had each served as portrayers and interpreters of transcendent formulations of order; in no sense had they served as originators of models, and surely in no sense as models themselves. Now the arts and especially literature had become chief agencies for the act of transforming existence into mind, and not simply the elucidators of the drama of self and history but intimate participants in it. The redoubtable Elizabethan Captain John Smith speaks in his *Generall Historie of Virginia* about the actor who becomes the relator. Even a bluff adventurer like Smith sensed, with Shakespeare and Donne, what Berkeley intimates so clearly in *The Practice of Human Knowledge:* history has become an act of thought. Acting and relating—the actor and the relator, the hero and the storyteller—have become one in the historical act. Smith might almost be said to have intuited that the colony of Virginia would directly produce the actions of thought that resulted in the American Revolution, the new republic, and the creation of the first trans-Allegheny state of the United States, Kentucky.

It was as an eminently self-conscious participant in the act of thought that was, and is, Kentucky that Elizabeth Madox Roberts achieved her extraordinary novels. Envisioning Kentucky as the result of the modern mind's transference of a wilderness into itself, she envisioned her own part in this act; of her own part—to apply to her case the language of Robert Penn Warren—in living and making "the big myth of history." Let us turn to some analysis of Roberts' vision in its leading manifestation, its embodiment in her heroines.

Four of these are figures of the artist and, to an appreciable degree, I believe, surrogates of the author. In each instance the heroine represents the mind—the consciousness—of the artist figure as the crux of the relation between self and history; each artist figure, moreover, represents the model of history in the consciousness of the feminine artist. The heroines I am referring to are Ellen Chesser in *The Time of Man* (1926), Theodosia Bell in *My Heart and My Flesh* (1927), Diony Hall Jarvis in *The Great Meadow* (1930), and Jocelle Drake in *He Sent Forth a Raven* (1935). A shadowy presence among these figures, it must be added, is a woman whose first name is Luce. The novelist had large intentions for Luce, evidently planning to make her the center of a Kentucky saga and call the whole "The Book (or Books) of Luce." But save for the prologue to *My Heart and My Flesh,* in which Luce is called Luce Jarvis, this idea remained unfulfilled.

I shall return to Luce. I shall also comment in a moment on one heroine who is outside the Kentucky books, the female spider who spins her web in the blackthorn bush in *Jingling in the Wind* (1928). But first let us consider Ellen Chesser and Theodosia Bell. In 1923, three years before *The Time of Man* was published, Elizabeth Madox Roberts set down a curious reflection on the "argument" (her term) she wanted to work out in the novel.

> It could never be an analysis of society or of a societal stratum because it keeps starkly within one consciousness, and that one being not an analytical nature of a "conscious" consciousness. There is a tryst here, a bargain between two, and two only, and these are Ellen and Life, and then there is Life. Life uses her. What is this unit, this not-life substance which Life uses and breaks to its end?
>
> Life runs in form, design, alike for all instances. Ellen is the variant, the ego, the wonder, the asking unit.[3]

Asserting a difference between the naturalistic life force and a transcending "not-life substance" that is yet "used" by life (symbolized by Ellen), the novelist seems to posit a spiritual power that, to use the Heideggerian term, is "radically immanent" in life. Although it is doubtful that she was directly acquainted with Heidegger's longing for transcendence within immanence, Roberts shows an affinity with the philosopher who in *Being and Time* distills the pervasive dilemma of a culture moving toward a final collapse of transcendence into immanence—toward the conviction that not only the earth and its inhabitants but the idea of God and the realm of the supratemporal is subject to historical analysis. *The Time of Man* turns on the tension present in the "unconscious conscious" attributed to Ellen by the author in her notes. She is a contrary presence in her world. She is incapable of analytical consciousness, yet her mind consciously registers the places and people that mark her encounter with life. The

3. Roberts Papers.

drama of Ellen's awareness of life, in other words, presents a symbolic situation far beyond her intellectual comprehension but germane to her creator's way of thinking and feeling: the problematic assumption that life transcends history comes up against the evidence that the tenant sharecroppers of the Kentucky tobacco country are immutably creatures of history. Neither peasants (self-supporting land laborers and cultivators living in small village communities) nor, in the European sense, a "folk" (a people who live in a traditionalist culture rooted in Christianity yet are more fundamentally rooted in the timeless thought patterns of a pre-Christian culture), the Kentucky croppers are the descendants of those who only a few generations back had emigrated from an older New World to a newer one to participate in the Jeffersonian dream of dividing a wilderness into self-subsistent freeholds, each freehold being in the Jeffersonian view a symbol of the free mind. But even in its representation in Jefferson, the mind that served as the model of the Republic was divided against itself. On the one hand it associated its freedom with the right to use slaves (or, later, sharecroppers) to work the land, and on the other it identified its freedom with the independence of the freeholder. The eventual result was a conflict of unprecedented ferocity. Permanently displaced by the political and economic circumstances of the American Civil War, the great-great-grandchildren of the original actors in the Jeffersonian dream appear in *The Time of Man* as uneducated tenant farmers. Wandering from farm to farm and landlord to landlord, they are unaware that the identity with the land known to their forebears has been lost. Actors in a dream turned nightmare, they do not know it. Connected to the land solely through the cash nexus, they have neither a sacramental nor an intellectual obligation to it.

But Ellen Chesser—called in the author's notes "the ego, the wonder, the asking unit"—has epiphanic moments of self-identity. Helping her father clear land for a field on a "virgin hill," she hears him remark, "No plow ever cut this here hill afore, not in the whole time of man." Later her father goes to get seeds to plant, and she is alone.

> She piled stones from the plowed soil and piled them in her neat mound, and the wind continued to blow off the hilltop. . . . To the northeast the hills rolled away so far that

the sight gave out, and still they went, fading into blue hazes and myths of faint trees; delicate trees stood finer than hair lines on a far mythical hill. The rocks fell where she laid them with a faint flat sound, and the afternoon seemed very still back of the dove calls and the cries of the plovers, back of a faint dying phrase, "in the time of man." The wind lapped through the sky, swirling lightly now, and again dashing straight down from the sun. She was leaning over the clods to gather a stone, her shadow making an arched shadow on the ground. All at once she lifted her body and flung up her head to the great sky that reached over the hills and shouted:

"Here I am!"

She waited listening.

"I'm Ellen Chesser! I'm here!"[4]

Completely attached to the society in which she lives, Ellen, who, as she must, becomes the wife of a tenant farmer, is yet strangely detached. At times, her beauty moving among the men and the animals, she resembles Eula Varner in Faulkner's *The Hamlet*. But unlike Faulkner in the case of Eula, Elizabeth Madox Roberts—although she suggests a certain ambiguity about whether Ellen is innocent of history or simply ignorant of it—does not quite allow the ambivalent suggestion that she is an earth goddess displaced in history. Ellen's innocence, or ignorance, of history simply confirms her immanence in history, her innocence or ignorance being only the reverse of the conscious awareness of history. Thus Ellen figures in *The Time of Man* not, as some of her interpreters would have it, as a symbolic representation of the restoration of the sense of wonder and mythic consciousness, but as a symbol of the isolation of the poetic self in history which occurred once the irreversible transfer of being and existence into mind and history began.

Underlying Ellen's presence in *The Time of Man* is the recognition of the pathos of any effort to restore the prehistorical consciousness. The time of man is the time of history. At the end of the novel, Elizabeth Madox Roberts obliquely but surely confirms her realization of this truth. Ellen and her sharecropper husband Jasper and

4. Elizabeth Madox Roberts, *The Time of Man* (Lexington, Ky., 1982), 89.

their brood are on the road at night, once again on the way, to a "somewheres" that will, they hope, be better for them. The children are watching the stars as the wagon moves along. One of the boys, Dick, observes to his brother Hen that you could learn the names of the stars if you had a book. Scientific knowledge, little Dick recognizes, is the power unto life. Longing for knowledge, which in all likelihood is in his case unattainable, Ellen's child ironically implies the pathos of a kind of ultimate isolation of the human spirit. Aspiring to be a self, the human spirit existing in the world of the sharecroppers—which is, after all, a part of the historical world created by the Baconian imperative—lacking both the power of mythic consciousness and the power of rational knowledge, cannot participate in the world of which it is a part.

While *The Time of Man* may be taken as a discovery of the defeat by history of instinctive wonder and delight, *My Heart and My Flesh* may be read as the discovery of a situation more profound and more distressing. "My protagonist here," Roberts comments in her notes, "is a more self-conscious person than my Ellen was, and thus the book moves in a more inward way."[5] An important but subordinate theme in *The Time of Man,* sexuality, is the dominant motive in *My Heart and My Flesh,* reminding us that Elizabeth Madox Roberts, like Joyce, Lawrence, and Faulkner, belonged to the age of Freud. Understanding what we may take to be Freud's central insight—namely, that the transference of being into mind has meant the transference of sexuality into history—Roberts grasped the possibility that the self-conscious, rational recognition of the implication of sexuality in history may be the leading aspect of modern historiography. Whereas sexual behavior—controlled by an elaborate, transcendent symbolism derived from an amalgam of classical and Hebraic-Christian myths—had been external to self-consciousness, in Freud it becomes integral to self-consciousness. Identifying self with the imperatives of sexuality, mind's search for the meaning of sexual behavior encloses the self in history with finality.

Among American novelists the struggle against the demythologizing of sex is written largest in Faulkner, being the core of his first great work, *The Sound and the Fury.* This novel was published in

5. Roberts Papers.

1929, but the first truly compelling depiction of the struggle against the demythologizing of sex by an American writer had appeared two years before *The Sound and the Fury* in *My Heart and My Flesh*. Possessing the refined self-consciousness of an educated and passionate artist, the heroine of this story is frustrated in her career as a violinist by a simple genetic impairment: her hands, it turns out, are not adequately structured for the instrument she plays. But the physical impediment to Theodosia Bell's career is no more than a symbol of a more absolute constraint: the deformation of her consciousness by the cruel sexuality of the demythicized historical society in which she strives for her identity as an artist. Sexual disasters multiply in Theodosia's life. Her true lover dies in a fire (and then is falsely accused of having fathered a bastard by one of the girls in the community); she learns that she has two half sisters and a half brother who are mulattoes (and at one point finds her half brother in bed with one of his sisters); her grandfather, with whom she has her sole secure relationship, dies; and as he is dying, she becomes aware that her own father has an incestuous desire for her. Emotionally shattered, Theodosia is on the edge of suicide. But she is saved—redeemed, so to speak, from the sexuality of history—by a moment of spiritual ecstasy. The "sudden spasm of movement" that would have taken her through the door to plunge into the dark waters of the pond is suddenly, miraculously transformed into an orgasmic entrance into a new life: "At once a vivid appearance entered her mind, so brilliant and powerful that her consciousness was abashed. Larger than the world, more spacious than the universe, the new apparition spread through her members and tightened her hands so that they knotted suddenly together. . . . Her body spread widely and expanded . . . and the earth came back, herself acutely aware of it."

Ellen Chesser experiences the infinite as "a sweet quiet voice" that, "harmonious and many-winged" and "released from all need or obligation," says, "Here I am." One might say that Theodosia's experience sexualizes Berkeleian metaphysics. Furthermore, it subtly asserts a reversal of the masculine and feminine power in the act of creativity. In her epiphanic moment, she not only experiences an orgasmic awakening to a new life but acquires a philliclike power to penetrate the womb of the universe: "She had shifted her gaze so that she looked now into the fire. She sat leaned forward, tense with new life, with the new world, and she penetrated the embers with her gaze and saw into the universe of the fire, the firmament of dimly glowing heat that receded, world on worlds, back into infinities, atoms, powers, all replete with their own abundance."[6]

After her resurrection Theodosia assumes the qualities of a fertility goddess. The birds on the farm where she is living sing "as if it were to celebrate the coming of Aphrodite among the herds, to announce the beginnings of fine desires and the passing of Aphrodite among the pastures." Her life merges with that of the cows—Queen, Mollie, Betty, Hawthorne, and Princess—creatures described in sensuous images that suggest that they, and Theodosia, bear a relation to the ancient mythology of the powerful, often aggressive, and terrifying cow goddesses like Io, Europa, and Pasiphae. How much more Roberts was up to in *My Heart and My Flesh* than a comforting pastoral resolution of Theodosia's sufferings is intimated in a note in her papers on the significance of Horace Bell, Theodosia's father: "Horace Bell is not an accurate [*i.e.,* actual?] portrait, but I have known men as brutal. During the process of writing I have always a great deal of machinery off stage which makes the performance move. Writing of him, then, I thought of him as a great Jovian thunderer lacking Jove's benignant paternality. He is the Don Juan ideal of freedom carried to the end of its logic. Beyond him lies the spider that is eaten by his female, and a new world."[7]

Engaged in writing the satirical fantasy *Jingling in the Wind* at the same time she was working on *My Heart and My Flesh,* Roberts must have had in mind the scene in *Jingling in the Wind* when Jeremy the rainmaker discovers an exquisite, enigmatic spider in a blackthorn bush by a pool and learns from her that she is spinning the whole design of life out of herself. Hurt because his beloved Tulip McAfee has derisively called him a "Rain-bat," Jeremy decides the masculine sex has been too submissive and that he will institute a "Masculine Renaissance." The spider says to go ahead, that this event, like all things, is woven into the web; but then she quietly announces that she will not be weaving tomorrow.

> "Tomorrow I expect to eat my husband."
> "Where is your husband?" Jeremy asked.

6. Elizabeth Madox Roberts, *My Heart and My Flesh* (New York, 1927), 255, 256.
7. Roberts Papers.

"I have not seen him yet," said the spider, "but he will turn up tomorrow. I will eat him down to the last mouthful. Then I will begin a new race of spiders, each one as complex as myself. It is all very intricate."[8]

What is actually woven into the web, it would seem, is the intricate and unceasing aggression of the female against the masculine will. Thus the overall design of existence makes Jeremy's idea of a masculine renaissance absurd. Although the spider deprecates Jeremy's commonplace moralism that "history teaches," she herself and her web constitute the emblem of an equation between the "life design" and history. Determined by the life design, history moves ruthlessly toward its fulfillment in the self-will of the feminine artist.

The closure of history in the life design spun out of the belly of the spider—the Supreme Author and Designer, the Ultimate Cause— is perfected at the end of *Jingling in the Rain*. Jeremy's delusion that he has restored chivalry and masculine domination and has returned woman to her proper and subordinate role (though he had yielded utterly to Tulip) is celebrated by the singing of old love ballads. The singing ended, "that most exquisite spider that crouched at the hub of the web that is the mind stirred, feeling a tremor pass over the web as if some coil were shaken by a visitation from without. Life is from within, and thus the noise outside is a wind blowing in a mirror. But love is a royal visitor which that proud ghost, the human spirit, settles in elegant chambers and serves with the best."[9] Although the human spirit with its capacity for love can still be visited by love, *Jingling in the Wind* implies, it is a ghost in the house of mind (or the house of history, or the house of the life design). The noise love makes in the house is as silent as the wind blowing in a mirror. The spider's web is finally a symbol of the separation of mind from spirit. It may be taken—I suppose more ominously—as a symbol of the isolation and death of love in the will to make the feminine the fulfillment of history.

In *Jingling in the Wind*, Elizabeth Madox Roberts reached a potential crisis in the relationship between making the little myth of poetry

8. Elizabeth Madox Roberts, *Jingling in the Wind* (New York, 1928), 236.
9. *Ibid.*, 256.

and living the big myth of history. Abstracting the drama of self and history in fantasy and allegory was a way of exploring the historical and philosophical implications of the stories of Ellen Chesser and Theodosia Bell, but it threatened to dissociate the author from her primary material, the matter of Kentucky. In *The Great Meadow* she turned toward providing a rationale for the stories of Ellen and Theodosia in the historical origin of their world, the settlement of Kentucky during the age of the American Revolution. The result was a historical fantasy, in which, far more than in *My Heart and My Flesh*, an ancient goddess is associated with the mind's interiorization of the historical will to power. I am speaking of Diony Hall Jarvis' reincarnation of Dione—"a great goddess . . . the mother of Venus by Jupiter, in the lore of Homer, an older report than that of the legendary birth through the foam of the sea . . . one of the Titan sisters, the Titans being earth-men, children of Uranus and Terra."[10] Diony's father, the blacksmith-scholar Thomas Hall, obviously an oblique personification of Roberts' own father, associates his daughter with Rhea, mother of gods, who signifies "succession." A disciple of Berkeley, Hall takes *The Principles of Human Knowledge* as his Bible and inculcates the philosopher's teachings in his daughter. He conceives that when Diony leaves her home in Virginia for Kentucky, the newest New World, with her new husband, Berk Jarvis, she is an instrument of the succession of history. A powerful goddess and a disciple of Berkeley, Diony is fulfilling the mission of "historic Man" to bring "such men as have no history to humble themselves and learn their lesson." Although neither Hall nor his daughter mentions Berkeley's "On the Prospect of Planting Arts and Learning in America," they are embodiments of Berkeley's dream of America.

Diony's representation of Berkeley—and of mind in the New World—is symbolized in her work at the loom, an act invested with an aura of sexuality.

> Her eyes followed the flaxen web which was a yellowish gray like some woman's hair, and as such it clung to her thought and twined gray spirals about any words her throat contrived but left unsaid. Her mind slipped to her father's books and

---

10. Elizabeth Madox Roberts, *The Great Meadow* (New York, 1930), 114, 75–76.

tried to bring this idolatrous devotion into relation with what she had read [in Berkeley], and she divided the several processes of willing, imagining, and remembering, and placed the supreme act in one governing Spirit where all unimagined and unwilled and unremembered acts are kept before they are called into being. Having come to the inmost thought, the inmost realization, she held it one instant before it slipped swiftly beyond her most penetrating reaching.

But in her art as a weaver Diony has penetrated the "governing Spirit." Judging from the resourcefulness with which she meets the supreme crisis of the story, she is even in a sense the custodian of acts not yet called into being. The resolution of the crisis is already within the fabric. When Berk returns to the frontier community, long after being given up for dead, to find Diony remarried, it is not the two men who, by fist or knife, decide whose wife she is. By the law of the wilderness—by the law of a new world—it is Diony who chooses between the two, both worthy fathers of her children. Although Berk left a squaw and Indian children behind when he escaped from captivity, Diony regards this as having been a physical necessity and admits it as no impediment to her decision. When she acknowledges Berk as her husband, she chooses squarely on the basis of his greater psychic strength, responding to her sense of a will that is mated to her own. And yet in the very act of choosing she asserts the dominance of her will—a will that is sanctioned by the law of the wilderness, by the basic nature of things. Figuratively speaking, she eats her mates. As the narrative consciousness of *The Great Meadow*—the interpreter of the motives and meaning not only of her husbands but of the leading figure in the legend of Kentucky, Daniel Boone, the prototype of the prime American hero Leatherstocking—she conceives her idea of the world and wills the idea into being. Choosing between Berk and Muir, she defies history as a naturalistic life design. Diony does not simply live the myth of history, she makes the myth she lives.

At this juncture in her career—having in *The Great Meadow* correlated civilization and the inward movement of history, having portrayed the heroic differentiation of history from chaos through the power of the feminine mind, having made a feminine literary imagination formed in Kentucky and the American South the model of American history—Roberts might well have turned toward assimilating her vision of history in the will, imagination, and remembrance of her dream character, the woman called Luce. According to indications in her papers, she had this in view at the beginning of her work as a novelist; for she had intended to introduce into *The Time of Man* two or three digressive episodes. In these passages Luce, I judge, would have appeared in the role Diony occupies in *The Great Meadow*. Relator of and actor in the heroic age of Kentucky, Luce would have served as a counterpoint to Ellen, their stories suggesting dramatic comparisons and contrasts, continuities and discontinuities between the heroic age and a time a century and a half later.

Having dropped Luce from the scheme of *The Time of Man,* Roberts brought her into the prologue of *My Heart and My Flesh.* Here she appears as a young girl named Luce Jarvis. But she is not the Luce of the pioneer period; she is one of Theodosia's childhood companions. Nobody seems to know quite what to make of this introductory portion of *My Heart and My Flesh.* Perhaps it conveys the notion that Theodosia is an aspect of Luce, just as Luce in the abandoned sections of *The Time of Man* may have served to suggest that the Luce of Kentucky's heroic era is an aspect of Ellen. But Diony is not an aspect of Luce. She is herself. Having in *The Great Meadow* created a strong character to replace the Luce of the early time, the novelist, one would think, would have been ready to develop an account of the generations between Diony Hall Jarvis and the Luce Jarvis of the twentieth century. If Roberts had stayed within Diony's imagination of history, she could have plunged ahead with an epic version of Diony's later life, and the years of the children and grandchildren; bringing in the coming of the Civil War, the war epoch, and the bitter aftermath, she could have given the epic story coherence and force by relating it to the original vision of a strong feminine actor and relator and its fulfillment in her successors. But as far as I can tell this was never a possibility. The Luce sketched in the notebooks had a firm hold on the imagination of her creator.

In Roberts' first conception of Diony, her story was to have been told as part of a larger reconstruction of the Kentucky past by the twentieth-century Luce Jarvis. One note in the Roberts Papers reads: "Luce Jarvis. Has in her possession or in their possession, one pewter spoon marked with a rude free hand, Diony, and a few leaves of a journal. Out of this Luce reconstructs the past. The ink faded into the brown of the paper which is burnt by air and light and time to be a frail dry chip. A strong fine hand is written. An Eighteenth Century hand writing an Eighteenth Century way of thought, setting it beside an Eighteenth Century anxiety." Elsewhere among the notes we find a more specific description of the spoon Luce will use as one way of reconstructing the past: "A spoon shaped to fit into a mouth. It has the hollow of a hungry tongue. It is fitted and cupped to meet the hunger of lips." (In its first form the last sentence read "fitted and cupped to meet the hunger of tongues," but *tongues* is scratched out and the less suggestive *lips* substituted.) [11] One has the impression that the novelist was contemplating a novel of more complicated dimensions than *The Great Meadow*. It would have been something like a Proustian quest for the past in the present and the present in the past, more specifically perhaps a Proustian effort to define the sexuality of modern history.

Among other jottings concerning Luce are two that invite juxtaposing. One is a declaration by Luce: "I will be something of my own right, of myself, I Luce Jarvis." The other is a conjuration of Luce by the author: "I look in the glass and I see a form having a clearly defined color against the dark of the watery air that hangs about me. I see Luce Jarvis myself." The *myself* can be taken merely as intensive, yet it has reflexive force. In the observations on Luce in the Roberts notes, we also come across a couple of attempts to estimate her personal qualities. One stresses Luce's "clarity" and "frankness," calls her "simple and honest" and "straightforward." But a longer entry suggests a much more complex Luce.

> She could find within herself little to identify with what she read of experience in love or family experience, little to coincide with the fixed emotions and patterns of the old stories. She thought she must herself be wrong and her way of life out of all relation to the truth as she read it. She could not find her way. This and that was continually true in her own flesh. She could not find the fixed pattern. She thought her life must not be real and herself wrong, her love wrong. [12]

11. Roberts Papers.
12. *Ibid.*

Some of the notes I have been drawing on may have been made as early as 1927. The novel that ultimately came out of them in 1935, *He Sent Forth a Raven,* is a story centering in Jocelle Drake and her father, Stoner Drake, a man who has taken a vow never to set his foot on the earth again. The chief characters were first conceived as Luce Jarvis and her father, Stone Jarvis. The conception of the father remained the same after he became Stoner Drake; but the conception of the daughter was altered considerably when Luce became Jocelle. Apparently the Luce Jarvis–Stone Jarvis novel would have responded to the elaborate concern for the past that the author demonstrated by her devotion to the genealogies of her fictitious Kentuckians. It would have responded to her vision of a saga based on the progression of a family out of the Old World into Virginia, then in a later generation across the dangerous Trace into Kentucky; then in still later generations the fate of the family as Kentucky entered into the history of the continental nation. Among the succession of family members would be William Jarvis, born in 1865. As one device in the story, Luce would have an old-fashioned loom. While her father stomped about overhead, blowing his horn and commanding his farm hands, she was to weave a tapestry symbolizing the heroic period of the Jarvises. Depicting a blockhouse within a stockade and Indians and their artifacts, the tapestry was to be a work of great care and devotion. Its woven-in title—replete with a large measure of irony between pastoral ideal and historical actuality—would be "The Great Meadow, 1774." But this concept of presenting the story of the settlement of Kentucky was drastically altered. The device of the tapestry was abandoned. The story of the settlement was assigned to the consciousness of Diony Jarvis. When she took this step, the author of the projected Book of Luce effectively abandoned both the book and its heroine. Her reason for rejecting Luce for Diony, I surmise, is basically that Luce was too close to the doubt and anxiety that haunted her creator's inmost consciousness. The heroic element in Luce was insufficient; she lacked the power to overcome the terror of modern existence. There is a stark gloss in Roberts' hand on one of the several genealogical charts in her papers: "Appalled at Life."[13] Like Faulkner, Elizabeth Madox Roberts was nearly overwhelmed by the disorder of history. Seeking a redemption from it, she sought

13. Roberts Papers.

a character who had what she thought she herself did not sufficiently have—an executive will, or, as one might say, an executive sexuality.

Roberts did not entirely relinquish Luce. She comes back as an aspect of Jocelle Drake. I think it is not farfetched to believe that the intention was through Jocelle to invest Luce with a commanding will. As in *My Heart and My Flesh,* the heroine of *He Sent Forth a Raven* is almost overpowered by the masculinity of her society, becoming at last the victim of rape committed by a cousin on his way to the war. Her redemption from this traumatic incident involves her becoming an embodiment, not of Dione, but, like Theodosia, of Aphrodite, a daughter of the primal goddess. Only this time the emblems of the heroine's state of renewal are not cows, nor even the doves usually associated with Aphrodite, but creatures without mythic status, white Plymouth Rock chickens. The pastoral realism contributes rather than detracts from the believability of Jocelle's discovery, in the epiphanic moment in *He Sent Forth a Raven,* that she is not isolated from being but shares what all human beings share: a "common mental pattern where individual traits merge," a community of the human spirit. Yet this comforting revelation is not so significant in the redemption of Jocelle as a force more fundamental than her attraction to "communal devotions and emotions": "the lonely will, the wish, the desire [for] . . . the underlying complexity reducible within itself and of itself to the one simple determinate, lonely among its fellows, aloof, arising now to a super-life, the will to believe, to live, to hate evil, to gather power out of emotion, to divide hate from love where the two are interlocked in one emotion, the will to love God the creator."[14]

Now anyone who is sensitive to the elementary themes of Christian theology will sense in Jocelle's vision of the will to the "super-life" the gravest heresy. In affirming the efficacy of the autonomous will in her redemption, Jocelle denies the efficacy of God's grace. One cannot deliberately will to love God without identifying the human will and God's will. Since Jocelle is not an artist, and may be taken as a rather ordinary Kentucky girl of her time, we may not readily relate her to the complicated quest for transcendence by the artist Elizabeth Madox Roberts. But let us set Jocelle's moment of

14. Elizabeth Madox Roberts, *He Sent Forth a Raven* (New York, 1935), 252–53.

illumination beside a kind of epiphanic moment that came to the writer herself. I refer again to a note in her papers.

There is finally and at first, last and first, the aesthetic requirement, the desire to be completed. Beyond theses and plot, beyond history and the daily real, is a thematic design—this final satisfaction to be met. The mind requires fulfillment. One cannot avoid the demand. Some ultimate and fit design beyond all the uses of the mind, some necessity inherent in human works, calls for the consummation. Shall we say the "categorical aesthetic." It is the message from beyond life. The hand of God writing on the walls of the cosmos.[15]

To declare a design beyond history—beyond the human mind— by drawing an analogy between the modern aesthetic imperative and the Kantian moral imperative is to appeal to Kant's mediation between the external and the internal, the objective and the subjective. But in the transference of existence into itself and of itself into itself, mind, as Roberts knew, had rejected Kant. In an account of her vision of art as the act of God, she had written: "The mind requires fulfillment. The tragedy must follow if it is begun. One cannot avoid the demand." No doubt aware that with this declaration she had established a highly ironic, a tragic, tension between the will of the artist to creative action and the action of God, the only creator, Roberts drew a line through "The tragedy must follow as it is begun." But she could not blot the implication. Present everywhere in her work, it is summed up in Theodosia Bell's cry of desperation: "O, God, I believe, and there's nothing to believe." This desperate plea occurs in a portrait of an artist who, whether she is called Luce or Theodosia, is also to be called Elizabeth.

Pursuing the manifestations of the artistic will in Elizabeth Madox Roberts, I find myself wondering if I am guilty of unduly denigrating the spirit of hope that, at least in the days in which she was still read, many found in her stories. I have intended, however, to pay tribute to an artist who, more or less misread in her own day,

15. *Ibid.*

presents the possibility of being read correctly in our day, when we discover her sense of history. Doing so we discover the significance of a series of novels in which in her struggle with history the author is the peer of William Faulkner, Allen Tate, and Robert Penn Warren. Of course she wrote stories other than the ones I have touched on. Some of these show a relaxation of the concern with the artistic will and the historical imperative. *A Buried Treasure* ends with an almost medieval delight in the garden of the world. The more complex *Black Is My True Love's Hair* poses the nostalgic possibility of recovering the balladic world. But even these novels turn on the sense of what intervenes between the self of the modern artist and a sacramental connection with "the simple and uncomplicated earth": to wit, a terrible intimacy with history that has dissolved both metaphysical and physical reality into illusions generated by the self-consciousness that is history and the history that is self-consciousness. Having modeled order on the society of science and history—on mind—Elizabeth Madox Roberts discovered what we are like: we believe in the idea but not in the fact: in the idea of the heart but not in the heart; in the idea of the flesh but not in the flesh; in the idea of the community but not in community; in the idea of responsibility for one another but not in the responsive, and thus responsible, act of sympathy; in the idea of love but not in the act of love.

IV

War and Memory
Quentin Compson's Civil War

Asked about his indebtedness to Sherwood Anderson, whom he had known personally in New Orleans in the early 1920s, William Faulkner replied, "In my opinion he's the father of all my generation—Hemingway, Erskine Caldwell, Thomas Wolfe, Dos Passos." Strictly speaking, Faulkner's sense of literary genealogy may have derived more from a personal regard for Anderson than from an informed appreciation of his wider literary influence. It was Anderson who had advised the young writer from Mississippi to give up his residence in the French Quarter bohemia of New Orleans, return to his native patch of earth, and write about what life was like there. Heeding this cogent admonition had made all the difference. But neither the advice nor the stories of the well-known midwestern writer account for the compelling creative impulse that led a literary novice from Mississippi to develop into the world-famous author of the Yoknapatawpha saga. Faulkner offered a more basic, less arguable assertion about American literary genealogy, and about his own literary descent, when he rounded out his comment on the subject by declaring that the writer who may be considered Anderson's literary father, Mark Twain, "is all our grandfather."[1]

Whatever he owed to Anderson, the author of the Yoknapatawpha stories might have been more accurate in his metaphor if, ignoring generational chronology, he had described himself as also a son of Mark Twain; for Mark Twain was more than a distant forerunner of Faulkner. He created the model of the crucial role Faulkner en-

1. Frederick L. Gwynn and Joseph L. Blotner, eds., *Faulkner in the University: Class Conferences at the University of Virginia, 1957–1958* (New York, 1965), 281.

acted: that of the southern author as at once a participant in and ironic witness to a drama of memory and history that centered essentially in the never-ending remembrance of the great American civil conflict of 1861–1865. The obligation of the writer to serve as a witness, not to the actual historical event, but to the remembrance of it, was a force in shaping the vocation of the writer in the South from Thomas Nelson Page to Ellen Glasgow to Faulkner, Allen Tate, Katherine Anne Porter, Robert Penn Warren, and Eudora Welty; to, in fact, all of the writers associated with the flowering of southern authorship, especially novelists, in the 1920s and 1930s. The prime testimony to the shaping power of remembrance on the identity of the southern writer is offered not in the actual lives of the writers themselves but in certain implicit portrayals of the figure of the writer in their fiction, two of the notable instances being Lacy Buchan in Tate's *The Fathers* and Jack Burden in Warren's *All the King's Men,* but the supreme example being a twenty-year-old Mississippian who appears in *The Sound and the Fury* and *Absalom, Absalom!,* Quentin Compson III. On the surface these two Faulkner novels seem to bear no more than a coincidental relation to the war; but in the second of them, Faulkner's most baffling yet possibly finest single work, the portrayal of Quentin brings the drama of southern remembrance to its culminating expression.

Mark Twain's most cogent definition of the postbellum southern sensibility of memory occurs in *Life on the Mississippi.* At one point in this autobiographical work, first published in 1883, Mark Twain remarks that in the North one seldom hears the recent American civil conflict mentioned, but in the South it "is very different." Here, where "every man you meet was in the war" and "every lady you meet saw the war," it is "the great chief topic of conversation." To southerners, Mark Twain declares, the war is in fact "what A.D. is elsewhere: they date from it." Thus "all day long you hear things 'placed' as having happened since the waw; or du'in' the waw; or be'fo the waw; or right aftah the waw; or 'bout two yeahs or five yeahs or ten yeahs befo' the waw or aftah the waw."[2]

Beneath the surface of the humor in *Life on the Mississippi,* the

2. Mark Twain, *Life on the Mississippi,* in *Mississippi Writings,* ed. Guy Cardwell (New York, 1982), 491–92.

author—who had been brought up as Sam Clemens in the semi-frontier Missouri extension of the southern slave society but had long since assumed the complex pseudonymous identity of "Mark Twain"—registers his realization of the profound effect of the war on his own consciousness of time and history. In his early manhood, before he became Mark Twain, Sam Clemens of Hannibal, Missouri, had permanently separated himself from the South when he withdrew from—or to speak less politely, deserted from—a ragtag volunteer company of Confederate Missourians and went adventuring on the new frontiers of Nevada and California. While in Nevada as a reporter for the Virginia City *Territorial Enterprise,* he adopted as his literary name the familiar cry of the leadsman on the Mississippi River steamboats he had piloted for three years prior to the war. It was as Mark Twain that after the war Sam Clemens went to live in the North and, later, having become a world traveler, at times in Europe. Although always haunted by a complex and troubled sense of his fundamental identity, in *Life on the Mississippi* Mark Twain writes out of a persistent, deeply empathic relationship with the South. It is in his identity as a postbellum southerner that the author speaks when he says that to grasp the significance of the war the stranger to the South must realize "how intimately every individual" southerner was involved in it. Ostensibly quoting a gentleman he had met at a New Orleans club—who, whether he was a real person or merely a convenient invention of the narrative moment, serves as an effective authorial persona—Mark Twain says that the experience of the calamity of war was so intense and encompassing in the South that each southerner, "in his own person," seems to have been intimately "visited . . . by that tremendous episode"—most notably by the "vast and comprehensive calamity" of "invasion." As a result, Mark Twain continues in the guise of the New Orleans gentleman, "each of us, in his own person, seems to have sampled all the different varieties of human experience." Inseparably connected to the war, the southern comprehension of time and history in Mark Twain's conception is such that "you can't mention an outside matter of any sort but it will certainly remind some listener of something that happened during the war—and out he comes with it." Even "the most random topic" will "load every man up with war reminiscences." As a result, "pale inconsequentialities" tend to disappear from southern conversation; "you can't talk" about business or the weather "when you've got a crimson fact or fancy in your head that you are burning to fetch out."[3]

Mark Twain's description of the effect of the Civil War on the southerner belongs to the account in the second part of *Life on the Mississippi* of his revisitation of the river in 1882. Although he had had his initial experience on the river only twenty-five years earlier, Mark Twain had returned to a world that bore only a superficial resemblance to the one he had known as a fledgling pilot, everything having been changed by the catastrophic internecine struggle that had erupted in the Republic of the United States of America in the seventh decade of its founding. Not to be generally known for a long time yet as the Civil War—often in the North still called the War of the Rebellion and in the South the War for Southern Independence—the unparalleled bloodletting that the grandchildren and great-grandchildren of the founders of the Republic were engaged in for four years had changed the meaning of time and history in the most fundamental sense. The civil slaughter and destruction had, to be sure, altered the very structure of American memory. Those Americans who had known the war intimately—and this in some way included all southerners, even those who like Mark Twain had removed themselves from the theater of war by going west—now, more self-consciously than the victors in the war, lived in two republics: the "Old Republic"—the remembered republic of the constitutional federation of self-liberated imperial colonies that had freed themselves in a war in that other time "befo' *the* waw"; and the actual republic—the integral union of states, the "Second American Republic," the "nation-state"—that had come into existence "aftah *the* waw." But for southerners, the defeated citizens of the aborted Confederate States of America, the sense of the displacement of memory was expressed in a more particular, in an essentially more intimate, historical terminology: the "Old South" and the "New South." Implying a displacement of memory different from that suggested by the terms Old Republic and New Republic, the southern effort to differentiate an Old and a New South emerged most simply and clearly, and it may be said most superficially, in the literary endeavor to create "local color" representations of the South. More deeply, the

3. *Ibid.*

terms *Old South* and *New South* reflected the search by postbellum southern novelists for characters and situations that would transcend the regional concept of the southern literary identity. In their cultural situation, southern writers were inclined to see the life of the individual southerner as always in a dramatic tension with history; they seemed almost incapable of imagining the rejection of the historical context of the individual life. As Robert Penn Warren once said, "History is what you can't / Resign from."[4]

Yet after the War for Southern Independence had ended in the massive invasion and complete defeat of the Confederacy, southern writers—in ironic reaction to the feeling of being imprisoned in history—had commonly envisioned what amounted to a southern resignation from history. Ignoring the historical actuality of the Confederacy—a nation that in its brief existence was ever contentious and divided—writers created a rhetorical image of a unified spiritual nation. The metaphysical southern nation had, according to the rhetoric of southern nostalgia, evolved out of a stable antebellum civilization centered in the harmonious pastoral plantation and the beneficent institution of chattel slavery. Accepting such a vision of the past—out of the fear, it may be said, of the alienation of memory by history—the southerner was, as Warren observed, truly "trapped in history." The metaphysics of remembrance being equated with historical reality, one questioned the ideal image of the past at the risk of being suspected of treason.

But the literary imagination in the South did not yield altogether to delusionary remembrance. Reality at times intruded itself even into the rhetoric of an apologist like Thomas Nelson Page, creating an implied dramatic tension between memory and history. Removed sufficiently from the motive of apology, this tension promised to become highly fruitful in the case of Mark Twain's younger contemporary George Washington Cable, but faded as Cable became more and more committed to the politics of promoting equitable treatment for the freedmen. Among the immediate postwar generation of southern writers the literary promise of the drama of memory and history reached notable fulfillment only in Mark Twain, and this in only one book, *Adventures of Huckleberry Finn.*

This was a novel Mark Twain had begun in the 1870s and put

4. Robert Penn Warren, *Selected Poems, 1923–1975* (New York, 1972), 159.

aside. When he had finished *Life on the Mississippi,* he almost immediately went back to the story of Huck and Jim and completed it in a
sustained burst of energy. Obviously the experience of returning to
the river and completing the book that he had begun earlier as "Old
Times on the Mississippi" with an account of the river and its world
fifteen years after the end of the Civil War had produced a tension
lacking in the initial book about Tom Sawyer and Huck Finn. Although *The Adventures of Tom Sawyer* (1876) has its dark moments,
in this book Mark Twain's recollection of life in Hannibal "befo' the
waw" (in the 1840s) is informed more by nostalgia than irony. But
in *Huckleberry Finn* the relationship between past and present—what
was "befo' the waw" and what was "aftah the waw"—has altered.
Always more significant in Mark Twain's imagination, and in the
southern mind generally, than what was "du'in' the waw," what was
"befo' the waw" and what was "aftah the waw" coalesce. In a novel
that is basically an exploration of the southern society that fought the
Civil War, Mark Twain strongly implies that history is what you
can't resign from.

Or, to put it more precisely, Huck Finn implies this. Although a
boy of no more than twelve or thirteen years of age, Mark Twain's
persona in *Adventures of Huckleberry Finn* is not merely the narrator;
writing in his own language, the vernacular of the Missouri back-
woods, Huck is the highly self-conscious author, the literary artist,
the authoritative maker of his own book. This is evident from the
beginning, when Huck says that "you don't know about me without
you have read a book . . . by Mr. Mark Twain [*i.e., The Adventures
of Tom Sawyer*]," to the final moment, when he says that if he had
"knowed what a trouble it was to make a book," he "wouldn't 'a'
tackled it." Invested with the authority of the author—in a day when
a "writer" was still an "author" and was presumed to have authority—Huck is fundamentally a reliable narrator. He tells it like it was
because, in terms of Mark Twain's philosophy of history, he could
not do otherwise. Much has been made of what seems to be Mark
Twain's trivialization of the logical climax of *Huckleberry Finn* when,
after his awesome declaration that he will defy every rule of society
and society's God rather than abandon his support of a "nigger" and
a slave with whom, in an act of ultimate impiety, he has entered into
a bond of brotherhood, Huck becomes a tool of Tom Sawyer's de-

votion to the rhetoric of the romantic novelists and participates in the resolution of the story in the cruel rigmarole of the "splendid, mixed up rescue." Yet, ironically, Huck's authoritative honesty is still basically present. He has come close to experiencing the delusion of an elevation to a moral level superior to that of the society in which he lives—a society indubitably marked by its subscription not only to the God-ordained right to own human beings but, according to Huck's witness, to the right to be aggressively ignorant, like Pap Finn; to carry on murderous and meaningless feuds, like the Grangerfords and Shepherdsons; to lynch defenseless bums like Boggs; and to tar and feather con artists like the Duke and the Dauphin. In a society, in short, that wholly betrays the ideal of the rule of reason that had informed the founding of the American Republic, Huck acquiesces in the historicity of his moral condition. Indeed, almost immediately after he has spoken the "awful words" affirming his allegiance to Jim, he qualifies his declaration by saying that he will "go to work and steal Jim out of slavery again," for this is the kind of thing he ought to do, "being brung up to wickedness."

In his seemingly unsophisticated yet subtle recognition of the immanence of the conscience in society—of the historicism of his own consciousness of good and evil—Huck displays an intuitive awareness of his situation. He cannot breathe at the level of transcendent moral choice. In his way Huck is profoundly aware of the irony of living in the semifrontier microcosm of a society that had had its origin in a statement to the world proclaiming the innate sovereignty of self—and heralding a "Great Experiment" in governance that amounted to an unprecedented experiment in human nature, this to test whether human beings are endowed with a sufficient capacity for rational thought and rational behavior to govern themselves as free "selves." Yet even as it came into being, half of the nation that had invented itself on the assumption of an affirmative answer to this question was already in the process of expanding into the largest slave society in modern times. Having made a book detailing his memory of his own effort to reject this society through an aborted flight to freedom with Jim, Huck asserts that he will now exercise the prerogative of the transcendent sovereign self and "light out for the territory" to escape being "civilized." He has "been there before." But even as he announces the second flight to freedom, Huck knows the desperate futility of his gesture. He cannot escape the burden of the historical actuality of his experience with Jim by referring it to the realm of nostalgic memory.

Yet if in his effort to penetrate the inner reality of southern society Mark Twain resolved the tension between memory and history in favor of history, the influence of his exemplary effort did not appreciably undercut the subservience of the southern literary mind to the metaphysics of remembrance. This reason is no doubt to be found in the fact that Mark Twain wore the comic mask but not altogether so. The multivolume compilation of southern literary piety called *The Library of Southern Literature* (prepared, the title page pointedly announces, under the "direct supervision of Southern men of letters") was published in the first decade of the twentieth century. While such an undertaking would not have been as feasible ten years later in the aftermath of World War I, the drama of the tension between memory and history created in the southern literary imagination by a war that had ended over fifty years earlier not only was still present but—in spite of the preoccupation with the before and after of the "Great War"—found its fulfillment as the definitive force in the writers of the Southern Renascence: in (to speak only of a few novelists) Allen Tate, Caroline Gordon, Andrew Lytle, Robert Penn Warren, and, most profoundly, Faulkner.

The question of how the memory of World War I enhanced the memory of the Civil War in the twentieth-century southern literary imagination is illuminated by a comparison of the difference between the attitude toward the memory of war assumed on the one hand by Faulkner and on the other by his precise contemporary Ernest Hemingway. Like Faulkner, Hemingway acknowledged the primary significance of Mark Twain, even to the point of saying in *The Green Hills of Africa* that "all modern American literature comes from one book . . . *Huckleberry Finn.* . . . There was nothing before. There has been nothing since."[5] But in this hyperbolic theory of American writing, the midwesterner Hemingway ignored entirely the question of Huck's historical context and made him into a "Hemingway hero," who, however incongruously, may be compared to Jake Barnes in *The Sun Also Rises*. A figure of the writer (or the "author")

5. Ernest Hemingway, *The Green Hills of Africa* (New York, 1954), 19.

and the chief actor in his own story, Jake, like all Hemingway heroes, finds the major motive of his life in the self-creation of a strangely stripped-down image of a world that, in contrast to the memory-obsessed world of Quentin Compson (in which "the past is not even past"), is preoccupied with the presentness of the present, even to the point of rejecting all traditional associations, including that of the family.

To speak of the role of Quentin in *Absalom, Absalom!* is to raise a much discussed problem. As we read the story of the Sutpens in its various reconstructions by the several narrators, do we discover any single character who serves as a focus of the authorial consciousness? On the face of it, is Quentin not simply one among the several characters in the novel, each obsessed by memory, each—including the third-person narrator—a self-conscious narrator (and actor), each the contributor of a highly subjective interpretative version of the fall of the House of Sutpen? The voluminous library of Faulkner criticism offers such different, and at times contradictory, responses to the narrators' interpretations of the story of the Sutpens that we may well reach the conclusion that the underlying motive of *Absalom, Absalom!* is contradictory: a strenuous effort to recover the past, the novel is yet a demonstration of the ambivalence of the effort. Yet in spite of the narrative maze we encounter in *Absalom, Absalom!*— which is further complicated, it should be added, by the presence of the unidentified third-person voice amid the identifiable voices— there is reason to interpret it as finding its ultimate focus in Quentin. "Ishmael is the witness in *Moby-Dick*," Faulkner once commented, "as I am Quentin in *The Sound and the Fury*."[6] It may be argued with some plausibility that Quentin not only is the chief participant-witness in *Absalom, Absalom!* but in his imaginative struggle to grasp the meaning of the lives of Henry Sutpen and his family, white and black, is—as a persona of Faulkner, the author, the maker, the ordering artist—the same enclosing presence in the story of the Sutpens that Faulkner had conceived him to be in his earlier story about the Compsons.

Powerfully established at the beginning of the novel, when Quentin sits with Miss Rosa in the September heat of the "dim airless

6. Joseph Blotner, *Faulkner: A Biography* (2 vols; New York, 1974), II, 1522.

room" of Sutpen's mansion—and powerfully reasserted at its end, when Quentin lies in bed talking with Shreve in the "iron" winter dark of a Harvard dormitory room—the presence of the twenty-year-old Mississippian in *Absalom, Absalom!* is more compelling than that of any other character. Hearing Miss Rosa's version of the story about the "demon" Sutpen in the initial scene of *Absalom, Absalom!*— listening to her speak "in that grim haggard amazed voice"—Quentin, a grandchild of the generation of Mississippi warriors who had fought in the Civil War, discovers after a time that he is no longer listening to the voice of Miss Rosa but is hearing "two separate" voices in himself: one voice is that of the "Quentin Compson preparing for Harvard in the South, the deep South dead since 1865 and peopled with garrulous outraged baffled ghosts"; the other voice in this inward dialogue is that of the Quentin "who was still too young to deserve yet to be a ghost, but nevertheless having to be one for all that, since he was born and bred in the deep South the same as she [Miss Rosa] was." The two Quentins talk "to one another in the long silence of notpeople, in notlanguage, *like this: It seems that this demon—his name was Sutpen—(Colonel Sutpen)—Colonel Sutpen. Who came out of nowhere and without warning upon the land with a band of strange niggers and built a plantation.*"[7]

At this point his dialogic interiorizing of the Sutpen story is interrupted when Quentin becomes aware that Miss Rosa is directly addressing him:

> Because you are going away to attend the college at Harvard they tell me. . . . So I dont imagine you will ever come back here and settle down as a country lawyer in a little town like Jefferson, since Northern people have already seen to it that there is little left in the South for a young man. So maybe you will enter the literary profession as so many Southern gentlemen and gentlewomen too are doing now and maybe some day you will remember this and write about it. You will be married then I expect and perhaps your wife will want a new gown or a new chair for the house and you can write this and submit it to the magazines. (5)

---

7. William Faulkner, *Absalom, Abasalom! The Corrected Text* (New York, 1986), 4–5. Hereafter references to this work will be made parenthetically in the text.

Why, Quentin wonders, does Miss Rosa need to suggest that he become a writer so that he can be the teller of her tale? If her need to tell the story of her relationship with Sutpen is so coercive, why does not she herself tell it? She is a writer, well-known as Yoknapatawpha County's "poetess laureate," who "out of some bitter and implacable reserve of undefeat" has frequently celebrated the heroes of the Lost Cause in odes, eulogies, and epitaphs published in the county newspaper. Quentin's question remains unanswered, at least explicitly. The implicit answer lies in Miss Rosa's recognition of Quentin as a potential literary witness in the first scene of *Absalom, Absalom!* Here Faulkner indicates his intention to repeat, in a more complex way, what he had done in *The Sound and the Fury* six years earlier, namely, to project Quentin as an incarnation of the fundamental, and inescapable, motive of the postbellum southern writer's imagination: the importunate sense, stemming from a compulsive memory of the Civil War, not simply of a personal intimacy with history but, as in the case of Huck Finn, of a connection with history so absolute that it is the very source of his being. When his father tells Quentin that Miss Rosa has a vengeful motive in her idea of involving him in the story of her dastardly treatment by the "demon"—this because she believes, or wants to believe, that her fateful association with Sutpen would never have occurred if the "demon" had not come to Mississippi as the consequence of a friendship with Quentin's grandfather—Quentin counters with an explanation of epic grandeur: "*She wants it told . . . so that people whom she will never see and whose names she will never hear and who have never heard her name nor seen her face will read it and know at last why God let us lose the War: that only through the blood of our men and the tears of our women could He stay this demon and efface his name and lineage from the earth*" (6).

Although Quentin himself immediately rejects his bardic explanation of Miss Rosa's solicitation of his pen, he is, as the third-person narrator indicates, not merely playing a game with his father. His conception of Miss Rosa's appeal to the "God who let us lose the War" indirectly reflects the fact that Quentin knows that he and Miss Rosa (and for that matter his father) are as profoundly entangled in the history of Sutpen's struggle to found the House of Sutpen as is Miss Rosa's older sister, Ellen Coldfield, the wife Sutpen takes from a prominent Yoknapatawpha family to be the bearer of his heirs; or

Henry and Judith Sutpen, the children Ellen bears; or Charles Bon, the son and heir Sutpen has earlier fathered in Haiti, only to reject him upon discovering that his mother is partly Negro; or Clytie, Sutpen's daughter by one of the "wild" slaves he brings to Yokna-patawpha. And Quentin knows that, in a larger sense, he and Miss Rosa and Mr. Compson are also implicated in the anomalies and ironies of a shaping cultural ethos that paradoxically at once com-memorates and celebrates the world-historical self-defeat of a house that was not only a part of that larger house Lincoln said could not stand divided against itself but was significantly in itself a divided house.

Without insisting at all on a literal correspondence between the House of Sutpen and the House of the South, one can hardly fail to discern implicit symbols of the southern divisiveness in Quentin's knowledge of the Sutpens. He knows, for one thing, that Miss Rosa had a father "who as a conscientious objector on religious grounds, had starved to death in the attic of his own house, hidden (some said, walled up) there from Confederate provost marshals' men and fed secretly at night by the same daughter [Miss Rosa] who at the very time was accumulating her first folio in which the lost cause's unre-generate vanquished were name by name embalmed." Quentin also knows the more fateful fact that Miss Rosa had a "nephew [Henry Sutpen] who served for four years in the same company with his sister's fiance [Charles Bon] and then shot the fiance to death before the gates to the house where the sister waited in her wedding gown on the eve of the wedding and then fled, vanished, none knew where" (6). And Quentin knows much more, too much for any peace of mind. Having "grown up" with all the names associated with the story of Sutpen, Quentin, the third-person narrator tells us, has become a symbolic repository of the memory of the destroyed House of Sutpen and the remembrance of the southern defeat. "He was a barracks filled with stubborn back-looking ghosts still recov-ering, even forty-three years afterward, from the fever which had cured the disease, waking from the fever without even knowing that it had been the fever itself which they had fought against and not the sickness, looking with stubborn recalcitrance backward beyond the fever and into the disease with actual regret, weak from the fever yet free of the disease and not even aware that the freedom was that of impotence" (7).

Described by the third-person narrator as "not a being, an entity," but, in metaphors of Shakespearean intensity, as a "barracks" filled with ghosts, or more expansively, a ghostly "commonwealth," Quentin emerges more clearly in *Absalom, Absalom!* than in *The Sound and the Fury* as a highly self-conscious, romantic, doomed embodiment of the lost Confederacy. Out of the deepest levels of his imagination of memory and history, he subtly transforms the story of the House of Sutpen into a deeply introverted, and deeply ironic, vision of the drama of the inner history of the War for Southern Independence. Even as southern society was engaged in a massive struggle to preserve itself as a slave society, the third-person narrator intimates in his description of Quentin, it had a secret motive, inarticulate, hidden even from itself: a desire to free itself from its enslavement to the "disease" of slavery. Yet, having been forced by military catastrophe to accept the fulfillment of its hidden desire, this society looks back with regret at having been freed by the "fever" of war from the "disease" of slavery. Until the South can openly accept the historical implications of its desire to be free from the social and economic institution of chattel slavery—which, although *Absalom, Absalom!* does not quite make this explicit, had been rationalized by antebellum southerners as their necessary source of freedom—the revolutionary shift from a slave society to a free society is historically "impotent." As the drama of the House of Sutpen unfolds through the witness of Miss Rosa and Mr. Compson, Quentin's struggle to interpret it almost half a century after the end of the War for Southern Independence becomes the focal revelation of this powerful irony. In an earlier age, Quentin would have been a bardic voice speaking of the glory of "olden times." But in the first decade of the twentieth century—not so much a grandchild as a ghost of the generation of the 1860s—a poet of the American South assumes not only the role of a witness to the unending drama of his own personal struggle to interpret the meaning of the vexed and tortuous history of the South but, like Faulkner, the self-conscious role of an actor in a drama he is both composing and enacting in his own consciousness.

The problem of interpretation that preoccupies Quentin in this drama is the central problem in *Absalom, Absalom!*: Why does Henry kill Charles Bon? Three poignant scenes are particularly illuminating. One occurs toward the end of the fifth chapter, when the third-person narrator interrupts Miss Rosa's narrative to present what he imagines to be Quentin's creation for himself of a part of the story of Sutpen's children, this being the moment when Henry, having just shot Charles Bon as the two soldiers arrive back at Sutpen's place after Appomattox, runs up the stairs and bursts into his sister's bedroom. Here he sees Clytie and Ellen, "the white girl in her underthings (made of flour sacking when there had been flour, of window curtains when not)." He sees too Judith's wedding dress,

> the yellowed creamy mass of old intricate satin and lace spread carefully on the bed and then caught swiftly up by the white girl and held before her as the door crashed in and the brother stood there, hatless, with his shaggy bayonet-trimmed hair, his gaunt worn unshaven face, his patched and faded gray tunic, the pistol still hanging against his flank: the two of them, brother and sister, curiously alike as if the difference in sex had merely sharpened the common blood to a terrific, an almost unbearable, similarity, speaking to one another in short brief staccato sentences like slaps, as if they stood breast to breast striking one another in turn neither making any attempt to guard against the blows.
> *Now you cant marry him.*
> *Why cant I marry him?*
> *Because he's dead.*
> *Dead?*
> *Yes. I killed him.* (139)

Another illuminating scene in *Absalom, Absalom!* occurs when Quentin, listening to his father's account of the relationship between Bon and Judith, sees the one letter Bon—at Henry's urging—wrote to Judith during his entire four years in the Confederate army. Taking the letter in hand, Quentin imagines as he reads "the faint spidery script"—written nearly fifty years before on elegant French notepaper from a gutted southern mansion with a pen dipped in stove polish captured from the Yankees—that he is listening to Bon's "gentle sardonic whimsical and incurably pessimistic" voice telling Judith in the final days of the Confederacy that he has come to believe they are, "*strangely enough, included among those who are doomed to live*"

(105). Although Bon's message is enigmatic, Judith takes it to be a proposal of marriage.

While Mr. Compson talks on about Henry and Bon—wondering whether Henry had warned Bon not to come back to Judith and describing the scene of their encounter outside the gate of the Sutpen place as they arrive back from the war ("the two of them must have ridden side by side almost")—Quentin, once again "hearing without having to listen," according to the intervening imagination of the narrator, is depicted as silently imagining the scene for himself.

(It seemed to Quentin that he could actually see them, facing one another at the gate. Inside the gate what was once a park now spread, unkempt, in shaggy desolation, with an air dreamy remote and aghast like the unshaven face of a man just waking from ether, up to a huge house where a young girl waited in a wedding dress made from stolen scraps, the house partaking too of that air of scaling desolation, not having suffered from invasion but a shell marooned and forgotten in a backwater of catastrophe—a skeleton giving of itself in slow driblets of furniture and carpet, linen and silver, to help to die torn and anguished men who knew, even while dying, that for months now the sacrifice and the anguish were in vain. They faced one another on the two gaunt horses, two men, young, not yet in the world, not yet breathed over long enough, to be old but with old eyes, with unkempt hair and faces gaunt and weathered as if cast by some spartan and even niggard hand from bronze, in worn and patched gray weathered now to the color of dead leaves, the one with the tarnished braid of an officer, the other plain of cuff, the pistol lying yet across the saddle bow unaimed, the two faces calm, the voices not even raised: *Dont you pass the shadow of this post, this branch, Charles, and I am going to pass it, Henry*). (105–106)

The conclusion of the scene is in Mr. Compson's voice: "and then Wash Jones sitting that saddleless mule before Miss Rosa's gate, shouting her name into the sunny and peaceful quiet of the street, saying, 'Air you Rosie Coldfield? Then you better come on out yon.

Henry has done shot that durn French feller. Kilt him dead as a beef'" (106).

Why does Bon want to marry his sister? Is he in love with her? If so, his love is clearly subordinated to his passion for revenge on a father who refuses to acknowledge him. Sutpen had a vivid chance to accept Bon as his son when the elegant and handsome New Orleanian came to visit Sutpen's Hundred as Henry's fellow student and friend at the University of Mississippi. He had a still more vivid chance to accept Bon as his son toward the end of the war when the unit Bon and Henry were in became attached to a regimental unit commanded by their father. If Sutpen had recognized Bon at either time, presumably things would have been different. But he cannot acknowledge an heir who has a tincture of black blood. Bon—with no trace of the negroid in his appearance, handsome, urbane, ten years older than Henry—becomes Henry's idol, and no less a fatal attraction for Judith. Undergoing the experience of war with Bon, Henry, who has known since 1861 that he and Judith are half brother and half sister to Bon (and has known as well, though this knowledge is of lesser import, that Bon is the father of a boy by a New Orleans octoroon), has, it would seem, overcome his revulsion against its incestuous nature and reconciled himself to a union between Bon and Judith. How has this incredible adjustment taken place? Has the war experience rendered Henry's feeling toward Bon an emotion transcendent over any other emotion? Or does Henry, unconsciously harboring incestuous feelings both for his brother and for his sister, somehow imagine their marriage as a consummation of his desire? Does Bon desire the marriage only for revenge on Sutpen? Or is he in love with Judith? For that matter, is Judith in love with Bon?

In any event it is not until the very end of the war that Henry learns of an impediment to the marriage of Bon and Judith that love, normal or abnormal, can in no wise blink. When he responds to a command to come to Colonel Sutpen's tent (Sutpen has organized a command and gone to the war not long after Henry and Bon), he is told by Sutpen that after Bon's birth he had discovered that Bon's mother, a planter's daughter he had taken as his wife while he was an overseer on a Haitian plantation, had Negro blood. Henry is given an injunction by his father that, issuing from the lips of his commanding officer, has something of the force of a military order: "*He must not marry her, Henry*" (283).

We do not know about the meeting of Henry and his father until the culminating, and concluding, scene in *Absalom, Absalom!* In their chilly Harvard dormitory room on a snowy night in January, 1910, Quentin and his roommate, the Canadian Shreve McCannon, discuss at great length the question of why Henry killed Bon. As they talk they engage in a speculative reconstruction of what led to this event. But significantly we learn about Sutpen's injunction to Henry not through Shreve's and Henry's speculative reconstruction of the meeting in Sutpen's tent. What happened there comes to us only in Quentin's unspoken re-creation. At first, Quentin imagines, Henry refused the order.

> —*You are going to let him marry Judith, Henry.*
> *Still Henry does not answer. It has all been said before, and now he has had four years of bitter struggle following which, whether it be victory or defeat which he has gained, at least he has gained it and has peace now, even if the peace be mostly despair.*
> —*He cannot marry her, Henry.*
> *Now Henry speaks.*
> —*You said that before. I told you then. And now, and now it wont be much longer now and then we wont have anything left: honor nor pride nor God since God quit us four years ago only He never thought it necessary to tell us; no shoes nor clothes and no need for them; not only no land to make food out of but no need for the food and when you dont have God and honor and pride, nothing matters except that there is the old mindless meat that dont even care if it was defeat or victory, that wont even die, that will be out in the woods and fields, grubbing up roots and weeds.—Yes. I have decided, Brother or not, I have decided. I will. I will. . . .*
> —*He must not marry her, Henry. His mother's father told me that her mother had been a Spanish woman. I believed him; it was not until after he was born that I found out that his mother was part negro.* (283)

Quentin's imagination of it is also the only source of the moment that follows immediately after the scene in Colonel Sutpen's tent, the encounter between Bon and Henry at the campfire.

> —*So it's the miscegenation, not the incest, which you cant bear.*
> *Henry doesn't answer.*

—And he sent me no word? He did not ask you to send me to
him? No word to me, no word at all? That was all he had to do,
now, today; four years ago or at any time during the four years.
That was all. He would not have needed to ask it, require it, of me.
I would have offered it. I would have said, I will never see her again
before he could have asked it of me. He did not have to do this,
Henry. He didn't need to tell you I am a nigger to stop me. He could
have stopped me without that, Henry. (285)

In Quentin's private re-creation of what happened next, Bon extends
a pistol and commands Henry to shoot him (Bon is also Henry's
superior officer), but Henry refuses, saying, "*You are my brother.*" He
continues to refuse even though Bon says, "*No I'm not. I'm the nigger*
that's going to sleep with your sister. Unless you stop me, Henry" (286).
Henry does not stop Bon until the two arrive at the very gate to
Sutpen's Hundred.

By this juncture in the novel Quentin's telling Shreve about his
going out to Sutpen's Hundred with Miss Rosa, discovering the dying Henry there, and then witnessing the burning of Sutpen's mansion can only come as an anticlimax. It is instructive to learn that in
the short story out of which Faulkner's novel grew, this is not the
case. Unpublished until Joseph Blotner's edition of *The Uncollected*
Stories of William Faulkner came out in 1979, this story, entitled
"Evangeline," like another Faulkner short story called "Mistral," is
developed through the use of an "I" narrator and the narrator's friend
Don Giovanni. Don has put the narrator onto a "ghost story" about
the mystery surrounding a decaying Mississippi plantation house belonging to a family named Sutpen. Although the details of the plot
are somewhat different and not nearly so elaborate, "Evangeline"
centers in the narrator's investigation of the story of Judith, Bon, and
Henry, and his discovery of Henry's presence in the Sutpen house,
where throughout the forty years since his fraticidal act he has lived
secretly under the protection of a black woman named Raby. Raby,
it turns out, is Sutpen's child by one of his slaves and the sister of
Judith, Bon, and Henry (she becomes Clytie in *Absalom, Absalom!*).
As though he was unable to assimilate the experience of verifying
the secret presence of Henry Sutpen in the Sutpen mansion, the narrator's account of the event is fragmentary and impressionistic. Yet

it is strangely emphatic; the narrator feels a certain identity with Henry:

> It was quite still. There was a faint constant sighing high in the cedars, and I could hear the insects and the mockingbird. Soon there were two of them, answering one another, brief, quiring, risinginflectioned [*sic*]. Soon the sighing cedars, the insects and the birds became one peaceful sound bowled inside the skull in monotonous miniature, as if all the earth were contracted and reduced to the dimensions of a baseball, into and out of which shapes, fading, emerged fading and faded emerging:
> "And you were killed by the lost shot fired in the war?"
> "I was so killed. Yes."
> "Who fired the last shot fired in the war?"
> "Was it the last shot you fired in the war, Henry?"
> "I fired a last shot in the war; yes."
> "You depended on the war, and the war betrayed you too; was that it?"
> "Was that it, Henry?"[8]

In *Absalom, Absalom!* Quentin's visit to the dark room of the Sutpen mansion where Henry lies dying is more ambiguous in its presentation. In the novel, in contrast to "Evangeline," Henry flees after he kills Bon and returns four years before Miss Rosa and Quentin find him there under the zealous protection of a "tiny gnomelike creature in headrag and voluminous skirts" with "a worn coffee-colored face," his sister Clytie. In the discovery scene in *Absalom, Absalom!* no reference is made to a last shot in the war; Quentin's interrogation of Henry is elliptical. But the scene brings to a subtle climax the increasingly close relationship the doomed Quentin feels with Sutpen's tragic children. The sealing of this relationship is indicated by so small a sign as the colon that marks the transition from the narrator's objective description of how Quentin enters the shuttered "bare stale room" where Henry lies dying to the portrayal of the interior scene in which the identity of Henry is established.

8. William Faulkner, "Evangeline," in *The Uncollected Stories of William Faulkner*, ed. Joseph Blotner (New York, 1979), 685–86. *Cf.* below, 176–81.

The bed, the yellow sheets and pillow, the wasted yellow face
with closed, almost transparent eyelids on the pillow, the
wasted hands crossed on the breast as if he were already a
corpse; waking or sleeping it was the same and would be the
same forever as long as he lived:
   And you are————?
   Henry Sutpen.
   And you have been here————?
   Four years.
   And you came home————?
   To die. Yes.
   Yes. To die.
   And you have been here————?
   Four years.
   And you are————? (298)

In the exact use of a colon instead of a parenthesis ["(—*the winter of '64 now, the army retreated*," etc.] to denote the shift from
the objective to the subjective mode (*i.e.,* the entry into Quentin's
consciousness), the subtle authority of the third-person narrator becomes explicit. His consciousness has become identical with Quentin's. For those who know "Evangeline" an anticipation of this moment may be seen in the "I" narrator's strange rapport with Bon,
Henry, and Raby [Clytie] in that story. When both the *Saturday Evening Post* and the *Woman's Home Companion* rejected "Evangeline,"
Faulkner put the story aside, but finding that it would not let him
alone, he came back to it after a couple of years and sought to make
it work better by replacing the "I" narrator and Don with two characters he called Chisholm and Burke. Eventually, the grip of the story
on him becoming stronger, he thought of transforming Chisholm
and Burke into Quentin and Shreve and making them interpreter-
participants in a story that, greatly expanded and far more sophisticated in technique, would have a suggestive frame of reference in the
Old Testament epic of David and his sons and be a major part of his
symbol of the history of the South, the fictional history of Yoknapatawpha County, Mississippi. The expanded story, in other words,
would have its center not in the account of Sutpen and the exploit-
ative invasion of the wilderness that in not much more than two
short generations produced the rise and fall of the Cotton Kingdom

but in a story allusive of the biblical story of King David and his sons. In this story the murder of Ammon by Absalom occurs just after the two brothers have concluded four long years of fighting against great odds for a common cause. Ironically, in a civil conflict that has often been called "the brothers' war"—and in which brothers, not only in a figurative but in some cases in a literal sense, were engaged on opposing sides—the sons of Sutpen were on the same side. Like most southerners, slaveholders and nonslaveholders, they fought to uphold the more or less official doctrine that the preservation of slavery was necessary for the preservation of a sacred guarantee of constitutional freedom that included their right to own slaves. Forcibly dispossessed of this right, they believed, they would become slaves themselves. The murdered brother and the murdering brother had no quarrel in this respect.

But the narrator in "Evangeline," asking Bon if he had been killed by the last shot fired in the war and Henry if he had pulled the trigger, was moved by the knowledge that Bon had died not in the war between the North and the South but in a struggle within a society that, even as it fought against the brothers with whom, only three generations earlier, it had made common cause in the American Revolution, was rent by its need for a more coherent, convincing definition of its historical character than the Revolution had provided. The southern struggle for historical self-representation was rendered all the more intense because of the fact that even as the South sought to express its destiny, the effort was repressed by the need to present the image of a society united in support of slavery. In its uncertainty about itself the southern slave society placed an extreme premium on an ideal of order that held above all, as Faulkner said in speaking of Andrew Jackson, that "the principle of honor must be defended whether it was or not because defended it was whether or not."[9] Equating the principle of family honor with the ideal of feminine chastity and the protection of the purity of the bloodline, Henry had finally to slay Bon, even though Mr. Compson says Henry loved Bon, and in "Evangeline" Don says the two were "close as a married couple almost."[10]

In their conversation in the cold dark after they finally go to bed,

9. Appendix to *The Portable Faulkner,* ed. Malcolm Cowley (New York, 1964), 738.

10. Faulkner, "Evangeline," in *Uncollected Stories,* ed. Blotner, 587.

Shreve keeps on baiting Quentin about the South. Referring to the Canadians, he says, "We dont live among defeated grandfathers and freed slaves (or have I got it backward and was it your folks that are free and the niggers that lost?) and bullets in the dining room table and such, to be always reminding us to never forget." When Shreve, warming to his subject, observes that the southern memory of General Sherman is perpetual, so that "forevermore as long as your children's children produce children you wont be anything but a descendant of a long line of colonels killed in Pickett's charge at Manassas," Quentin at once corrects Shreve's factual error about the battle in which Pickett's charge occurred, adding, in the second most famous statement in the novel, "You cant understand it. You would have to be born there." But when Shreve—in a passage not often noticed in the voluminous critical interpretation of *Absalom, Absalom!*—continues to challenge Quentin about the southern culture of memory, "Would I then? [*i.e.,* have to be born there]. . . . Do you understand it?" Quentin equivocates: "'I dont know. . . . Yes, of course I understand it.' They breathed in the darkness. After a moment Quentin said: 'I dont know'" (289).

When Shreve presents his most dramatic challenge to Quentin: "Now I want you to tell me just one thing more. Why do you hate the South?," the heir of the Compsons replies "quickly, at once, immediately," in the best-known words of the novel. "'I dont hate it,' he said. *I dont hate it* he thought, panting in the cold air, the iron New England dark; *I dont. I dont! I dont hate it! I dont hate it!*" (303). If, as has been said, Quentin protests Shreve's challenge too much, he has reason to. His very identity, in a way his very existence, is suddenly and irrevocably at stake.

"Ishmael is the witness in *Moby-Dick* as I am Quentin in *The Sound and the Fury*": If in his imagination of his authorial role, Faulkner identifies with Quentin in the comparatively simple structure of the story of the doomed Compsons, he does so even more surely, if more subtly, in the intricately structured story involving the relationship between the memorial reconstruction of the doom of the House of Sutpen on the one hand and the doom of the House of Compson on the other. Thought of by Faulkner as a symbol of the second—or, it may be said, the first full—literary generation of the postbellum South, Quentin (born 1890) could scarcely have been conceived by a writer of his own generation. A symbolic embodi-

ment of the culmination of the drama of memory and history in
Faulkner's generation (Faulkner was born in 1897)—the generation
that became the post–World War I generation—Quentin incarnates
more powerfully than any other character in southern fiction the
drama of the ironic equivocation of the southern literary mind in its
quest to discover in the southern memory a postbellum southern
identity. The revelation of the inner civil war in the South in the
story of Henry, Bon, and Judith reveals how, in his effort to come to
terms with the South, Quentin, a romantic southern Puritan, is the
doomed reincarnation of an earlier young southern Puritan, Henry
Sutpen. In the last moment of a difficult journey back from the war,
obeying the southern mode of the murderous defense of family
honor—defending an abstract principle that had to be defended lest
the order of the world be lost—Henry had not only killed his brother
and made himself into a ghost, he had made Quentin, who would
not be born for another fifteen years, into a ghost. "'I am older at
twenty than a lot of people who have died,' Quentin said" (301).

Before he called on Quentin Compson to be a witness to, and an
actor in, the drama of Henry Sutpen's desperate and despairing defense of the principle of honor in *Absalom, Absalom!*, Faulkner had of
course in *The Sound and the Fury* already depicted the ultimate fate of
his surrogate. Drowning himself in the Charles River in Cambridge,
Massachusetts, on June 2, 1910, Quentin had signaled the despair of
those bound by the poetry of memory to a world no longer believed
in. In this case it was the world the slaveholders—and, however
unwillingly, the enslaved themselves—had made in the American
South. Equating freedom with the defense of an illusory principle
that they nonetheless conceived to be the vital basis of order, the
slave masters had littered battlefield after battlefield with the sacrifi-
cial victims of a War for Southern Independence. Like the subtly
ironic pathos of Mark Twain's representation of Huckleberry Finn's
memory of the antebellum South, the still more refined distillation
of pathos in Faulkner's representation of Quentin's memory of the
Confederacy, and of the postbellum South, does not simply reflect
the drama of the literary representation of the inner history of the
Civil War, it is part and parcel of this history. If, moreover—and we
must admit the possibility—either Mark Twain's or Faulkner's representation of the war be deemed at times to be misrepresentation, it
is not less integral to the war's inner history.

V

The Tenses of History
Faulkner

Like Thomas Hardy's Wessex, William Faulkner's Yoknapa-tawpha County originated in the imagination of a young writer reared in a provincial community. In both instances a youthful mind endowed with literary genius discovered that the small, remote world of his nativity in its own way represented the major experience of modern Western civilization: the almost complete displacement of a society of myth and tradition by a novel society of history and science. In either case a youthful writer entered into the knowledge of this phenomenon through an unacademic but intensely self-conscious and sustained process of reading in a variety of literary and philosophical works; and in either case, during the struggles of his self-education, a youthful writer became a self-elected member of the cosmopolitan order of poets, critics, and literary prophets that since the end of the age of ecclesiastical dominion has thought of itself as having a moral mission to the evolving secular civilization of the West.

Foreshadowed by Petrarch and Chaucer, clearly represented by Shakespeare and Cervantes, this realm has been perpetuated by myriad literary figures, great and small, to the present day—when it may be that its sense of purpose is becoming so attenuated that the vocation of the writer in the West is failing for lack of an assumed rationale. But in the first half of the twentieth century the literary vocation was still a basic cultural assumption wherever appreciable reading and writing skills extended. A Faulkner in Lafayette County, Mississippi, or a Thomas Hardy in Devonshire, England—no less than a James Joyce in Dublin or a T. S. Eliot in London—self-consciously conceived of his interest in literature in terms of a moral obligation to fulfill the image of the writer as both literary artist and "clerk," as both storyteller and prophetic voice. He might think of his commitment to literature, even as the young Eliot and the young Faulkner did, as being no small thing—as being potentially at least a historical transaction involving the past, present, and future of civilization.

Although the literary vocation had suffered a severe constriction in the American South during the years dominated by the slavery issue, and by the War for Southern Independence and its aftermath, a writer in the twentieth-century South stood in relation to such cosmopolitan figures of his own region as Thomas Jefferson (the poet-philosopher-prophet who wrote the Declaration of Independence), Edgar Allan Poe (who had a larger influence in Europe than in America), and Mark Twain (who walked on the world stage for at least half of his career). In his own time the writer of the twentieth-century South stood, or would come to stand, in relation to a panoply of writers associated with a sophisticated literary movement that included John Crowe Ransom, Allen Tate, Donald Davidson, Andrew Lytle, Robert Penn Warren, Caroline Gordon, Katherine Anne Porter, and Eudora Welty. Indeed, by virtue of a civilized commitment to letters that was still taken for granted, the writer of the twentieth-century American South bore a relation to the large body of writing, imaginative and critical, which for five centuries recorded the complex story of the conquest of the older community by the modern order—and in so doing created out of the drama of differentiation the large, many-faceted secular myth of the self's encounter with history. The modern writer participates in this myth both as author and (in various guises of alienation from modernity) as actor. The literary myth of modern history, to be sure, is in an important sense a myth of the modern literary vocation. As demonstrated by his efforts to express and define it in his early writings and by his complex realization of it in the creation and peopling of Yoknapatawpha County, Mississippi (a more audacious undertaking than Hardy's creation and peopling of Wessex), Faulkner's involvement in this myth is the major aspect of his career.

Some of the sources of his initial experience of the drama of cultural differentiation in the history of modern Western civilization may be deduced in part from the fragmentary records of his voluminous reading. At the age of twelve or thirteen, for example, Faulkner began a life-long devotion to *Moby-Dick,* of all nineteenth-century American novels the largest and most complicated treatment of the disjunction of the sacramental world of medieval Christendom from the secular modern world. But the influence of Melville on the early Faulkner was less powerful than direct and comparatively simple visions of cultural transformation: for example, those implicit, on the one hand, in A. E. Housman's ironic, Stoic pastoralism and, on the other, in Swinburne's lush, despairing farewell to the Greco-Roman gods. Young Faulkner was also strongly drawn to the earlier nineteenth-century poets, especially Shelley and Keats. Keats, to be sure, became a crucial influence on the young Faulkner, serving not only as a prime model of literary attainment but as an image of literary apprenticeship. Remarkably like the aspiring Keats, in fact, Faulkner grasped the problem of the imagination in the time between boyhood and manhood. "The imagination of a boy is healthy, and the mature imagination of a man is healthy," Keats says in the Preface to "Endymion," his first long poem, "but there is a space of life between, in which the soul is in ferment, character undecided, the way of life uncertain, the ambition thick-sighted."[1]

Cultivating the possibilities of the "space between" even more assiduously and in more complicated ways than Keats, the youthful Faulkner endeavored to project into it a series of symbolic figurations of the young poet Faulkner himself seeking his identity. These include the image of the poet as the dispossessed faun in *The Marble Faun,* sighing for "Things I know, yet cannot know, / 'Twixt sky above and earth below." More significantly, they also include the oblique image of the poet presented in the remarkable twinned exemplars of modern sexual narcissism, Pierrot and Marietta, the chief characters in Faulkner's youthful play *The Marionettes.* "I desire— what do I desire?" Marietta asks, and in his seduction of her the vain Pierrot echoes the same futile question.[2] In both *The Marble Faun* and *The Marionettes* the formal garden setting suggests that the poetic spirit has become confined in history or, more broadly put, that the literary imagination in general is imprisoned in a world in which all

1. John Keats, Preface to "Endymion," in *The Poetical Works of Keats* (Boston, 1975), 48.
2. William Faulkner, *"The Marble Faun" and "A Green Bough"* (New York, 1960), 12; *The Marionettes: A Play in One Act* (Charlottesville, Va., 1972), 51.

the mythic and traditionalist—the sacramental—attitudes toward human existence are becoming historicized. More significantly, in the figure of the poet represented by the twinned image of Pierrot and Marietta, Faulkner suggests a major symbol of modernity in the differentiation and specialization of sex, or the historicizing of sexuality.

Faulkner's preoccupation with this symbol and its bearing on the role of the poet (a preoccupation increased and enlarged, it would seem, by his reading of Freud) is evident in various other poems written in the early years of his career and collected in 1933 in *A Green Bough*. A short poem entitled "Eros and After" in one typescript and "And After" in another (published as poem number XXVI in *A Green Bough*) depicts the withdrawal of Selene, Greek goddess of the moon, from the world.

> Still, and look down, look down:
> Thy curious withdrawn hand
> Unprobes, now spirit and sense unblend, undrown,
> Knit by a word and sundered by a tense
> Like this: Is: Was: and Not. Nor caught between
> Spent beaches and the annealed insatiate sea
> Dost myriad lie, cold and intact Selene,
> On secret strand or old disastrous lee
> Behind the fading mistral of the sense.

Perhaps this poem is a metaphor of the psychic state of the spent lover; possibly it is a symbol of the Cartesian crisis. In any event its portrayal of the sundering of sense and spirit represents Faulkner's sense of the historicizing of time—his awareness of the remorseless historical demarcation in modernity of *is* from *was*. The tension between this recognition and the nostalgic impulse to restore the ancient sense of cyclical wholeness is placed in the ironic context of the Hebraic-Christian conception of history in another *Green Bough* poem (XLII).

> Beneath the apple tree Eve's tortured shape
> Glittered in the Snake's, her riven breast
> Sloped his coils and took the sun's escape
> To augur black her sin from east to west.

In winter's night man may keep him warm
Regretting olden sins he did omit;
With fetiches the whip of blood to charm,
Forgetting that with breath he's heir to it.

But old gods fall away, the ancient Snake
Is throned and crowned instead, and has for minion
That golden apple which will never slake
But ever feeds man's crumb of fire, when plover
And swallow and shrill northing birds whip over
Nazarene and Roman and Virginian.[3]

Obviously written under the influence of Keats's "Ode on a Grecian Urn," a poem that always served Faulkner as an emblem of the vocation to art, "Twilight" (designated as poem number X in *A Green Bough*) is about a precociously self-conscious youth who, forced to strive "with earth for bread" in the day, upon the approach of night forgets "his father, Death" and "Derision, his mother" and yields himself to an evening vision of nymphs and fauns rioting in the dusk,

Beyond all oceaned Time's cold greenish bar
To shrilling pipes, to cymbals' hissing
Beneath a single icy star
Where he, to his own compulsion
—A terrific figure on an urn—
Is caught between his two horizons,
Forgetting that he can't return.[4]

The young Faulkner's notion of the poet caught between his self-imagined horizons of myth and history reminds us that each major writer since the end of the sixteenth century has had to situate himself with reference to these two horizons. Writing his poems (and several prose sketches not discussed here) in the first half of the 1920s, Faulkner repressed the poetic differentiation of the historical from the traditionalist-mythic, or sacramental, mode of conscious-

3. Faulkner, *A Green Bough*, 48, 65.
4. *Ibid.*, 30.

ness. The initial, or poetic, phase of his career, in other words, cogently represents the literary myth of modern history: the story of the self trying through the power of the literary art to cope with its irresistible identification with history. But his recapitulation of the drama of differentiation would not be completed until Faulkner took the path of Cervantes rather than the one of Shakespeare. Although with the decline of the principle of sacramental unity the poets, such as Shakespeare and Donne, came to embody the disappearance of the image of the poet as bard in the image of the poet as alienated self, novelists were verily created by the loss of the unified society. Beginning with Cervantes, they have exhaustively explored each successive stage of the movement out of the old society into the new, projecting endless images of the historical self in quest of its meaning. Although Faulkner says that he gave up being a poet because he found that his proficiency in poetic techniques was too limited, the inner reason would seem to be his discovery that if he was to write the myth he was living—the drama of self and history, the story of the Knight of the Pale Countenance in quest of his historical identity—he must shift his conception of his vocation and think of himself as a novelist rather than a poet. The transformation of the Yocona River country with its red clay hills and fertile bottomlands into Yoknapatawpha County was not Faulkner's fundamental motive in writing his novels. Nor, for that matter, is the creation of the history of Yoknapatawpha County to be construed as his basic novelistic subject.

In 1944, when Malcolm Cowley became engaged in editing *The Portable Faulkner* and decided to represent the Yoknapatawpha stories as possessing an epic unity in that taken together they comprise a legend of the South, Faulkner agreed with the editorial concept yet observed in a letter to Cowley:

> As regards any specific book, I'm trying primarily to tell a story, in the most effective way I can think of, the most moving, the most exhaustive. But I think even that is incidental to what I am trying to do, taking my output (the course of it) as a whole. I am telling the same story over and over, which is myself and the world. Tom Wolfe was trying to say everything, get everything, the world plus "I" or filtered through "I" or the effort of "I" to embrace the world in

which he was born and walked a little while and then lay down again, into one volume. I am trying to go a step further. This I think accounts for what people call the obscurity, the involved formless "style," endless sentences. I'm trying to say it all in one sentence, between one Cap and one period. I'm still trying, to put it all, if possible, on one pinhead. I dont know how to do it. All I know to do is to keep on trying in a new way. I'm inclined to think that my material, the South, is not very important to me. I just happen to know it, and dont have time in one life to learn another one and write at the same time. Though the one I know is probably as good as another, life is a phenomenon but not a novelty, the same frantic steeplechase toward nothing everywhere and man stinks the same stink no matter where in time.[5]

In his statement to Cowley, Faulkner essentially says that to give the impression that the Yoknapatawpha stories constitute a collectivity distorts his motive in creating them. The stories are in his own view a series of discrete endeavors, each motivated by the inner compulsion on his part to render the story of the self as literary artist attempting to confront and to order a desacralized world, in which all—everything and everybody, every aspect of nature and of human existence as apprehended by the human consciousness—has become historical. The telling of this story demands an art of storytelling more strenuous and complex than that of a Thomas Wolfe: an art of the word that may appear to be formless but is designed to seize human existence in history in the tight and irrevocable grasp of one long sentence. Although Faulkner's remarks to Cowley may be partly a spoof, they give us a less distorted view of his purpose as a novelist than the view that conforms his intention to the Balzacian standard of diversity and monumentality. As Faulkner indicates in the same letter to Cowley, his desire "to put all mankind's history in one sentence" accords with Joyce's motive in *Ulysses*—that is to say, through the strength of art to make the novel an intricate metaphor of the differentiation of the historical self.

5. William Faulkner to Malcolm Cowley, [early November, 1944], in *Selected Letters of William Faulkner,* ed. Joseph Blotner (New York, 1978), 185.

Faulkner wrote his first novels not—as he himself sometimes said with all too self-conscious, heavy-handed irony—for fun. Both *Soldiers' Pay* and *Mosquitoes* represent committed efforts by a fledgling novelist to get his hands on his subject—the same subject he had failed to get his hands on as a poet: the relation of self, history, and art in a society divested of the sacramental. In the first novel Faulkner daringly uses a fictitious town in Georgia called Charleston as a quasi-wasteland setting. Donald Mahon, a wounded and comatose World War I aviator who is in truth a faun, and Januarius Jones, a plumpish satyr at loose in the twentieth century, are among the characters who appear on the scene as symbols of alienation. In the second novel the scene of the wasteland, more appropriate if less imaginatively daring, is New Orleans. An ambitious effort to encompass the whole subject of artist, critic, and patron under the modern condition, *Mosquitoes,* like *Soldiers' Pay,* does not develop the drama of differentiation beyond a superficial symbolic level. The self's experience of historical existence fails of embodiment in any character, though Faulkner makes a half-convincing try in the case of Gordon, the sculptor.

The imperative need of a maturing literary artist for a way to embody the experience of the modern self brought Faulkner to the matter belonging to the land of his nativity. In a memoir of Sherwood Anderson published in 1953, Faulkner acknowledges his motive in pursuing the South as his material; but he does so in a typically curious and indirect manner, attributing to Anderson's influence what he himself indubitably perceived.

> I learned . . . from [Anderson] . . . that, to be a writer, one has first got to be what he is, what he was born; that to be an American and a writer, one does not necessarily have to pay lip-service to any conventional American image. . . . You had only to remember what you were. "You have to have somewhere to start from: then you begin to learn," he told me. "It dont matter where it was, just so you remember it and aint ashamed of it. Because one place to start from is just as important as any other. You're a country boy; all you know is that little patch up there in Mississippi where you started from. But that's all right too. It's American too; pull

it out, as little and unknown as it is, and the whole thing will collapse, like when you prize a brick out of a wall."

"Not a cemented, plastered wall," I said.

"Yes, but America aint cemented and plastered yet. They're still building on it. That's why a man with ink in his veins not only still can but sometimes has still got to keep moving around in it, keeping moving around and listening and looking and learning. That's why ignorant unschooled fellows like you and me not only have a chance to write, they must write. All America asks is to look at it and listen to it and understand it if you can. Only the understanding aint important either: the important thing is to believe in it even if you dont understand it, and then try to tell it, put it down. It wont ever be quite right, but there is always next time; there's always more ink and paper, and something else to try to understand and tell. And that one probably wont be exactly right either, but there is a next time to that one, too. Because tomorrow America is going to be something different, something more and new to watch and listen to and try to understand; and, even if you cant understand, believe."[6]

Whatever basis it may have in fact, Faulkner's account of Anderson's sage advice to him is another one of his fables about his career. An ignorant American country boy who wants to be a writer learns from a successful writer, also of country origin, that the way to be a genuine literary artist is to keep on being an ignorant American country boy. Faulkner is talking about how a relatively sophisticated, highly gifted, widely read young writer, from an educated and locally prominent family resident in the southern university community of Oxford, Mississippi, realized that what he knew as actuality—the life in the community of his rearing, the life of his own family, his own life—embodied the subject he had been pursuing. His comprehension of this subject was not, as he had assumed in his first writings, to be derived from literary records. He had already comprehended it in his inner consciousness of himself and the world. He was inside the drama of differentiation, both as participant and

6. William Faulkner, "A Note on Sherwood Anderson," in *Essays, Speeches and Public Letters,* ed. James B. Meriwether (New York, 1965), 8–9.

as observer. Like Anderson, and no doubt partly because of his association with the author of *Winesburg, Ohio,* Faulkner intuited in the American microcosm of the Western society of history and science a profound intimacy between self and history. Like no other American writers save Poe, Mark Twain, and Wolfe, he intuited that this intimacy assumed its typical form—an internalization of history in the self—with a singular intensity in the microcosm of American culture, the South.

Flags in the Dust, the first of the Yoknapatawpha novels (published in abridged form as *Sartoris* in 1929 and published in the original form in 1973), essays a full-scale version of the matter of north Mississippi as the embodiment of the drama of differentiation. The setting of this novel is a South that is not, and never was, the traditionalist society represented in the standard literary image of the South. The southern society represented in *Flags in the Dust,* specifically that of Mississippi in the years right after World War I, is a society which, like that of the older, eastern seaboard South, has harbored an illusion of itself as a perpetuation under New World conditions of the traditional European landed order. But as the novel makes plain, modern history would not for long tolerate the existence of such an illusion. The Civil War killed the South, leaving it to live its death in history, of which its experience of World War I is an integral part. Although in the society depicted in *Flags in the Dust* the connections among individuals give the impression of being assumed and formalistic—of being unspoken save in the public voice of the orator and storyteller—these connections are in truth deeply personal, for each person in Faulkner's southern society experiences his personal existence in history as a story that must be told.

This compulsion is not autobiographical or, at any rate, not confessional. It is a historical, or biographical, imperative. Faulkner once described its influence on the novelist—by clear implication on his own method as a novelist—as follows: "But then, every time any character gets into a book, no matter how minor, he's [the author is] actually telling his own biography, talking about himself, in a thousand different terms, but himself."[7] This comment was a reply to a question about Quentin Compson, the richest distillation of Faulk-

---

7. Frederick L. Gwynn and Joseph L. Blotner, eds., *Faulkner in the University: Class Conferences at the University of Virginia, 1957–1958* (New York, 1965), 275.

ner's method of novelistic development. He attempted this method in his first two novels; but he came into possession of it only when he took Sherwood Anderson's advice and yielded his imagination to discovering an image of self and history implicit in his north Mississippi homeland. A case in point: *Flags in the Dust* begins with a scene in which Old Man Falls is once again subjecting Bayard Sartoris to the recital of an often-told story about Colonel John Sartoris and the Civil War. But as the novel progresses it becomes apparent that while Old Man Falls's story seems to represent merely a bardic garrulity often said to be characteristic of southern culture, it may be seen as the manifestation of a more important characteristic of this culture, its tendency to hide under a masking flow of words a deeply introverted world enclosed in a long series of illusions about self and history that ultimately derive from illusions shared by European forebears.

In *Flags in the Dust* Faulkner successfully emblematizes this fact through his emphasis on what may be called the biographical mode of southern culture. Consider the scene in which old Bayard goes to a secluded upper room of the Sartoris home, opens the chest of family memorials, and contemplating the faded list of Sartoris names in the back of the brass-bound Bible, thinks about the list as a gesture made in the name of an illusory destiny. Old Bayard thinks, too, about the ultimate illusion, that of the heaven that is claimed as part of man's destiny: "heaven, filled with every man's illusion of himself and with the conflicting illusions of him that parade through the minds of other illusions." Feeling his way into the self-contained and reclusive world of the Sartorises—a world dominated not by *is* but by *was*—Faulkner discovered in the history of his little postage stamp of a world the same motive he had sought to define in *Soldiers' Pay* and *Mosquitoes,* the deep narcissism of the modern self. In other words, he regarded *Flags in the Dust* not as the inauguration of a saga of the South but as a more successful attainment of what he had tried to do in his earlier works, which were, he said strangely, the "foals" of *Flags in the Dust.* He had, he believed, paradoxically created the immature offspring before he brought into visible existence the mare that had given them birth, a novel, that is, in which the characters are no longer symbols of history but its flesh and blood creatures, complex human beings who interiorize history in the passions of human nature. It is no wonder Faulkner declared to his publisher, Horace Liveright, that *Flags in the Dust* "is the damndest best book you'll look at this year, and any other publisher."[8]

Liveright unfortunately did not think so. Failing to understand Faulkner's intention to create a drama based on the biographical structure of history, he turned the novel down with the suggestion that it was so lacking in plot and character development that it was unpublishable. In spite of his disappointment about the rejection of *Flags in the Dust*, however, Faulkner plunged more deeply into the matter of the South. In his exploration of its novelistic possibilities he had not only discovered a novelistic method in the biographical mode of southern culture but had found in himself, a southern self, an example of the embodiment of history in the modern literary consciousness.

Now Faulkner's struggle to encapsulate the self and the world (implicit in the self-consciousness of history he had been seeking to express since he conceived the poems in *The Marble Faun*) came into its most intense phase. Within a period of about seven years he wrote the five greatest Yoknapatawpha novels: *The Sound and the Fury, As I Lay Dying, Sanctuary, Light in August,* and *Absalom, Absalom!* Each of these works is distinctly marked by its character as an autonomous experiment in novelistic composition, yet each finds its focus and movement in characters who, directly or indirectly, tell their own biographies. In each novel there is one character who serves to some degree as a surrogate of the authorial figure: Quentin Compson in *The Sound and the Fury* and *Absalom, Absalom!*, Darl Bundren in *As I Lay Dying*, Horace Benbow in *Sanctuary*, and Gail Hightower in *Light in August*. Both as participant in and observer of the biographical movement of a given novel, the surrogate serves not so much as a voice of the author but as eyes through which he looks at the inside of his story. Then, too, he serves to suggest that there is an authorial self, a literary artist, a controlling authorial presence in the story. This presence may be as explicit as that of Quentin in *The Sound and the Fury* and *Absalom, Absalom!* or it may be as tenuous as that of Darl in *As I Lay Dying*. Yet it is there, an assertion, in the negative

---

8. William Faulkner, *Flags in the Dust*, ed. Douglas Day (New York, 1973), 81–83; William Faulkner to Horace Liveright, October [16, 1927], in *Selected Letters*, ed. Blotner, 38.

sense, that Yoknapatawpha is no more an un-self-conscious traditionalist culture than is the culture of the Old Testament; in the positive sense, that a self-conscious, poetic, historical, perhaps prophetic
imagination is intrinsically existent in Yoknapatawpha County.

Pursuing meaning in human history through the biographical
mode, Faulkner was, to be sure, adhering to a major source of the
post–Civil War culture, the modern interpretation of the biblical sense
of history, especially as this is expressed in what Erich Auerbach in
Mimesis terms the "biographical element" of the Old Testament. Unlike the heroic or epic mode, Auerbach observes, the Old Testament
charges the lives it records with "historical intensity." Even when a
life is no more than a fragmentary legend, even when a life is plainly
a composite of different legends, it becomes historically credible in
the context of other biblical stories. As Auerbach says:

> The claim of the Old Testament stories to represent uni-
> versal history, their insistent relation—a relation constantly
> redefined by conflicts—to a single and hidden God, who yet
> shows himself and who guides universal history by promise
> and exaction, gives these stories an entirely different perspec-
> tive from any the Homeric poems can possess. As a compo-
> sition, the Old Testament is incomparably less unified than
> the Homeric poems, it is more obviously placed together—
> but the various components all belong to the one concept of
> universal history and its interpretation. . . . The greater the
> separateness and horizontal disconnection of the stories in re-
> lation to one another, compared with the *Iliad* and the *Odys-
> sey,* the stronger is their general vertical connection, which
> holds them all together and which is entirely lacking in
> Homer. Each of the great figures of the Old Testament, from
> Adam to the prophets, embodies a moment of this vertical
> connection.[9]

In the composition of each of the five Yoknapatawpha novels after *Flags in the Dust,* Faulkner's commitment to an autonomous the-

9. Erich Auerbach, *Mimesis: The Representation of Reality in Western Literature,* trans.
W. R. Trask (Garden City, N.Y., 1957), 14.

matic and artistic endeavor was in a strong tension with the sense of a larger endeavor that was beginning to take on a compulsive aspect in his imagination—a many-dimensioned story about all kinds and conditions of Yoknapatawpha inhabitants, red, white, black, through the several generations, from the time of the antebellum South's expansion into the north Mississippi wilderness to the present. Faulkner became quite aware of the deepening interrelation of the Yoknapatawpha novels; as early as 1933 he thought of making a Golden Book of Yoknapatawpha, in which he would record the genealogies of his characters. But he had no impulse during the period of their origination (which was also the period of Faulkner's triumph as a literary artist) to conform the Yoknapatawpha tales to a chronological scheme, not even to the simple narrative pattern of legend. Imprecisely yet assuredly Faulkner's historical sensibility imposed on the evolving Yoknapatawpha saga a structure resembling the vertical structure of the Old Testament. Just as the biblical characters respond to the will of the hidden God, the Yoknapatawpha people respond to the artist's will to make history yield its meaning in the intensity of their lives. In their inward images of themselves as historical beings, in the historical images other characters make of them, and those the author himself may make of them, they become representative moments in the vertical connection of the great Yoknapatawpha novels.

The climactic moment is embodied in the character of Quentin Compson in *Absalom, Absalom!*, in which the biographical mode is brought into full play as Miss Rosa Coldfield, Mr. Compson, and Quentin tell the biography of Thomas Sutpen, and in the telling reveal their own biographies. As the talking proceeds, wandering around and around, it discloses with the force of fate the burden of Yoknapatawpha's history: the introverted illusion of itself as a representation of the old, familial, corporate, sacramental community. The truth that is Sutpen comes out: the origins of Yoknapatawpha (and of the South) lie in the ruthless drive of the modern historical ego, which, unleashed from all societal bonds, has founded a modern slave society in a wilderness; and yet in its isolation must seek to emulate not the substance but the appearance of the old community. Witnessing the incredible struggle of Quentin to assume the whole burden of the South's tangled psychic history, Shreve McCannon, the Canadian interrogator and commentator, exclaims, "The South.

Jesus. No wonder you folks all outlive yourselves by years and years and years." And Quentin says, "I am older at twenty than a lot of people who have died."[10]

Although *Absalom, Absalom!* is the closest Faulkner would come to getting history, figuratively speaking, onto a pinhead, his will to comprehend its intricate complexities in the modern age dictated his motive and method in each Yoknapatawpha novel through *Go Down, Moses* (1942). But the historical emphasis is altered and diminished in the later Yoknapatawpha works. Auerbach, in connection with his remarks on the Old Testament structure quoted above, also observes that the Hebraic "classification and interpretation of human history is so passionately apprehended" that it "eventually shatters the framework of historical composition and completely overruns it with prophecy." An analogous phenomenon influenced the course of the Yoknapatawpha saga. Not long after *Go Down, Moses* appeared in the year in which America actively entered World War II, Faulkner became fascinated with a legend about the identity of the French Unknown Soldier of World War I. His interest resulted in ten years of labor on *A Fable,* a work he often called his "big book." When he finished *A Fable* in 1954, Faulkner believed it to be the one work that unqualifiedly confirmed his genius. Although not many of his critics have supported the author's high opinion of it and have ranked it as inferior to most of the Yoknapatawpha novels, *A Fable* is the logical outgrowth of Faulkner's fervent examination of the drama of differentiation in the Yoknapatawpha stories. In its own way a study of history, a philosophy or humanistic theology of history, this singular book is primarily a work of prophecy. Its message is the triumph of mankind over modern historical society—with its destructive divisions into self-interpreted nation-states—through the eventual acceptance, not of the Son of God, but of the Son of Man. *A Fable* proclaims the triumph over history of a humanistic myth of man. The hero of this myth transcends the consequence of the differentiation of the historical from the sacramental order, the closure of history in the narcissistic modern society, the kind of society so graphically represented in the Yoknapatawpha image of the South.

Yet withal, *A Fable* is a dark book. To redeem history from its

10. William Faulkner, *Absalom, Absalom!* (New York, 1986), 301.

descent into the self, Faulkner identifies the Unknown Soldier with a Christ who as the Son of Man is the son of Satan, the fallen angel, who is not only in his passions the symbol of man but in his function in the novel a surrogate of the author. Unable to control the endless ramifications of this portentous identification, Faulkner ends up with a passionate but unconvincing assertion of man's capacity to transcend his historical condition, and, by paradoxical implication, with a passionate and convincing assertion that he never will. The reason for this passionate irresolution in *A Fable* can hardly be stated simply, but it amounts to the fact that the Old General (Satan) becomes an autobiographer of such eloquence and conviction that his story (as that of Satan in Milton) submerges that of his son, the Corporal (the Christ figure).

Faulkner's struggle to give desacralized history a transcendent spiritual quality in *A Fable* demarcates a line between the Yoknapatawpha novels through *Go Down, Moses* and the ones that follow. We may indeed appropriately speak of a first and second cycle of Yoknapatawpha tales. The second begins in 1948 with the publication of *Intruder in the Dust* and includes *Requiem for a Nun, The Town, The Mansion* (the latter being the second and third volumes of the Snopes trilogy), and *The Reivers: A Reminiscence.*

This is by no means to suggest that the second cycle of Yoknapatawpha stories may be distinguished from the first by an inclination to prophetic frenzy in the second. Faulkner's large-scale and prolonged adventure in prophecy during the writing of *A Fable* did not overwhelm the Yoknapatawpha saga. It simply quietly shattered Faulkner's sense of its temporal structure. In the novels of the second cycle the assignment of the South to the condition of a world living its death in history—a world composed, as Charles Bon said, of those "doomed to live"—is significantly modified. There is an assimilation of *was* to *is*. When Chick Mallison in *Intruder in the Dust* thinks "yesterday today and tomorrow are Is: Indivisible" and recalls Gavin Stevens' celebration of the great, always present moment in the mind of every fourteen-year-old southern boy—the living instant right before the Battle of Gettysburg began ("Its all *now* you see. Yesterday wont be over until tomorrow and tomorrow began ten thousand years ago")—he speaks for the Faulkner of the second cycle. This is the Faulkner who talked about the strategy of his long sentences: "There is no such thing really as was because the past is. It is a part of every man, every woman, and every moment. . . . And so . . . a character in a story at any moment of action is not just himself as he is then, he is all that made him, and the long sentence is an attempt to get his past and possibly his future into the instant in which he does something."[11]

Regarded as the expression of a mutant moment in history conceived as *is* the long sentence no longer bears the burden (as it did in the earlier Faulkner's imagination) of serving as an integral symbolic recapitulation of man's history conceived as a sundering of the tenses. Abolishing the fatality of *was,* Faulkner abolishes the differentiation of the historical self and the narcissism of history, thereby abolishing the grievous burden of the alienation of the self from the world, and so leaving his imagination free to conceive of Yoknapatawpha as the embodied design of *is*—as a microcosm of the universal, a fictional yet timeless structure of reality created by the literary artist.

Several times the later Faulkner affirms the *is* with a sense of exultation, nowhere more so than in the famous vision of the scope and meaning of his fiction he projected in a widely quoted interview with Jean Stein Vanden Heuvel in 1956:

> Beginning with *Sartoris* I discovered that my own little postage stamp of native soil was worth writing about and that I would never live long enough to exhaust it, and that by sublimating the actual into the apocryphal I would have complete liberty to use whatever talent I might have to its absolute top. It opened up a gold mine of other people, so I created a cosmos of my own. I can move these people around like God, not only in space but in time too. The fact that I have moved my characters around in time successfully, at least in my own estimation, proves to me my own theory that time is a fluid condition which has no existence except in the momentary avatars of individual people. There is no such thing as *was*—only *is*. If *was* existed, there would be no grief or sorrow. I like to think of the world I created as being a

---

11. William Faulkner, *Intruder in the Dust* (New York, 1948), 194; Gwynn and Blotner, eds., *Faulkner in the University,* 84.

kind of keystone in the universe; that, small as that keystone is, if it were ever taken away the universe itself would collapse. My last book will be the Doomsday Book, the Golden Book, of Yoknapatawpha County. Then I shall break the pencil and I'll have to stop.[12]

Faulkner's serene, retrospective vision of Yoknapatawpha as a transcendent autonomous world created by the artist implies all the pathos of the literary myth of modern history—of the drama so powerfully expressed in Melville's Ishmael—of the differentiation of the artist as a historical self. The vision reveals what it denies: Faulkner's awareness of the unremitting tension between self and history. Yoknapatawpha is in truth no sublimation of the actual but a representation of the profoundest reality: the terrifying subjectification of man and nature, God, world, and universe. When he refers to Yoknapatawpha as "my apocryphal county," or calls the Yoknapatawpha stories "my apocrypha," Faulkner means more than "my fictions." He means "my stories in which there are hidden things," and notable among the things he hides in his tales is the story of the artist and his struggle against modern history. In this struggle Faulkner follows the defiant Joycean dream of sacramentalizing the role of the artist by means of grace self-bestowed. But Faulkner at the same time knew, perhaps more surely than Joyce, that the artist cannot transcend his implication in history. He understood this as an American, and especially as a southerner. In his last novel, *The Reivers,* subtitled *A Reminiscence,* he finally surrenders to the pathos of the self's effort to escape from history: creating a Yoknapatawpha existing neither in the *was* of Quentin Compson nor in the *is* of Gavin Stevens but in the ineffable *is-was* that, transcending all tense, is yet the truest time reference for Americans, that of nostalgia—the source of the timeless image Americans appeal to when they speak of America as "home sweet home": a place beyond history, a place beyond all grief and sorrow.

12. Malcolm Cowley, ed., *Writers at Work: The Paris Review Interviews* (New York, 1958), 141.

VI

The Poetry of Criticism
Allen Tate

During the last twenty-five years of his life Allen Tate was a literary presence both at home and abroad. He served as a tenured professor at the University of Minnesota (retiring in 1968 as Regents' Professor), filled numerous visiting lectureships, collected several honorary degrees, received various prominent literary awards, held the presidency of the National Institute of Arts and Letters, and, by no means least, continually conducted a large literary correspondence. It is a surprise when, looking at the record, one discovers that from 1953 until his death in 1979 Tate was hardly more than a nominally active poet or critic, the publication of *The Forlorn Demon: Didactic and Critical Essays* in 1953, when he was only fifty-four years of age, having marked the virtual end of his productive career. This is not to say that Tate ceased publication. Ten more books appeared under his name. Several of these were edited volumes, among them the distinguished *T. S. Eliot, The Man and His Work: A Critical Evaluation* (1966). But Tate's most important publications were collections of his own previously published writings: in 1955 *The Man of Letters in the Modern World* (save for the prefatory essay, the essays all belonged to the years before 1955); in 1959 *Collected Essays* (with one new major essay, "A Southern Mode of the Imagination," written in 1959); in 1968 the omnibus collection *Essays of Four Decades;* and in 1977 *Collected Poems, 1919–1976* (with two short poems written after 1953). Another book published in the 1970s, *Memoirs and Opinions, 1926–1974,* collected a few more cogent critical pieces, one being Tate's last attempt to define the myth of the South, "Faulkner's *Sanctuary* and the Southern Myth" (1968).

Memoirs and Opinions is notable chiefly because it contains two chapters of an aborted "book of memories." Tate gave up on this project, he explains, because he could not bring himself "to tell what was wrong" with his friends and acquaintances "without trying to tell what was wrong with myself"—a subject, he says wryly, he felt uncertain about. A deeper reason is disguised significantly as an afterthought: "Then, too, I fell back on authority: I couldn't let myself indulge in the terrible fluidity of self-revelation."[1] While Tate does not indicate specifically the authority he appealed to, he clearly suggests an aversion to the modern compulsion to self-confession. His abandonment of the autobiographical project is, to be sure, consistent with a fundamental theme in Tate's criticism: the need to subject the willful self to the authority of a culture rooted in a great moral and religious tradition. Tate's whole career had been distinguished by a desire to recover the power of such a culture as it had once existed in Western civilization. Since he believed that what remained of the Greco-Roman Christian culture—what he at times awesomely referred to as "The Tradition"—was rapidly disappearing, his desire bore the quality of desperation. In 1950 Tate conclusively ratified his support of a major tradition of authority by being confirmed in the Roman Catholic faith. As in the earlier instance of Eliot, one of his chief mentors, the act of religious conversion was implicit in the initial phase of his career; but, unlike Eliot, Tate failed to discover in the experience of conversion itself and in its aftermath a poetic and critical inspiration equal in power to that of the spiritual struggle toward conversion. The resolution of Tate's long quest for faith is reflected in three poems of the early 1950s: "The Maimed Man," "The Swimmers" (possibly his greatest poem), and "The Buried Lake." But it is no more than reflected: Tate did not explicitly live his conversion in an "Ash-Wednesday." Nor did he, like Eliot, objectify his conversion by issuing a manifesto to Western civilization comparable to *The Idea of a Christian Society* (1939).

Eliot was inclined, as Elisabeth Schneider has said in *T. S. Eliot: The Pattern in the Carpet,* to think about his poetry as a personal statement and to consider his criticism, marked by a doctrinaire tone and pruned at least of outward evidence of hesitation and self-doubt, as a

---

1. Allen Tate, *Memoirs and Opinions, 1926–1974* (Chicago, 1975), ix. See above, "A Fable of White and Black," 29–31, 52–53, for a fuller discussion of this book.

public declaration. But even though John Crowe Ransom had proclaimed that the modern poet is without laurels, for Tate the poetic task was still invested, if ironically, with the aura of public responsibility. This may be why, reversing Eliot's attitude, he looked on the critical essay, although written for the public, as being a comparatively personal form of expression, in which the writer (although Tate the essayist was at times as boldly doctrinaire as Eliot the essayist) conducts a debate or even a quarrel with himself, asking questions he can answer only conjecturally and even confiding his self-doubts to his reader. Yet of five remarkable essays Tate wrote in the early 1950s, four—"To Whom Is the Poet Responsible?," "The Symbolic Imagination," "The Angelic Imagination," and "Is Literary Criticism Possible?"—hardly reflect a personal experience of conversion. In an effort to a grasp the significance of his conversion for his vocation as poet and man of letters, perhaps it is not altogether incongruous for us to compare the other essay of the early 1950s—the dramatic analysis of the character of the man of letters in the title essay of *The Man of Letters in the Modern World*—with Eliot's effort in "Ash-Wednesday."

Tate had first collected "The Man of Letters in the Modern World" in *The Forlorn Demon*. Although he implies that *The Forlorn Demon* is a personal expression, possibly an intellectual and spiritual self-portrait, he undercuts the suggestion by overplaying it. I refer to his explicit identification of the literary vocation with Poe's lugubrious, melodramatic self-image in the poem "Alone," which describes the poet as having had since "childhood's hour" a "demon" in his "view." In *The Man of Letters in the Modern World,* associating the literary role with a conventional image, Tate provides a more encompassing identification of his role than that offered by linking it to Poe's narrowly focused, bizarre image of the poet as a demonic self. Yet from the seventeen essays in *The Man of Letters in the Modern World,* representing the most productive span of Tate's career, the dominant image that emerges is not of Allen Tate as the man of letters, but of the man of letters as Allen Tate. Although less obviously than Poe's or Eliot's, his own career, Tate suggests, illustrates a reversal of the emblematic, the mythic, function of the man of letters that occurred when this figure ceased to seek an image in the cultural ideal of the man of letters (represented by Samuel Johnson or, later, with less assurance, by Matthew Arnold) and began to accommodate the image of the literary vocation to his existential condition in history. Representing, in fact, an advanced stage of this accommodation, *The Man of Letters in the Modern World* may well be considered Tate's focal work. Concerning the struggle of the modern quest for literary identity, this compilation of essays, while it hardly constitutes an autobiography, is in effect a revealing autobiographical drama. The plot of the drama centers in the uncertainty and instability—the terrible fluidity—of the critic's identity. The theme of the drama is essentially the failure of the critical, or more broadly of the critical and poetic, the literary, will. Or to put it another way: the theme is criticism as a tragic mode.

I am speaking about the character of the critical will in Tate that may be discerned when we stand at some remove from the intimidating actuality of his presence. Both when he was actively writing and later when he was engaged primarily in lecturing or reading his poems, Tate incarnated the image of literary authority. A small personal recollection of the force of his presence occurs to me with some vividness. Over a year after Allen's death in the bitter and snow-filled winter of 1979, George Core, Louis D. Rubin, Jr., and I made a visit to his grave in the cemetery behind the chapel at Sewanee. It was a luminous morning in April on the "mountain" and the birds were singing. We had stood silently for several moments at the plot where Allen and his infant son are buried when, with a quiet intensity, Louis suddenly said, "Colonel Tate!" This hail and farewell was, I suppose, at once a social and a literary gesture. It recalled the anachronistic convention in the southern local community of making captains, majors, colonels, and generals out of citizens held in regard whether they had worn a uniform or not. In a more profoundly ironic sense the salutation was a gesture made in the name of those of us who in one way or another belong to the second and third generations of the twentieth-century southern literary scene, and for whom, more than any other figure, Tate had worn the aspect of a field commander of the literary troops. Maybe this was because he had inherited from his Virginia ancestry the "natural habit of command" Henry Adams attributed to all Virginians. In any event, his investment with command had nothing to do with service in the Great War; unlike John Crowe Ransom and Donald Davidson, he was too young to serve in the trenches on the Western Front during 1917–1918. And it was distinctly not because of the time of World War II that Tate had displayed the patriotic disposition typical of southerners. As a matter of fact, still imbued with the Agrarian disdain for both capitalism and communism, Tate took a skewed and largely negative attitude toward the war against the Axis powers. In the period between the German invasion of Poland and the Japanese attack on Pearl Harbor, he held (to judge from what he said in his correspondence with John Peale Bishop) a "strong" political and economic, though not "cultural," sympathy for the Germans. His ambivalence left him, he said, in a state of "perfect neutrality." Although he declared he would if necessary fight for "our sort of fascism vs. the German," he would not fight for "democracy," a form of "laissez-faire capitalism."[2]

The line Tate drew at this time between politics and economics on the one side and culture on the other is not clear, nor is his concept of the American brand of fascism. It is apparent that, even after the nation became fully engaged in the conflict, he felt little commitment to the American war policies. He envisioned America as having become, like imperial Rome, pledged to fight endlessly on distant frontiers. Thinking about the possibility of being drafted in the summer of 1942, he wrote to Bishop: "We shall be like some of Tiberius's legions on the German frontier—toothless, our hair long and gray, and so decrepit that we shall scarcely be able to march, yet we shall still be in the army." Tate predicted that at the age of sixty-seven he would be "assigned as a private, to the inspection of whorehouses in Sumatra."[3] One doubts how much his fantasizing about being drafted expressed an actual apprehension. Not unlike Faulkner, who once said that the ideal life for a writer would be that of the manager of a bordello, Tate, imagining himself to be an ancient private in the medical corps of the American army, was by self-deprecation exalting his militant, transcendent dedication to the literary profession. A testimony to Tate's sense of the desperate cultural situation of the man of letters, his fantasy inversely asserted the authority of the literary mind. While World War II and its implementation of the con-

2. Allen Tate to John Peale Bishop, May 24, 1940, July 8, 1940, in *The Republic of Letters in America: The Correspondence of John Peale Bishop & Allen Tate,* ed. Thomas D. Young and John J. Hindle (Lexington, Ky., 1981), 166, 167.
  3. Tate to Bishop, August 28, 1942, *ibid.,* 191.

cept of the "total war" increased his anxiety about the ineffectuality of the man of letters, it intensified Tate's vision of the *real* war of modernity: the widespread conflict between the "dehumanized society of secularism . . . and the eternal society of the communion of the human spirit." This concept of the modern situation, as stated in "The Man of Letters in the Modern World" in 1950, may be placed not only in the context of Tate's religious conversion but in that afforded by his writings during the decade of the war and its immediate aftermath. This period of Tate's career was marked by a series of essays that in one way or another are concerned with making a self-conscious definition of the critic's capacity as a strategist and tactician in the war between the secular and the spiritual.

A key essay in this effort, collected in *The Man of Letters in the Modern World,* is the brilliant "causerie" on the imagination and the actual world, "The Hovering Fly" (1943). In this Tate constructs a military image of the critic.

> Armies used to besiege towns by "regular approaches"; or they took them by direct assault; or they maneuvered the enemy out of position, perhaps into ambuscade. These strategies are used today, for in war as in criticism the new is merely a new name for something very old. When Caesar laid waste the country, he was using a grand tactics that we have recently given a new name: infiltration, or the tactics of getting effectively into the enemy's rear. When you have total war must you also have total criticism? In our time critics are supposed to know everything, and we get criticism on all fronts. Does this not outmode the direct assault? When there are so many "problems" (a term equally critical and military) you have got to do a little here and a little there, and you may not be of the command that enters the suburbs of Berlin.[4]

Equating total war with the triumph of the "positivist program for the complete government of man" and seeing the modern totali-

---

4. Allen Tate, "The Hovering Fly," in *Essays of Four Decades* (Chicago, 1968), 107–108. In *Mumford, Tate, Eiseley: Watchers in the Night* (Baton Rouge, 1991), Gale H. Carrithers, Jr., explores the implications of the military metaphor in Tate's criticism more fully than I do. See especially 107–30. Hereafter references to Tate's *Essays of Four Decades* will be made parenthetically in the text.

tarian impulse as altogether the triumph of the assumed self-sufficiency of science, Tate (drawing on Scott Buchanan's terminology)
regards the positivist test of reality as having usurped all other tests
by performing an "act of occultation"—a hiding away of other tests,
or an ascription to them of "dark motives" and "black arts." How
does literature reveal the positivist act of occultation? The exemplary
illustration Tate appeals to in "The Hovering Fly" is the scene in
Dostoevsky's *The Idiot* in which Myshkin stands at the bed on which
lies the corpse of the murdered Nastasya, completely covered by a
white sheet save for the protruding toes of one foot. Suddenly in the
silence Myshkin hears a fly buzz and sees it light on the pillow. What
is the significance of Dostoevsky's introduction of such a casual detail
as the presence of a fly?

> The fly comes to stand in its sinister and abundant life for the
> privation of life, the body of the young woman on the bed.
> Here we have one of those conversions of image of which
> only great talent is capable: life stands for death, but it is a
> wholly different order of life, and one that impinges upon
> the human order only in its capacity of scavenger, a necessity
> of its biological situation which in itself must be seen as neu-
> tral or even innocent. Any sinister significance that the fly
> may create for us is entirely due to its crossing our own path:
> by means of the fly the human order is compromised. But it
> also extended, until through a series of similar conversions
> and correspondences of image the buzz of the fly distends,
> both visually and metaphorically, the body of the girl into
> the world. Her degradation and nobility are in that image.
> Shall we call it the actual world? (119)

Once, Tate observes, we might have done so. But in the modern
world we have no heart for "the consideration of actual worlds." We
are in "an occult world, from which actualities, which in their nature
are quiet and permanent, are hard to find." The "very instruments
of our daily economy have more and more dictated our ends." They
have virtually obscured the "human powers"—powers "by no means
yet depleted" but that cannot exert themselves when, captivated by
our attraction to "operational techniques," we obtusely or even will-

fully occult them, exclude them as unreal. The "function of the imagination as a black art" will grow more and more powerful unless by a "miracle of gift or character, and perhaps of history also, we command the imaginative power of the relation of things" (120–21).

The necessities of command are the three liberal arts: grammar, rhetoric, and philosophy. "The grammarians [the men of letters] of the modern world," Tate asserts, "have allowed their specialization, their operational technique, to drive the two other arts to cover, whence they break forth in their own furies, the one the fury of irresponsible abstraction, the other the fury of irresponsible rhetoric." Following the imagination of the "modern positivist," we have as men of letters imagined "ourselves out of humanity." We have become capable of being mere spectators even at a scene like that of the fly hovering about the dead Nastasya. We know actuality only as process, and so do not know it at all. "The fiction that we are neither here nor there, but are only spectators who, by becoming, ourselves, objects of grammatical analysis, can arrive at some other actuality than that of process, is the great modern heresy: we can never be mere spectators, or if we can for a little time we shall probably, a few of us only, remain, until there is one man left, like a solitary carp in a pond, who has devoured all the others" (123). The burden of "The Hovering Fly" is that the man of letters is inextricably both a participant in and an observer-reporter of the conflict between the historical and the spiritual (120–23). Switching from the metaphor of the writer as strategist, Tate compares him to the painter Philippoteaux, "who placed himself under a tree in his picture of the Battle of Gettysburg to warn you that what you see is only what he sees, under that tree." From his observation post on a hill or under a hill, a tree, a log, or a leaf, the reporter may be "less than heroic," but he makes it clear that he is reporting not only what he sees but what he "infers, merely guesses" (109). Paradoxically, in his recognition of the limitations of his vision, he has a commanding vision of the relation of things.

The image of the solipsistic self as the devouring carp in the pond in "The Hovering Fly" forcefully reminds us of the jaguar that leaps for his image in the pool in "Ode to the Confederate Dead." Composed in 1927, Tate's most famous poem was not considered by its author to be finished until 1937, the year in which he wrote his well-known essay about its structure and meaning, "Narcissus as Narcissus." In this comment, the only formal analysis Tate wrote about one of his own works, he explains that he imagined the scene of the predatory animal leaping to "devour himself" as a more effective way of suggesting the Narcissus theme than a direct reference to a youth gazing into a pool. In the next passage in the poem, which begins "What shall we say who have knowledge carried to the heart?," it becomes clear, if it has not been earlier, that even though the poem is called an ode, its setting is not a public celebration but the mind of the visitor to the cemetery—the "lone man" by the gate. The drama enacted in the consciousness of the lone man concerns the failure of the old culture of "heroic emotion," symbolized by the Confederate dead, and the consequence, embodied in the visitor, attending this failure: the decay of the "whole man"—of the individual as a physical and spiritual entity—and the emergence of the modern "fragmented personality." (Tate often used the term *personality* in its old and proper sense. We can still find the definition in Webster's: "the quality or state of being a person and not an abstraction, thing, or lower being.")

In "Narcissus as Narcissus" Tate only partially dissociates the author from the "meditating man" at the gate, declaring parenthetically that he "differs from the author in not accepting a 'practical solution'" to his solipsistic tendency. This difference distinguishes the maker of the poem from his persona, the poet's "personal dilemma perhaps being not quite so exclusive" as that of the man at the gate. But how much less exclusive was Tate's personal situation than that of the lone man? His sensitivity to such a question is indicated obliquely at the beginning of "Narcissus as Narcissus" when he rebukes the commonplace notion that the poet is a man who, lacking the capacity for real life, makes up a fictional life for himself. According to some of his critics, Tate says, "my one intransigent desire is to have been a Confederate general, and because I could not or would not become anything else [an automobile salesman, for example], I set up for poet and began to invent fictions about the personal ambitions that my society has no use for" (594). His refutation of the nonsensical accusation makes us predisposed to accept the idea that the poet's dilemma is not so "exclusive" as the persona's, when in truth the identity of the poet and persona is the basic subject of the poem. If this is not obvious in the poem itself, it becomes so in "Narcissus as Narcissus," in which the identification of the critic with the man by the gate becomes virtually explicit. While this exclusive commitment to literature—his obsessive dedication to literature as an institution—led him to charge that scientists deliberately follow the strategy of occulting literary knowledge, Tate, even as he opposed the literary realm to the scientific, implicitly accepted occultation as the necessary practice of the literary profession.

The resulting stress is manifest in the ardent endeavor Tate made to answer the question "Is Literary Criticism Possible?" In the essay bearing this title, written in 1950, he deals with the degradation of rhetoric and the attending disciplines, grammar and logic. Defining rhetoric as "the study and use of the figurative language of experience as the discipline by means of which men govern their relations with one another in the light of truth," he says that it has been reduced to the "pragmatic dimension of discourse." Employed "to move people to action which is at best morally neutral," rhetoric is perpetuated today only as it was corrupted by Greek sophistry. Having lost the rhetorical tradition of Aristotle and the Christian rhetoricians, a tradition in which rhetoric was understood as "the study of the full language of experience," the critic no longer has available to him the language known to Dante and Shakespeare. Scarcely capable of conceiving the "full language of the human situation," deprived of the capacity to believe in "a higher unity of truth," the critic assumes that literature "has nothing to do with truth, that it is only an illusion, froth on the historical current." He languishes in "the pragmatic vortex where ideas are disembodied into power," losing sight of the fact that criticism "cannot in the long run be practiced apart from what it confronts"; that it is "always *about* something else." He cannot comprehend that if criticism "tries to be about itself and sets up on its own, it initiates the infinite series: one criticism within another leading to another criticism progressively more formal looking and abstract"; that it becomes "progressively more irrelevant to its external end as it attends to the periphery, the historical buzz in the ear of literature."

There are, Tate says, three "great sects" of criticism, having in common the ideal of devotion to a "pure" critical method: aesthetics, stylistics (analysis of literary language), and historical scholarship.

Subscription to any of these "techniques of purity" is a form of critical idolatry. Under the spell of the idol of purity "the critic achieves a coherence in the logical and rhetorical orders which exceeds the coherence of the imaginative work itself in these orders." Falling into the snare of "the logicalization of parts discreetly attended," he replaces the "elusive order of the imagination" with "a dialectic" not only leading him to commit the gravest of sins, intellectual pride, but leading the reader, "dazzled by the refractions of the critic's spectrum," like the critic, to "worship his own image." Tate deems historical scholarship to be the "purest" form of criticism because it "offers the historical reconstruction as the general possibility of literature, without accounting for the unique, miraculous superiority of *The Tempest* or *Paradise Lost.*" Returning to the doctrine of miraculous superiority elsewhere in "Is Literary Criticism Possible?," he asserts that "a work of the imagination differs from a work of theological intellect in some radical sense that seems to lie beyond our comprehension." It is not subject to improvement by another work. "Shakespeare does not replace Dante, in the way that Einstein's physics seems to have 'corrected' Newton's." No competition exists among poems; criticism, on the other hand, is constantly subject to revision by other criticisms (30–44).

But Tate's avowal of the suprahistorical permanence of high literary art and the impermanence of criticism seems curiously ambivalent in the light of his theory of the source of modern imaginative work developed in three essays in the late 1920s and the early 1930s: "Emily Dickinson," "A Note on Donne," and "The Profession of Letters in the South." Tate's theory, which asserts an integral relationship between art and history (the "perfect literary situation" is perfectly historical; it occurs at the moment of the historical encounter between "an old and a new order"), is first stated in the graphic essay on Emily Dickinson (1928): "A culture cannot be consciously created. It is an available source of ideas that are imbedded in a complete and homogeneous society. The poet finds himself balanced upon the moment when such a world is about to fall, when it threatens to run out into looser and less self-sufficient impulses. The world order is assimilated, in Miss Dickinson, as medievalism was in Shakespeare, to the poetic vision; it was brought down from abstraction to personal sensibility" (293–94). Comparable to the historical situation that existed in the time of Shakespeare and Donne, the situation in nineteenth-century New England was such, Tate says, that there was "no thought as such at all," nor was there any "feeling"; there was only that "unique focus of experience which is at once neither and both." At the precise moment a culture was poised on the brink of its historical doom it was incarnated in the "personal sensibility of a poet."

In the same year that Tate published the revised version of his essay on Dickinson (1932), he refined and expanded his concept of literature and the culture of crisis in a brief but fertile essay on Donne, in which he relies considerably on the authority of Eliot's statement that Donne's "learning is just information suffused with emotion . . . rather a humorous shuffling of the pieces; and we are inclined to read our own more conscious awareness of the apparent unrelatedness of things into the mind of Donne." The reason we feel an affinity for Donne, Tate elaborates, is that we acknowledge expressly what the seventeenth-century poet understood but could not articulate, save in the indirect language of the conceit: the revolutionary "rise of the historical consciousness." Self-awareness of history results, Tate says, in the deprivation of the poetic vocabulary; it loses the "ultimate, symbolic character of myth." It is "the peculiar fascination of Donne that he presents the problem of personal poetry in its simplest terms. There is the simple awareness, complicated at the surface by his immense intellectual resources, of frustration and bewilderment—to which, for us, is added the frustration of historical relativity. Milton stood for the historical absolute, which is the myth." Just before this comment Tate points out that when the poetic vocabulary loses "the ultimate, symbolic character of a myth," the poet becomes aware of the "intricacy of personal sensation as the center of consciousness." From this awareness "it is but one more step, for the philosophical egoist, to the dramatization of oneself against the background of society or history." If he were alive today, Tate says, Donne would take this step; but Tate is of course describing the step he himself had taken (245–46).

Three years after he revised his essay on Emily Dickinson and wrote his essay on Donne, Tate refined still further his concept of literature and the culture of crisis. Referring to his "considerable achievement"—we now envision it as a "Southern Renascence"—

Tate sees the twentieth-century southern writer as having "left his mark upon the age." But "it is of the age." This formulation is well known:

> From the peculiarly historical consciousness of the Southern writer has come good work of a special order; but the focus of this consciousness is quite temporary. It has made possible the curious burst of intelligence that we get at a crossing of the ways, not unlike, on an infinitesimal scale, the outburst of poetic genius at the end of the sixteenth century when commercial England had already begun to crush feudal England. The Histories and Tragedies of Shakespeare record the death of the old regime, and Doctor Faustus gives up feudal order for world power. (533–34)

In accounting for the Southern Renascence, Tate no longer describes the transitional state that produces a renascent situation as one in which thought and feeling exist in a state of equilibrium. The fructifying relationship between what he describes in his comment on Donne as the "historical mentality" and the creative imagination is considered to be quite direct, whether it is regarded as occurring in Elizabethan or Jacobean England or in the contemporary American South. The perfect literary situation is one in which the writer has become peculiarly, or absolutely, aware of history.

Although there is no overt evidence that the arrangement of the essays in *The Man of Letters in the Modern World* constitutes a deeply meditated reflection on his troubled, at times anguished, self-consciousness of history, the overall structure suggests that Tate had an intention beyond the nominal placement of the essays in three groups: the first devoted to issues in criticism, the second to specific writers, and the last to essays centered in literary regionalism ("The New Provincialism," "The Profession of Letters in the South," and "Narcissus as Narcissus"). Perhaps the nonchronological organization of the collection is a deliberately inverse arrangement. Instead of ending, as we might well expect, with the Christian vision set forth in 1952 of the man of letters dedicated to the "communion in time through love, which is beyond time," and to the fostering of "the eternal society of the communion of the human spirit," *The Man of*

Letters in the Modern World begins with the vision of 1952 and concludes with the vision set forth in 1937 of the man of letters as Narcissus. Actually, the essays collected in *The Man of Letters in the Modern World* do not in themselves represent the total contents of the volume because the initial essay is in fact the brief but heavily freighted preface. In its light the chronological inversion of the essays that frame the collection takes on a provocatively ironic significance. Observing in his preface that he has never written a "formal critical enquiry . . . of book length" and is in fact "a casual essayist of whom little consistency can be expected," Tate nonetheless points out that his essays from first to last show a "long development" in the sense that they represent "the gradual discovery of potentialities of the mind that must always have been there." He adds: "Whether one is made better, or is only made aware of greater complexity, by this discovery, is a question that cannot be answered by the person who asks it about himself." Does the revelation of the complex potentialities of the mind that came with rereading his essays account for putting a late essay first and an earlier one last? Something approaching such a revelation would seem to be suggested by the compacted argument that concludes the preface.

> A critical skeptic cannot entirely imagine the use of a criticism in which the critic takes the deistic part of absentee expositor. To take this role is to pretend that a method can accomplish what the responsible intelligence is alone able to do. The act of criticism is analogous to the peripety of tragedy; it is a crisis of recognition always, and at times also of reversal, in which the whole person is involved. The literary critic is committed, like everybody else, to a particular stance, at a moment in time; he is governed by a point of view that method will not quite succeed in dispensing with. After the natural sciences began to influence literary criticism, scholars held that a point of view without method led inevitably to impressionism. This need not follow; it is obvious why I prefer to think that it need not. Impressionism—"what I like"— is never more intractable than when it is ordered to dine perpetually at the second table. The first table is usually an historical or a philosophical "method"; but this is by no

means the same as historical or philosophical criticism. I
should like to think that criticism has been written, and may
be again, from a mere point of view, such as I suppose myself
to be possessed by. Of the range and direction of a point of
view, and why a point of view exists in some persons, nobody can be certain. It seems to take what little life it may
have from the object that it tries to see. There is surely little
impropriety in describing it negatively, by what it cannot
see. Whatever certainties one may cherish as a man—religious, or moral, or merely philosophical—it is almost certain
that as literary critic one knows virtually nothing. (625–26)

If this crosshatched vision of the act of the critic as at once an act
of tragic dignity by the "responsible intelligence" and a mind that
knows virtually nothing is taken to be the actual beginning of *The
Man of Letters in the Modern World,* the termination of the collection
with "Narcissus as Narcissus" becomes darkly logical. In my beginning as a critic—in my recognition of the historical consciousness—
Tate seems to be saying, is my end. He rounds out "Narcissus as
Narcissus" with the observation that the writing of it has been an
anticlimactic exercise in futility. Anyone who wants to find out more
about "Ode to the Confederate Dead" than he can interpret for himself, he says, is probably "still in the dark." One is tempted to say of
The Man of Letters in the Modern World what Tate says about the
"Ode": it is "about solipsism, the philosophical doctrine which holds
that we create the world in the act of perceiving it; or about Narcissism or any other *ism* that denotes the failure of the human personality to function objectively in nature and society." Moreover, one is
tempted to gloss this adaptation of Tate's statement with a marginal
note: *The Man of Letters in the Modern World* is fundamentally about a
historical situation in which consciousness is imprisoned by the self-
consciousness of history; while the self-consciousness of history can
never be transcended, it is possible to recognize the situation it has
created through the self-interpretation we call criticism, and even to
describe it through the self-interpretation we call art. Tate says of the
"Ode" that it is not about a thesis that may be abstracted as statement. The poem is a drama involving "fundamental conflicts that
cannot be logically resolved," conflicts that we can state "rationally"

but are not thereby "relieved" of, save when they are rendered coherent in their "formal re-creation" in art. Rendered as art, they are frozen "permanently as a logical formula, but without, like the formula, leaving all but the logic out" (595–97).

Disregarding his professed view of his own criticism, yet supported by reason beyond logic, or logic beyond reason—the logic embodied in his ironic portrayal of himself in his writings, either directly or through personae—we may conceive Tate's criticism to be integral with his work as a poet. Clinging to the sense of a necessary distinction between the poet and the critic, Tate apparently did not explicitly recognize himself in the image of the "poet-critic" until he wrote the preface to *Essays of Four Decades* in 1968. Here he overtly describes himself as "the poet-critic, who is not concerned with consistency and system, but merely with as much self-knowledge as he needs to write his own verse." Tate plainly is not referring to self-knowledge in the sense of intimate self-revelation. In the name of the myth of the whole man in a whole society, as he says in his essay on Emily Dickinson, Tate resisted the substitution of self-confession for transcendent religious truth as an act of blasphemy. This was the sin of Donne and Dickinson: "self-exploitation," or "egoism grown irresponsible in religion and decadent in morals." In the interest of the redemption of the man of letters from the modern secular "society of means without ends"—in which he takes on the character of society, and like everyone else busily engages in a "plotless drama of withdrawal" from the spiritual substance of his humanity—Tate confesses in "The Man of Letters in the Modern World" that "he has not participated in the world with the full substance" of his humanity. As a competitor in the "dissemination of distraction and novelty" the modern man of letters, he says, is like the cultish votary of the "*parvenu* gods" of "decaying Rome" (15–16). When he opposes the amorphous drama of modernity by seeking to isolate himself from it, he compounds his idolatry by self-imposed alienation. Nor does self-knowledge of this self-imposed condition enable the man of letters to transcend his alienation: this for the reason that this very knowledge is his literary subject, and he cannot deprive himself of his subject.

Insofar as *The Man of Letters in the Modern World* is Tate's implicit acknowledgment of the limitations on the poet imposed by self-knowledge—that is to say, insofar as the book implies Tate's self-recognition of an irreconcilable tension between his experiential knowledge of the crossing of the ways as the source of imaginative power and his commitment to the belief that the true source of art is "The Tradition"—the volume enacts the crisis of recognition that distinguishes the tragic mode. This tension, whether symbolized by the situation in seventeenth-century England or nineteenth-century New England or the twentieth-century American South, was the one and only motive in the drama of the man of letters as Tate simultaneously wrote and enacted it. When he decisively altered the motive, or tried to, by accepting a transcendent "self-contained objective system of truths," he brought order to what seemed increasingly to be a "plotless drama of withdrawal." But in his refusal of the tragic self-knowledge of history he frustrated, or partially frustrated, his sense of the proper performance of the vocational role he had conceived for himself from the moment of his precocious beginning as a poet-critic in the days of the Nashville Fugitives.

Save in wordless moments (we want to believe he had such moments), Tate never transcended the concept of his role in the perfect literary situation. Within two or three years of his conversion he became engaged in a lengthy repetition of the drama of the crossing of the ways. He added little to the story he had already written except a tendency to single out the critic from the poet-critic and condemn him. But it was the man of letters, Allen Tate, who in his self-consciousness, his self-knowledge, as the poet-critic of history had discerned the stress during the last five hundred years between a society of myth and tradition and an emergent society of science and history as the controlling situation in the literary imagination, and had dramatized himself against this background. At times Tate condemned the poet-critic's role in the drama of the crossing of the ways by giving it a melodramatic twist, associating it—as in two of the best-known essays in *The Man of Letters in the Modern World,* "The Angelic Imagination" and "Our Cousin, Mr. Poe"—with the role envisaged by his "cousin," Edgar Allan Poe. In *Eureka,* Tate says, Poe identified himself with the demonic role played by the "angels of omnipotent reason," who, devoid of the human attribute of feeling, act only in the interest of the willful intellect with its desire to achieve an "angelic" command of the relations of things. "When criticism thinks it has proved anything, it has become angelic," Tate pronounced. Yet, while he seemed to ignore the angelic tendency of the criticism of criticism, he was fully aware of the irony of dogmatic critical assertion. At times Tate the poet-critic degraded Tate the critic by declaring that the critic ignores his own awareness, that he is in truth an ignoramus. This was a tactical way of redeeming the critic, and himself, from self-occultation as a demon, or an angel. It goes without saying that such a tactic may well seem less meaningful at the present literary moment, when more than one critic appears to have become powerfully moved by a demonic angelism, equating himself fully with the poet and scarcely less fully with God.

VII

The Loneliness Artist
Robert Penn Warren

One morning a few years ago Charles East—the southern editor, journalist, and storyteller, an old friend and near neighbor in the Southdowns section of Baton Rouge—picked me up at my door, and we set forth on a selective journey into the literary past of Louisiana's capital city. Our specific purpose was to see the three houses Robert Penn Warren lived in while he was associated with Louisiana State University in the 1930s and early 1940s.

Accompanied by his first wife, Emma Brescia (always called by a nickname, Cinina), Warren came to LSU in 1934 from Vanderbilt, where he had taught for three years with the title "acting assistant professor of English." Now twenty-nine years old, he had behind him a varied experience. While at Vanderbilt as a precocious under-graduate in the early 1920s, he had been a member of the Fugitive group. Later he had participated in the activities of the Agrarian group, including the publication of the 1930 manifesto *I'll Take My Stand,* although by the actual time of this event he was a Rhodes scholar at Oxford University, where he received the B.Litt. degree in the same year. Earlier Warren had been at the University of California at Berkeley (M.A., 1927) and after that at Yale University as an advanced graduate student. All of this time he was serving a dedicated apprenticeship to writing. By the time he arrived in Baton Rouge he had, over a span of twelve years, published poems, critical essays and reviews, and a substantial short fiction, "Prime Leaf," from which his first novel, *Night Rider,* developed. Warren had also published his first book, *John Brown: The Making of a Martyr* (1929), a biographical study that announced his lifelong preoccupation with the tension between ideality and reality in American history.

During his stay at LSU, Warren solidified the foundation he had laid for his lengthy career as a man of letters. He not only became an editor of the *Southern Review* (with Charles Pipkin and Cleanth Brooks) but in the same year the magazine was established (1935) published *Thirty-Six Poems,* his initial volume of poetry. The next four years saw the publication of Warren's first textbook, *An Approach to Literature* (with Brooks and John T. Purser); his edited gathering of fiction, *Southern Harvest: Short Stories by Southern Writers;* the first of the many editions of his classic collaboration with Brooks, *Understanding Poetry: An Anthology for College Students;* and *Night Rider.* By 1942, with another volume of poems in print and his second novel nearing completion, Warren was being generally recognized as a prominent addition to the remarkable list of writers who had emerged in the South in the twenties and thirties. His success seemed to confirm the wisdom of his decision in 1932 to return to the South and stay. But Warren now suddenly reversed his decision and departed for the University of Minnesota. His intention was to leave the South for good. He reconfirmed his design when, after six years at the University of Minnesota, he became a member of the faculty at a major New England bastion, Yale University. Yet, although after 1942 he was not to be in the South again save as a visitor, and then for no extended stays, Warren continued to be preoccupied with the South, past and present. Until Charles East and I made our little journey, I had never quite appreciated the complex irony of this fact.

It was a fine day with a blue sky. There was a hint of autumn in the air, the welcome intimation in a country where summer heat lingers on and on that we would soon have cooler days and could even begin to look for the minor miracle of fall coloring amid the perennial greenery of south Louisiana. Leaving my home, we had driven only about six blocks before we pulled up in front of the cottage Warren had rented at the time of his settlement in Baton Rouge. The oldest surviving dwelling in the Southdowns area of Baton Rouge, it is located on Hyacinth Avenue, a street known as Park Drive when Warren moved into Southdowns. Terminating at the edge of what was then the southernmost edge of Baton Rouge, Park Drive was not much more than a graveled country lane. Built in the late 1880s, Warren's first home in Baton Rouge had originally been the home of a dairy keeper. Today the home is the only place on Hyacinth set off by an old-fashioned picket fence. Unpainted and a little shabby, the fence, together with the ragged foliage in the small front yard, contributes to a certain aura of decadence that hovers about the modest cottage, an atmosphere accentuated by the presence of an old barn situated on something like an acre of former pastureland behind it.

If the rural ambience of Warren's first home in Baton Rouge reflects his lifelong distaste for urban living, his second home during his LSU period, which he lived in from 1937 to 1941, reflects his aversion even more strongly. At least this is plain to someone who, like me, has been in Baton Rouge long enough to have a feel for the history of its expansion from a small to a medium-size city. Otherwise it would be difficult to imagine the experience of turning off Old Hammond Highway into the ten-acre compound of a wealthy Baton Rouge family named McMains, crossing a pretty little creek—now spanned by a concrete bridge but in Warren's time by a primitive frame one—into a large stand of water oaks and red oaks, and there discovering, in the midst of residential opulence, a tiny wooden house with a sheet-metal roof. Hardly more than a cabin, the austere little house rests on simple concrete blocks, its one commanding exterior feature being a substantial red brick chimney. With, he said, the assistance of an out-of-work carpenter, Warren built his second Baton Rouge dwelling himself. Probably he designed it also. Joints and windows that seem a little awry suggest that he and his assistant were imperfect carpenters; but the interior of the house reflects a more exacting attention to detail. Particularly noticeable is the touch of rustic elegance given to the small living room by pine-paneled walls and a plain yet attractive fireplace.

After Warren had bought his own plot of Louisiana ground—acquiring the six acres for one thousand dollars during the liquidation disposal of a local bank that had gone under during the Great Depression—he built his cabin on it, one would suppose, in anticipation of the day when he would grace his woodland dominion with a more spacious home. But in reality he had no intention of settling permanently on the Hammond Highway land, regarding it, he said, merely as a stop on the way to a south Louisiana dreamplace. Save in the negative sense that his subscription to the anti-Brahmin Agrarian philosophy no doubt precluded the standard dream of the white-columned southern mansion, one cannot be very certain about what Warren imaged as an ideal place. Probably he himself had no absolute vision of it. But in 1941 he found a place that obviously satisfied his dream.

Located about eighteen miles south of Baton Rouge in a community called Prairieville, this property, known as the Frank Opdenweyer Home Place, consisted of a sizable story-and-a-half bungalow located on twelve acres of land. A removal to the new location meant Warren would have to make a daily round trip of thirty-six miles to and from the LSU campus. But the prospect of the journey back and forth to Baton Rouge was not intimidating; Warren had lived out in the country and driven the same distance while he was teaching at Vanderbilt. Nor did the prospect of taking on a larger financial obligation seem imprudent. By 1941 Warren was beginning to have some income from publishing. *Understanding Poetry* was exciting considerable attention, and he had achieved some success with *Night Rider*. Then, too, although its circulation was limited, the *Southern Review* was bringing significant acclaim not only to its young editors but to its sponsoring institution, and Warren could assume that LSU would reward him accordingly.

It must have been with considerable confidence in the future that on September 10, 1941, he signed an agreement with Tom Dutton, a prominent Louisianian and member of the LSU Board of Supervisors, to purchase the Opdenweyer Place for $6,750. Putting $675 down and making arrangements to pay off a note over an extended period of time, he moved to what he might well have expected would become "the Warren homeplace." Yet within nine or ten months he had put his newly acquired property up for sale and left Louisiana and the South for good.

I had known that his decision to depart had cost Warren a good deal of pain, but until I saw his briefly-held Prairieville domain I had never quite realized how deep the hurt must have been. A cluster of homes of varying age and character, Prairieville is located between Baton Rouge and Gonzales on what was then the meandering Jefferson Highway, the road that had replaced River Road between Baton Rouge and New Orleans and that, at this stretch, would itself be replaced by Huey Long's Airline Highway. We found the Opdenweyer Place by following Charles' recollection that Warren lived across the highway from the home of the late Margaret Dixon, managing editor of the Baton Rouge *Morning Advocate,* which he had visited in the 1950s when he was a young reporter. Turning into a road more or less directly opposite the Dixon home, we could not see a house at first because of the trees and shrubs. But as someone had told us to expect, we did see a large "For Sale" sign. At this point the drive split into two lanes, one leading to the back of the house, the other to a parking area on the side. Pulling into this area, we stopped in front of a gallery that had once extended the length of this side of the house but now ended at a point where, without benefit of architectural refinement, three or four rooms had been added. The original structure appeared to us to be fully intact. When we got out of the car and walked around to the front of the house, we discovered a still more spacious gallery. Looking out from this vantage point on an expanse of lawn bounded by the precipitous bank of a south Louisiana bayou—over the dark waters of which brooded ancient live oaks abundantly festooned with gray moss—I remembered the first lines of a Louisiana poem by Warren, "Bearded Oaks":

> The oaks, how subtle and marine,
> Bearded, and all the layered light
> Above them swims . . .

The grounds immediately surrounding the house, we remarked, had obviously been cared for, though not meticulously. We noted in particular a sadly dilapidated gazebo on the edge of the bayou bank; and, close by, what might be taken as a pathetic reminder of the ruined gardens of the Greek and Roman South, a discolored, moldy statue of Hebe and her water jug. We wondered if the gazebo and the statue had been there fifty years ago when Warren came to the Prairieville house.

As we were standing under the oaks, with Charles engaged in taking views of the house and grounds, a pickup truck sped up the drive and stopped at the back of the house. The driver was cordial to us and, when we indicated the purpose of our intrusion, said his wife had charge of selling the house for a bank in Gonzales. He also said that he had never heard of Robert Penn Warren. Feeling that we had no claim to do so, we did not ask if we could see the interior of the house. Satisfied that we had been well rewarded, nonetheless, we drove back to Baton Rouge.[1]

Walking beneath the oaks in Prairieville, I had recalled a reminiscence Warren had sent for inclusion in a small pamphlet that I edited in 1980 commemorating the *Southern Review* of 1935–1942. I had solicited only a limited number of brief reminiscences, for the available printing space was small. The responses I received included interesting comments by Cleanth Brooks and Eudora Welty, but as the reader of the commemorative pamphlet will find, the most spirited, and altogether most interesting one, is Warren's. Saying that his time with the *Southern Review* was "glorious and challenging," and altogether "one of the most educational experiences of my life," Warren concludes:

> War came. And the end for us. The administration couldn't afford the *Southern Review*. They preferred the tiger, mascot of the football team. Well, first things first. But one could scarcely suppress an inward smile of irony. Not that I—or I suppose my colleagues—cared very much, except in principle. We all felt, I suppose, that we had skimmed the cream of excitement in editorial work. We were older, and editing should be a young man's job. Each of us had his own fish to fry, his own vocation. We were to scatter. I, for good and sufficient reason, to leave my grove of live oaks, bayou, and windmill in Prairieville, which I had looked forward to enjoying for keeps. I fled to Yankee Land. But that is another story, and I look back gratefully on those years in our messy office as a gift of God—and accident.[2]

Remembering his memorial declaration about the *Southern Review* that morning in Prairieville (incidentally, the windmill is no

1. My indebtedness to Charles East is, I think, obvious, but I should like to acknowledge it specifically and to express my gratitude for both the information and the inspiration he has with typical generosity provided in this study of Warren.

2. *The Southern Review, Original Series, 1935–1942: A Commemoration, 1980* (Baton Rouge, 1980), 17. When Warren says "they preferred the tiger" to the *Southern Review*, he is referring to a rather elaborate cage LSU built to house Mike the Tiger, the mascot of the football team.

longer on the property Warren bought), I recalled a letter from him in which, referring to an essay I had written on Malcolm Cowley and the theme of literary exile in twentieth-century American writing, he had said that he too knew about exile. It had, he said, been a continuous part of his own experience. Unfortunately, when I looked for this letter after the trip to Prairieville I could not find it; nor could I find a copy of a response I distinctly remember having made, in which I invited Warren to write something for the *Southern Review* about his sense of exile. I remember this the more distinctly because I was sensitive to the fact that he did not reply, and felt that perhaps I had been unduly intrusive.

In searching for the lost letters I did come across a note that illuminates Warren's remark about his personal knowledge of exile. Dated October 10, 1979, it is a request concerning his 1980 volume of poems entitled *Being Here: Poetry, 1977–1980*. (During the 1970s and early 1980s, Warren, as Cleanth Brooks said to me once, "was writing poems by the yard.") Mentioning his interest in a chapter on southern fiction since 1945 that I had written for the *Harvard History of Contemporary American Literature,* Warren said he was intrigued by the brief quotation from St. Augustine's *Confessions* that I had used as an epigraph for the chapter: "I thirst to know the nature and power of time." The reason was that these words seemed more appropriate as the epigraph for a new book of poems bearing the aspect of a "shadowy autobiography" than another quotation from Augustine he presently intended to employ. Since he had not readily located the quotation I had used, he requested—if I did not mind his "stealing" it—that I spot it for him. I was flattered that I knew something Warren did not, even if it was only the location of one partial sentence from Book IX, Chapter 23, of Augustine's *Confessions,* and I did not mind in the least Warren's appropriation of my appropriation from Augustine. I sent the information promptly, but I refused to yield to the temptation to ask Warren to comment further on what he meant when he said that the new book of poems was in one sense a "shadowy autobiography." I still had a feeling of disquiet about possibly having trespassed on his privacy in my response to his unexpected note concerning his sense of exile. But when *Being Here* came out in 1980, I found that Warren had not exactly been making a private communication to me in his remark about its being autobiographical. He had taken the unusual step, I discovered, of adding a prose "Afterthought" to the volume, and in his letter to me was simply echoing the theme of this little essay on the rationale of the poems he had collected from his teeming output during the previous three years. This reads in part:

> The order of the poems is not the order of the composition. . . . The order and selection are determined thematically, but with echoes, repetitions, and variations in feeling and tonality. Here, as in life, meaning is, I should say, often more fruitfully found in the question asked than in any answer given. The thematic order—or better, structure—is played against, or with a shadowy narrative, a shadowy autobiography, if you will. But this is an autobiography which represents a fusion of fiction and fact in varying degrees and perspectives. As with question and answer, fiction may often be more deeply significant than fact. Indeed, it may be said that our lives are our own supreme fiction.[3]

Even after the hour beneath the oaks at Prairieville had recalled to me the reminiscent moment Warren had contributed to the commemorative pamphlet and the cryptic comment on exile in the lost letter, I knew that there was something else of some substance he had said about leaving the South that I could not quite seem to recall. A bit later on, Charles East came to my aid, calling my attention to a joint interview with Warren and William Styron that Louis D. Rubin had conducted in the late 1970s. At one point in the exchange Rubin asked the crucial question why two writers always referred to as "southern writers" had largely lived outside the South. Styron's response was that "the magnet was northward" and that he did not resist its pull because he did not want to. But Warren said that in his case in effect the pull was southward and that this made for a "difference" between him and Styron.

> I wanted to live in the South, you see; I'm a refugee from the South, driven out, as it were. The place I wanted to live, the

---

3. Robert Penn Warren, *Being Here: Poetry, 1977–1980* (New York, 1980), 107–108.

place I thought was heaven to me, after my years of wandering, was Middle Tennessee, which is a beautiful country, or *was* a beautiful country—it's rapidly being ruined. But I couldn't make it work. When I went back to teach for three years there, I enjoyed living in the country, and driving in to do my teaching, and this was fine. But I was let out of Vanderbilt University, and had to go elsewhere for a job. I went to Louisiana State University, which was quite fortunately a very exciting place. And I left Louisiana only because I felt I wasn't wanted. I felt pressure to leave. It wasn't a choice. I had settled myself down and bought a house in the country—settled down for life, I assumed. I left, shall we say, under pressure of some kind or another. I wasn't fired. I left out of pride. I went to Minnesota, which I enjoyed.

I've quit teaching several times—"never again." But I fell in love with teaching along the way, so I always drifted back in again. I was out as long as six years one time, two years another time, and again a year or so at a time. But that's not the point. The point is that I, unlike Bill, didn't make a choice of living outside the South. I always felt myself somehow squeezed out of the South, which is a very different thing from Bill's conscious choice. This is a generational matter, perhaps; I don't know.[4]

Why this dramatic statement, the most explicit and frankest Warren ever made, at least publicly, about leaving Louisiana, had not firmly registered on my mind when I originally saw it, I am not sure. But until I saw the little house Warren had built in the woods off Old Hammond Highway and walked in what was once, if only briefly, his own moss-shrouded oak grove in Prairieville, I had not had a sufficient intimation of the complex crisis in his sense of identity in the spring of 1942. I can hardly say even now that I have transformed intimation into perception. But in trying to define the crisis, I have found, as Warren says in the "Afterthought" to *Being Here,* that a question may be more important than an answer, and that fiction

4. Louis D. Rubin, Jr., ed., *The American South: Portrait of a Culture* (Baton Rouge, 1980), 307–308.

may be more important than fact. Do we detect in Warren's writing a fundamental element of the autobiographical? If so, is this to be defined in terms of the motive of exile? Is it to be read finally as the fulfillment of a vocation to exile? More specifically, if we seek the meaning of Warren's work in the motive of exile, is the primary revelation of this motive, as Warren himself seems to say, only in his writings that appear on the page as "poems"; or may we think of *Being Here* and *All the King's Men* as belonging alike to the comprehensive dominion Warren appeals to in his essay on *Democracy and Poetry*, that of "art in general"?

The most specific problem in pursuing the question of the autobiographical element in Warren's writings, I have discovered, is that of its presence in his greatest novel, *All the King's Men*, and in two subsequent novels, *Flood: A Romance of Our Time* and *A Place to Come To*. At the risk of ignoring other works that may be germane to my subject (notably the two versions of *Brother to Dragons*), I will focus my remarks on these works, believing them to have more implications than any of Warren's other writings for what I take to be the central question concerning his autobiographical motive: his sense of "being here" in relation to his sense of being of the South. To be sure, if we assume (somewhat contrary to Floyd Watkins in *Then and Now: The Personal Past in the Poetry of Robert Penn Warren* [1982]) that the autobiographical inference in Warren's work yields its most fundamental meaning not to categorical analysis but to "poetic" comprehension, *All the King's Men, Flood,* and *A Place to Come To* take on the character of "shadowy" autobiographical responses to Warren's experience of leaving Louisiana and the South in 1942.

It was not as though at this point Warren had undergone no prior experience of displacement. In his youth he had left the South to go to California, then to New England, then to England. As he said to William Styron, if somewhat overdramatically, his earlier life had been marked by years of wandering. He had, moreover, become a still more expansive wanderer after he came to LSU, spending so much time abroad, in fact, that there was some concern on the part of the LSU administration about the frequency of his leaves of absence. Even as we recognize that Warren felt rejected by the South, we become aware, I think, that his need, a lifelong one, to travel and even to live abroad implies the larger context of his alienation from the South: namely, his involvement in the sensibility of exile and deracination that, anticipated long before in Dante, had by the time of Melville and Flaubert become general in the Western literary life, and by the century of Conrad, Yeats, Joyce, Mann, Stein, Pound, Eliot, Hemingway, and Faulkner had become endemic. All the writers who have come of age in the twentieth century, Harry Levin has observed, whether they have known actual exile or not, have been affected by emotions associated with *dépaysement,* or the nostalgic yearning for a lost homeland. All bear the generic name the Alsatian poet Iwan Goll conferred on the modern author, Jean Sans Terre, or John Landless.[5]

As strongly as anywhere else—in the London of Pound and Eliot, in the Paris of Hemingway and Faulkner—Jean Sans Terre was a presence in the little circle of Nashville, Tennessee, poets who published *The Fugitive* in the first half of the twenties. He was a still larger presence in the more diverse and loosely knit group who published *I'll Take My Stand* in 1930. The determined effort of the Agrarian advocates to conceive of the South as the homeland of a preindustrial culture—when in historical fact, with the advent of the cotton gin and the steamboat in the early nineteenth century the South had become an inextricable part of the modern worldwide industrial culture—cannot be understood outside the context of *dépaysement.* An ironic case in point is Warren's taking on the task of writing an essay defending racial segregation for *I'll Take My Stand.* Sitting in his quarters at Oxford in 1930, he did turn out the essay, but it was such a halfhearted go at the subject that Donald Davidson thought it should not be included in the manifesto. Davidson's reaction is not surprising in view of the fact that Warren, who the year before had published his first book, *John Brown: The Making of a Martyr,* was already engaged in forging an imagination of history centered in the problem of the freedom and responsibility of the individual in a world in which the individual is conceived as at once the maker and the product of history.

Searching for the character of history—yearning to know its power and nature—Warren, in a comparatively late development in his career, acquired an intense interest in the novel, the literary form

5. Harry Levin, "Literature and Exile," *Listener,* LXII (October, 1959), 613–14.

that arose in response to the modern concept that history originates in the minds of men rather than in the divine mind. Out of this interest came not only the two novels Warren wrote while he was at LSU, *Night Rider* and *At Heaven's Gate,* but the seven novels that followed after he had "fled" from the South and, as he said, his life had become "another story"—this other story being partly at least that of an exile telling stories about his homeland. When he began writing fiction, Warren once remarked, it "never crossed" his mind that he "could write about anything except life in the South"; and save to a degree in his last novel, which appeared nearly forty years after the first, he never found another setting that "nagged" him "enough to stir the imagination."[6]

If it seems to accept as literal truth Warren's essentially metaphorical description of his permanent departure from the South, my reading of his northward move finds justification, I believe, when it is viewed in the light of the pervasive compulsion of the modern poet and novelist, as a necessity of being in the world, to establish an identity through self-portrayal in a figure of exile. The effort to do so is perilous. It may result in the creation of an eminently compelling identification of author and persona, as in the case of Melville and Ishmael or Joyce and Stephen Dedalus or Faulkner and Quentin Compson III. But if the distance between author and persona is either too great or too close, the drama of identification is weakened. How much so Warren himself argued in 1935 in a scorching critical evaluation of Thomas Wolfe's gigantic effort at self-understanding. Wolfe's massive autobiographical novels *Look Homeward, Angel* and *Of Time and the River,* Warren commented, show what happens when an author attempts "to exploit directly and naïvely the personal experience and the self-defined personality in art." Wolfe would do well, Warren harshly admonished, "to recollect that Shakespeare merely wrote *Hamlet;* he was *not* Hamlet."[7]

What I am up to may by now be suspected—that is, preparing the way for suggesting that in his third novel, *All the King's Men* (published in 1946, four years after he went to Minnesota and con-

6. Floyd Watkins and John T. Hiers, eds., *Robert Penn Warren Talking: Interviews, 1950–1978* (New York, 1980), 30.

7. Robert Penn Warren, "A Note on the Hamlet of Thomas Wolfe," in *Selected Essays* (New York, 1958), 183.

tinuously in print ever since), Warren created in Jack Burden, as Faulkner had in Quentin Compson, a sensitive and powerful self-interpretation of the modern literary artist. I am, I realize, interpreting Jack Burden in a way that Warren would have dismissed at the time he wrote *All the King's Men*. Yet, as I have indicated, I think that the later Warren would have been less inclined to say without qualification that Shakespeare is not Hamlet. Besides the illuminating moments I have referred to in his later thought when he recognized the pervasive autobiographical element in his work, we may well refer to a another moment, when, having observed that poetry, "however deep and obscure even to the writer," is always "an autobiography," he asks, "Isn't it William James who once said that any man who creates a philosophical system is really writing an autobiography?" It was not James who said this but Nietzsche, though James, copying from Nietzsche, did say something similar. If we don't take the term *philosophical system* technically, we may assume that Warren—like Conrad, often referred to as a "philosophical novelist"—came to the conclusion that in writing a novel, if not in quite the same way as in writing a poem, he was engaged in making "a hazardous attempt at the self-understanding" that is "the deepest part of autobiography."[8]

At the hazard of being melodramatic—a risk one should not, I suppose, worry about too much in the instance of a writer who regarded melodrama as a fundamental mode of expression—I would suggest that we may find a clue to the creation of Jack Burden in that dark moment of Warren's life when as a twenty-one-year-old student at Vanderbilt in 1924 he evidently made a serious attempt to take his own life. Although the fact of his self-destructive effort was known to some of his friends, the motive has remained obscure. Only in his last years did Warren himself explain that the provocation was a severe state of depression caused by the fear that he was doomed to

8. Robert Penn Warren, "Poetry Is a Kind of Autobiography," *New York Times Book Review*, May 2, 1985, p. 10. Also see Warren's Foreword to James A. Grimshaw, Jr., *Robert Penn Warren: A Descriptive Bibliography, 1922–1979* (Charlottesville, Va., 1981), ix–x; Warren's "special message for the first edition," the unpaged prefatory note to the Franklin Library edition of his *New and Selected Poems, 1923–1985* (Franklin Center, Pa., 1985); James Olney, "Parents and Children in Robert Penn Warren's Autobiography," in *Home Ground: Southern Autobiography*, ed. J. Bill Berry (Columbia, Mo., 1991), 31–47. Olney's essay points out Warren's mistake in attributing Nietzsche's statement to William James.

blindness as the result of a childhood eye injury. Having apparently no knowledge of his younger friend's visual difficulty, Allen Tate in a letter to Donald Davidson—dismissing as a possible motive "a maudlin self-pity working itself into the hysteria of suicide"—attributed Warren's attempt to kill himself to "a frustration" of his "emotional needs" by the Vanderbilt environment, dominated as this was, not by the poetic aspirations of off-campus Fugitives, but by the deadly genteel philosophy personified by Edwin Mims, the longtime head of the English department. Try to keep Mims away from the stricken Warren, Tate urged Davidson. "There is no reason why Red shouldn't survive in an intelligent environment, and if he doesn't survive there it will be a tremendous indictment of our whole system of ideas . . . [Warren] isn't persecuted by persons, but by hostile ideas, and the persecution is of course a mere figment in the popular mind but very real to an intellectual mind like Red's."[9] When we look into the depths of the autobiographical motive in Warren's writings, it does not seem too much for us to say that his transformation of a subminor character in a verse play called "Proud Flesh" into the highly sensitive, alienated young southerner who is the narrator and chief character in *All the King's Men* echoes the crises in Warren's personal life at Vanderbilt in 1924 and at LSU in 1942.

In 1943, the year after he left the South, Warren began once again to "fool with" a play he had written mostly in Mussolini's Rome the year World War II began. His idea was to transform this play about a dictator named Talos into a novel. Needing a novelistic narrator in order to effect the transformation, he turned a convenient plot device in "Proud Flesh"—"an unnamed newspaper man, a childhood friend of the assassin"—into a great deal more than "an excuse . . . for the assassin" of Willie Stark "to say something before he performed the deed." The nameless reporter became Jack Burden, who, Warren says, "gave me the interest I needed to write the novel," what Jack "thought about the story" being "more important than the story

---

9. Warren's reference to the suicide attempt is in David Farrel, "Poetry as a Way of Life: An Interview with Robert Penn Warren," *Georgia Review,* XXXVI (Summer, 1982), 322. Tate's letter to Davidson is quoted in Marshall Walker, *Robert Penn Warren: A Vision Earned* (New York, 1979), 54. *Cf.* Allen Tate to Donald Davidson, April 17, 1924, in *The Literary Correspondence of Donald Davidson and Allen Tate,* ed. John Tyree Fain and Thomas Daniel Young (Athens, Ga., 1974), 104. (The letter quoted by Walker does not appear in this collection.)

itself."[10] Although, like Melville and Faulkner, Warren avoided the direct exploitation of experience and personality that had trapped the genius of Wolfe, in creating Jack Burden he indubitably identified himself with his own Hamlet. Like the Hamlets of Melville and Faulkner, Ishmael and Quentin Compson, the Hamlet of Robert Penn Warren embodied the experience of the estrangement of the modern man of letters—at once intellectual and artist, critic and poet—from his native place.

When Jack Burden, having learned that Anne Stanton is Willie Stark's mistress, flees "west from the fact" and lies on a bed in a hotel in Long Beach, California ("at the end of History, the Last Man on that Last Coast"), is not his dream of suicide by drowning "in the comforting, subliminal ooze on the sea floor of History" a hidden symbol of the most critical moment in the life of the youthful Warren? Like Warren, Jack returns to life an "ex-suicide." (All "serious" writers are ex-suicides, Walker Percy once remarked.) Making his famous declaration, as World War II begins in 1939, that he and Anne are going out of the house at Burden's Landing "into the convulsion of the world, out of history into history and the awful responsibility of Time," Jack not only offers a kind of parallel to the sense Warren had of an end and a beginning in his exodus from Prairieville (six months after Pearl Harbor, incidentally) but prophesies his own reappearance as Warren's surrogate in other characters: Jeremiah Beaumont in *World Enough and Time* (1948), Brad Tolliver in *Flood: A Romance of Our Time* (1964), and Jed Tewksbury in *A Place to Come To* (1975). But if these characters suggest reembodiments of Jack Burden, they hardly suggest the Jack who is committed to a highly dangerous idea about assuming moral responsibility for Time. We discover that, insofar as Jeremiah, Brad, and Jed may be said to reflect the autobiography of Warren's thought and emotion, Warren's vision of the capacity of the self—of the self of the poet, the storyteller—to deal with history takes on a negative cast. Experiencing the South, past and present, not, according to convention, as a place of family and community but as a place of devastating loneliness, Jeremiah, Brad, and Jed become emblems of a southern expression of the modern isolation of the human spirit.

10. Watkins and Hiers, eds., *Robert Penn Warren Talking,* 44.

"Hell, the whole South is lonesome," Brad says. "It is as lonesome as coon hunting, which has always been a favorite sport, and that is lonesomer than anything except frog-gigging on a dark night in a deep swamp and your skiff leaking, and some folks prefer it that way." The Confederacy, he adds, "was founded on lonesomeness." Southerners "were all so lonesome they built a pen around themselves so they could be lonesome together," and the Confederate armies fought as long as they did "against overwhelming odds" because "everybody felt that it would just be too damned lonesome to go home and be lonesome by yourself."[11]

Jed Tewksbury, brilliant and cynical Dante scholar at the University of Chicago and Vanderbilt whose origins are Alabama poor white, is the most literal reembodiment of Jack Burden. In a way even more suggestive of Warren than Jack, he may indeed be regarded as the end of Warren's quest for a symbol of the southern writer as exile. Seeing the American West for the first time from the window of an airliner, Jed experiences "a new kind of loneliness." This new kind, the western kind, he decides, "comes because all the distance is fleeing from you, bleeding away from you, in all directions, and if you can't stop the process you'll be nothing left except a dry, transparent husk, like a cicada's with the ferocious sunlight blazing through it." In contrast, the kind of loneliness Jed had "known so well, the Southern kind," is "a bleeding inward of the self, away from all the world around, into an internal infinitude, like a pit." "Bred up" to the southern loneliness, Jed says that he had taken "full advantage" of the opportunities it offered: "I was the original, gold-plated, thirty-third-degree loneliness artist, the champion of Alabama."[12]

At the end of *A Place to Come To* the champion loneliness artist believes he has found his place to come to. But not in a return to Alabama; he will go back to Chicago, where he hopes to be blessed by the renewal of the warming love of his son and of the woman who bore the boy. Yet somehow we are not convinced—any more than in the case of Brad Tolliver—that Jed has a place to come to, or ever will, save in wistful wish and dream. Maybe, Jed thinks, like his

11. Robert Penn Warren, *Flood: A Romance of Our Time* (New York, 1964), 143–44.
12. Robert Penn Warren, *A Place to Come To* (New York, 1975), 93–94.

ignorant and debased father—killed during Jed's boyhood when, standing up in his wagon to pee on the back of his horse, he was thrown from the wagon as the horse spooked—he, the professor and Dante scholar, might have been better off if he had ridden with General Nathan Bedford Forrest and been killed in some obscure, long-forgotten action against the Yankee invaders.

In looking again at *All the King's Men, Flood,* and *A Place to Come To,* and in thinking generally about Warren and the South, I have been led to come again also to his meditation on Jefferson Davis. Entitled *Jefferson Davis Gets His Citizenship Back* (published in 1980 in the *New Yorker* and later under the same copyright date by the University Press of Kentucky as a small book), this is the last historical essay Warren wrote before the illness that eventually silenced his voice.

Its immediate origin lay in a minor historical event of the year 1978, the restoration by voice vote of the Congress of the United States of Jefferson Davis' right to vote. By this time the leader of the lost Confederacy had been dead for almost ninety years. As Warren tells the Davis story, following the surrender the leader of the Confederacy briefly became a fugitive and then, under rather grim conditions, a prisoner of the Federal government and finally, released from physical imprisonment, an inmate of the prison of internal exile. Although in the last years of his life he was generally revered and even celebrated in the South, Davis was never released from this bondage. Nor did he want to be. Warren's chief point is that Davis accepted his exile as his justification. Had he had a voice in the matter of the restoration of his rights, he would have once again renounced the Republic of the United States, Warren says, desiring only to keep his "eternal franchise in that shadowy, long-ago-established, rarely remembered, nation of men and women who in their brief lives learned the true definition of honor": this being that there can be no pardon for wrongdoing when it can be said that "in honor and principle" no wrong had been committed. The Davis story, to use a term Warren does not quite employ, is about a man who may be called the loneliness champion of the South.

When I told him I had found the essay on Davis fascinating, Warren replied cryptically and perhaps a little defensively that it was "an indulgence." He was aware, of course, that he had written what may be taken as altogether his most sentimental essay on the South. But it was more than that: Warren's telling of the Davis story was an old exile's symbolic reidentification with his homeland.

The interest that prompted Warren to write *Jefferson Davis Gets His Citizenship Back* was not new. He had, as he once observed, found the "germ" of the Cass Mastern episode in *All the King's Men* in the life of the young Davis, who like Cass attended Transylvania College and was established as a Mississippi planter by an older brother. Warren had, furthermore, made Jefferson Davis a character in the story-within-the-story. It is Davis, a neighbor of Cass's brother Gilbert, a Transylvania alumnus, who suggests that Gilbert send Cass there. Although this is not so in the more lurid details of his life and death, Cass is like the Davis in *Jefferson Davis Gets His Citizenship Back* in his bookishness and in his poetic quality of mind, in his possessing essentially what Tate referred to in Warren's case as an "intellectual mind." The identification of Cass with Davis is given a larger, more incisive meaning in *All the King's Men* through the device of bringing Cass and Davis into contact just before the beginning of the Civil War. Cass now lives in the Mississippi capital, having left the plantation because of his increasing scruples about slavery; Davis has come to Jackson after resigning from the Senate of the United States because war is imminent. Gilbert asks Cass to call on Davis, and having done so, Cass reports to his brother that Davis has said that he has been given "a very fine coat with fourteen brass buttons in the front and a black velvet collar" but no modern rifles. Later Cass sees Davis again on the steamboat *Natchez* as Davis is proceeding from Brierfield, his plantation, to Montgomery, Alabama, to assume the presidency of the Confederacy. Cass records in his journal—a journal Jack Burden the historian broods on until it becomes a part of his own life—that when Gilbert congratulated Davis on his election to lead the Confederacy, he said he "could take no pleasure in the honor," having "in the present moment only the melancholy pleasure of an easy conscience." When Davis retires to his cabin and Cass remarks that he is a good man who still hopes for peace, Gilbert says that Davis is a fool to so hope. "'What we want now they've got us into this is not a good man but a man who can win, and I am not interested in the luxury of Mr. Davis's conscience.' Then my brother and I had continued our promenade in silence, and

I had reflected that Mr. Davis was a good man. But the world is full of good men, I now reflect as I write these lines down, and yet the world drives hard into darkness and the blindness of blood, even as now late at night I sit in this hotel room in Vicksburg, and I am moved to ask the meaning of our virtue. May God hear our prayer!"[13]

As Jack meditates on the meaning of Cass Mastern, he does not specifically refer to Cass's own meditation on Davis. But Cass's reflections about the good man he sees incarnated in Davis—the man of honor, of virtue—are implicitly central in *All the King's Men,* which turns on the story of Jack and his real father, Judge Irwin, a good man whom Jack, following Willie's ruthless orders, exposes as a betrayer of his own ideal of virtue—the ideal, according to Warren, that Davis so preeminently exemplified: obedience to honor and principle.

Entangled with associations arising from the fact that Jefferson Davis was born in Warren's native place, Todd County, Kentucky, Warren's empathy with the president of the Confederacy is especially evident in the final part of *Jefferson Davis Gets His Citizenship Back.* Here he effectively joins a description of the celebration held by the people of Todd County from May 31 through June 3, 1977, to honor Davis' recovery of his national identity and two events of a month or so later. One is a visit Warren made to the graves of his parents and of two close friends in the local cemetery in his hometown of Guthrie, the other a visit he made to the Jefferson Davis Monument and the adjacent park. (Made possible by the purchase of a site by the United Confederate Veterans in 1917, the construction of the memorial, delayed by World War I and financial problems, was not completed until 1924. Some veterans would have preferred to hold off on topping the shaft until it was higher than the Washington Monument in the national capital.)

While at the cemetery, Warren's brother, his companion on the visit, pointed out to him a grave located in an adjacent potter's field. Located close to the railroad tracks, on which "the heavy freights groaned up a long grade eastward," this "unmowed strip of weeds and grass," Warren learned from his brother, was the last resting

13. Robert Penn Warren, *All the King's Men* (New York, 1970), 185–86.

place of "Old Jeff Davis," a town character he remembered from his youth. Apparently a namesake of the Confederate president, Old Jeff, who seemed to have arrived in Guthrie from nowhere, had taken up residence in an abysmal shack by the railroad track. A legend of fecklessness and poverty, he "had entered into the common speech of the region," a well-known expression in Guthrie being "as pore as Old Jeff Davis." Now Old Jeff was buried beneath a "little stone, commercial-made—the kind of monument a grateful government sets up to commemorate its penniless veteran." Old Jeff, it turns out, had served in the Spanish-American War, though whether "in heroism or quaking fear . . . is not recorded." Leaving the obscure monument to Old Jeff (adjacent to it is a crude concrete slab Old Jeff had made for his wife, who had preceded him in death by several years), Warren made his way to the monument that had been erected in honor of the other Jeff Davis. Ironically, it was a monument, Warren's grandfather had said, to the man who lost the war for the South. But the grandson preferred to characterize it as a memorial for one who in the war between the United States and Mexico had "received enemy lead into his own body and continued to sit his mount while a boot filled with blood." There, in Warren's own native place and the native place of the president of the Confederacy—who had once spilled his blood for the Union—the stone shaft stood before Warren in all its loneliness: "blank, whiter now, after a refurbishing for the commemoration: preternaturally white against the slow, curdling grayness of clouding sky, and somehow, suddenly, meaningless."[14]

Fusing fact and fiction, Warren sketched in *Jefferson Davis Gets His Citizenship Back*—if only partially, and at times in dim, slantwise lines—another portrait, deeply autobiographical, of the white southern loneliness artist. (Only white southerners know loneliness, Brad Tolliver says.) Searching for a place to come to, Warren fled the South in 1942, yet he was always to hold in his vision of history, as he puts it in *The Legacy of the Civil War,* the "City of the Soul that the historical Confederacy became." Seeking to discern the self-biography in his writings, we are reminded of the remark Warren made to Styron a year or two before he wrote the essay on Jefferson Davis,

14. Robert Penn Warren, *Jefferson Davis Gets His Citizenship Back* (Lexington, Ky., 1980), 12–14, 108–10.

that the response the southern writer makes to his homeland is perhaps "a generational matter." Warren recognized that he belonged to the last generation of white southerners whose childhood had a full context in the lives of grandfathers and grandmothers who had personally known the war of 1861–65. In the tension between implanted pieties and historical realities he carried on a long quarrel with himself about his relationship to his homeland—a quarrel dramatized not only in his fiction but in his nonfiction, in neither form more explicitly than in his essay on segregation in *I'll Take My Stand* in 1930 and, thirty years later, in *Segregation in the South: The Inner Conflict*. Warren would seem finally to have relieved his loneliness, if not redeemed it, by "indulging" in at least a momentary identification with the ineffable community of the lonely in which Davis held "eternal franchise"—that invisible Confederacy created by the southern imagination after the collapse of the visible prison white southerners had built around themselves in 1861 so that, as Brad Tolliver said, "they could be lonely together."

We may well ask, I think, if in his visionary treatment of Jefferson Davis, Warren did not reach the climactic point in the "shadowy autobiography" he had been writing for sixty years. We may, I believe, even ask the question—the question being more significant than the answer—does Jefferson Davis become the last persona, the last shadowy Hamlet, of Warren? At the same moment we must temper our asking with the realization that, although the portraits of his southern Hamlets and southern loneliness artists responded to his deep, compelling need to discover his identity, Warren had been obedient to his preemptory admonition to Thomas Wolfe about confusing art and self. In Wolfe's confusion Warren recognized his own strong temptation to reduce the world to the self. He came implicitly to acknowledge that his advice to Wolfe had been directed to himself. Resisting Wolfe's indulgence of the self, Warren found the large governing tension in his work in a larger autobiographical motive, a tragic opposition between the love of home and the necessity of exile.

One cannot escape the feeling that a certain symbolic resolution of these contraries was effected when, on October 8, 1989, Warren's ashes were quietly buried in a lonely country cemetery not far from his summer home in West Wardsboro, Vermont. Warren had come to love deeply this place he had finally come to. The farewell that accompanied the act of opening New England earth undisturbed for a hundred years to receive the burial urn included a reading—amid the burgeoning color of a New England autumn—of Warren's Louisiana poem "Bearded Oaks." There was a certain appropriateness in the ceremonial and the place of burial. A storyteller for whom the mystery of personal identity was deeply fused with the mystery of place—a storyteller who was southern to the bone yet was haunted after he left the South by the knowledge that, like Wolfe, he could never come home again—was now at home with exiles from the same homeland the southerners had left.

When that all-American loneliness artist Henry James returned to his native land in 1904 for the first time in twenty years to make a tour of the nation from which he had in effect made a personal secession, James came into the South for the first time in his life. The "palpitating pilgrim" of the chapters on Richmond and Charleston in *The American Scene* (1907) was immediately aware of the loneliness in which the antebellum southerners had been invisibly imprisoned. "It came over one," he says, "that they *were* there, in the air they had breathed, precisely lone—even the very best of the old Southerners . . . the real key to one's sense of their native scene was in that very idea of their solitude and isolation." In his empathy with the postbellum southern scene, James experienced it as the "melancholy void" of a people more "disinherited of art or of letters" than any he had ever seen. Yet he had intimations that when southern writers grasped the key to the southern condition—to their heritage of solitude and isolation—and defined themselves and their vocation in the image of loneliness, they would richly "garnish" and "people" the "void."[15]

With remarkable intuitive perception, the Yankee expatriate prophesied the image of the southern loneliness artist as it would be consummately incarnated in William Faulkner, Warren, and Tate; embodied exquisitely, if less directly, in Andrew Lytle, Caroline Gordon, and Eudora Welty; figured forth in haunted attenuation in Styron, Elizabeth Spencer, Reynolds Price, Walker Percy, Shelby Foote, and Cormac McCarthy; emerge in resurgent form in John

---

15. Henry James, *The American Scene*, ed. Leon Edel (Bloomington, Ind., 1968), 374, 386–87.

William Corrington, but as a fainter image still in Corrington's contemporaries Barry Hannah and Charles East; finally, as memory has reached the limits of attenuation, to become no more than a scarcely discernible impression in southern writers of the last two decades, as for instance, Bobbie Ann Mason, Clyde Edgerton, Jill McCorkle, Lee Smith, Mary Hood, and Padgett Powell. No longer defined by the image of a lost homeland—the ineffable vision of a place to come to—the image of the southern loneliness artist has passed beyond evocation, having yielded to the universal modern phenomenon of the alienation of memory by history.

VIII

The Last Casualty of the Civil War
Arthur Crew Inman

With the brutal actuality of the War for Southern Independence appreciably fading by the 1880s, southerners, Robert Penn Warren says, "mystically converted" the "human disorder" of the Confederate States of America into a "City of the Soul," and, "absolving" the leader of the fallen Confederacy from blame for their defeat, elevated Jefferson Davis to the presidency of this transcendent dominion. At the same time the former rebels, redeemed but unforgetting, and slow to forgive, accorded Jefferson Davis' beloved daughter Varina Anne—more frequently than her mother Davis' companion on ceremonial occasions—to the status of "Daughter of the Confederacy." But unfortunately, having become a symbol of the Lost Cause, "little Winnie" (as her family called her) fell in love with a young lawyer from Syracuse, New York. Although Winnie's suitor was, Warren says in his remarkable essay on Davis, a gentleman possessed of "every virtue, every grace," he was by unalterable fact of birth and rearing not only a Yankee but the grandson of a well-known abolitionist. To ask for the hand of the Daughter of the Confederacy her lover courageously confronted the proud leader of the lost war at Beauvoir, the palatial cottage at Biloxi, Mississippi, where Davis had found refuge following his imprisonment for treason and where he had written *The Rise and Fall of the Confederate Government*. Davis, as he must, refused Winnie's suitor. Later, seeing her desperate unhappiness, he indicated that he would relent, but it was too late.

Educated both at home and abroad, fluent in German and French as well as English, Winnie filled her empty days pursuing a literary inclination, writing among other things two romantic novels, an essay entitled "The Women of the South before the War," and, after his death in 1889, an essay on the virtuous character of her father. Yet, while her writings, according to one biographer, shone with "the moonlight" of the "idealism" of a "beautiful pure soul," Winnie Davis did not find the sublimation of her lost love in literary labor. Having undergone a lengthy "decline" (as they used to say), she died in 1898, by then, according to the social convention of the day, an old maid. Ironically, at the time of her death the Daughter of the Confederacy was living in the North, where she and her mother (also a writer) had gone several years earlier in search of brighter literary opportunities. That Winnie died in voluntary exile in the land of the conqueror contributes an additional note of poignancy to Warren's epitaph for her: "the last casualty of the Civil War."[1]

But in memorializing Varina Anne Davis, Warren sounds a note that neither she herself nor the members of her generation of southern writers generally would have quite understood. Although born either during the years of the fighting or in the early part of the bitter Reconstruction era, the writers of the Winnie Davis generation were singularly conformist and unimaginative. Numbering in their ranks Julius Madison Cawein, Frances Boyd Calhoun, Molly Elliot Seawell, C. Alphonso Smith, and Edwin Anderson Alderman, they scrupulously equated pious allegiance to the Lost Cause with a faithful adherence to a stifling genteel social and literary decorum. Judging by their literary tone as preserved in that egregious monument to the Lost Cause mentality published in the first decade of the twentieth century, *The Library of Southern Literature,* we may almost think that they were self-conscious parodists of the late nineteenth-century sentimental manner. The one exceptional mind of little Winnie's generation was the founder and first editor of the *Sewanee Review,* William Peterfield Trent. Leaving the South for a position on the Barnard College faculty at Columbia University, and eventually becoming an editor of *The Cambridge History of American Literature,* Trent anticipated the possibility Ellen Glasgow (born in 1873) first truly envisioned, that through the subjection of piety to the scrutiny of irony southern literary talent might be redeemed from the prison-

---

1. Robert Penn Warren, *Jefferson Davis Gets His Citizenship Back* (Lexington, Ky., 1980), 90–93; Chiles Chilton Ferrel, "Varina Anne Jefferson Davis," in *The Library of Southern Literature,* ed. Edward Anderson Alderman, Joel Chandler Harris, and Charles William Kent (1907–1909), 1334.

house of piety symbolized by *The Library of Southern Literature*. But Glasgow had no immediate contemporary, no other major southern writer being born during the three decades after 1861 except for John Crowe Ransom.

In the next twenty years or so after Ransom's birth in 1888, we find the birth dates of a whole cluster of important twentieth-century southern writers, including Katherine Anne Porter, Donald Davidson, Caroline Gordon, Allen Tate, William Faulkner, Andrew Lytle, Robert Penn Warren, and Eudora Welty. The Ransom generation— the second generation of post–Civil War writers and the first post-Reconstruction generation—repudiated the literary conservatism of the Brahmin South presented by Winnie Davis and her peers. Discovering a fundamental literary resource in their self-consciousness of survival in a defeated society, writers like Tate and Porter might at times specifically identify themselves as personal representations of the southern experience of defeat. More often, southern poets and novelists created personae to serve as incarnations of the fallen South, the most graphic instance being no doubt Faulkner's Quentin Compson III. Southern writers might also suggest their sense of personal involvement in the ethos of defeat through an empathetic portrayal of historical figures, as Warren does in treating Varina Davis and her father. But whatever their strategy of representing their relation to the southern pieties, the writers of the Ransom generation (if we allow for a possible exception in the case of Donald Davidson) identified themselves as survivors of a war that, whether explicitly or not, they impiously acknowledged that the South not only could not have won but should not have won, and, moreover—this was the crowning impiety—perhaps had not wanted to win.

I have been briefly sketching a possible historical context in which to locate the significance of Arthur Crew Inman (1895–1963), a startling recent addition to the post-Reconstruction generation of southern writers. A prime example of the kind of poet the Vanderbilt Fugitives fled from—a mediocre talent, wholly lacking in the sophisticated literary and philosophical education of the Ransom generation—Inman is nonetheless revealed in *The Inman Diary: A Public and Private Confession,* edited by Daniel Aaron (1985), to be a uniquely arresting and complex representative of the southern writer as at once survivor and victim of the Civil War.

An only child and scion of a prominent Atlanta family, Inman

was born in the capital of Georgia on May 11, 1895, and died a suicide in Boston on December 5, 1963. He began the record that he
called his "Diary" in 1919 and wrote in it almost daily until his death.
An invalid (possibly a self-willed one) during his forty years in Boston, Inman made his home for the most part on one floor of Garrison
Hall, a "somewhat seedy but respectable apartment hotel" in the
Back Bay area. Here, where he mostly confined himself to one per-
petually darkened room, he lived a reclusive yet not a solitary life,
having an attractive wife and a small retinue of servants and, beginning in 1924, a constant flow of visitors to his door. He arranged for
the visitors by the simple expedient of advertising in the "Help
Wanted" column of the Boston *Evening Transcript* for persons willing
to talk to an invalid for a fee of one dollar per evening. For the dollar,
or more often out of curiosity or a lonely need on their own part for
someone to talk to, applicants in considerable number either tele-
phoned or called on Inman personally, and soon he was seeing visitors nearly every evening. Some of them he called "talkers"; others,
asked to read to him, he called "readers." Some became both talkers
and readers. Thus it was that after a period when he had almost given
up his Diary for lack of subject matter, he came "into contact," as
Inman says, "with new thoughts, new emotions, new viewpoints,
new experiences." He had, moreover, found a way not only "to re-
stock the empty storehouse" of his mind but to provide an endless
flow of materials for his Diary. One cannot improve on Aaron's description of the lengthy drama of Arthur Inman's life with his talkers.

> After a few years of floundering, he acquired the knack
> of imparting the personalities of his talkers vividly and suc-
> cinctly and sketching their physical and mental attributes in
> swift, comical strokes. He would receive them in a heavily
> curtained room from which all light had been blotted out;
> and in this black sanctum they submitted to his highly per-
> sonal interrogations. Did they believe in God? Did they love
> their wives or husbands? Did they take drugs? Perhaps the
> anonymity created by darkness was conducive to confession.
> Perhaps his nonjudgemental responses to the most hair-rais-
> ing confidences relaxed inhibition. Whatever the reason, Ar-
> thur Inman, like some ghostly doctor-priest in a Hawthorne

tale, listened to the outpourings of heads and hearts: accounts of alcoholism and incest, of disastrous marriages, of abortions, of picaresque adventures, of adolescent tragedies and epiphanies, of catastrophic illnesses and religious faith. More often than not his informants were from the lower-middle or blue-collar class: young people on the loose and hungry for experience, people on the fringes who had once known better days, people living squalidly but often swollen with glory and pride, each flattered by the attentions of a strange and sympathetic man who said he wanted to improve them and make them successful and happy and was always ready with advice. Taken collectively, their revelations comprise a gritty tragicomedy and disclose aspects of American life only sporadically touched upon in contemporary fiction.[2]

But talking and reading were not the only activities that went on in Inman's shadowy domain. Almost from the beginning his experiences with his female talkers included physical as well as mental encounters. The first seems to have occurred in January, 1925.

I certainly guessed right concerning the sex part of the Mrs. Merriman woman. Last night she gave me the complete freedom of her body. Think she would have been in the bed if I hadn't taken pains to explain how my side had incapacitated me sexually for the last three months. According to her, she is desirous physically most of the time. She surely acted it. Never met anyone so frank to admit her desire towards and enjoyment in physical sensation. She was proud of her smooth skin, of the strength in her legs, of her large breasts. The latter, she was careful to explain, were her especial pride because the looks and feel of them always aroused men's passions. (I, 261)

Although the numerous accounts of his erotic experiences are often rendered ludicrous by his acute awareness of his infirmities, Inman

---

2. Arthur C. Inman, *The Inman Diary: A Public and Private Confession*, ed. Daniel Aaron (2 vols.; Cambridge, Mass., 1985), I, 259, 3–4. Hereafter references to this work will be cited parenthetically in the text.

describes each episode with complete frankness. As he emphasizes over and over, his desire was to be absolutely honest with the readers who would someday marvel at his great masterpiece of self-revelation.

But while Inman had a passionate fondness for women, particularly young ones, his predominant interest in his visitors, male and female, was in their thoughts and most of all in their life stories. In fact, whether his visitors were talkers or readers, he soon came to call all of them "characters," a term he extended to his servants in whose life stories he became interested, notably two manservants, Jason Flood and Ten Broek. Feeling that he had an obligation both to his characters themselves and to the future readers of his chronicle to record in detail their histories, Inman believed—as a growing number of diverse persons sat with him and confided in him—that he was creating a great chronicle of his age. Like Hakluyt "gleaning his collection of voyages," he said, he was limning "a picture of the world as men saw it in his day." He "may not stir from Boston," Inman says, "yet people who have dwelt or travelled in other parts of this broad America, people from every walk and condition of life [though, as Aaron points out, the spectrum was not so broad as Inman claimed] relate to me their experiences and observations that I may record a picture of this wide land and the customs and actions and thoughts of the folk who dwell therein for posterity to read" (I, 490).

At the same time, Inman continued to think that his primary task as diarist was to write his own thoughts and life history. Maintaining himself in his massive story as at once the observer and the leading character, the controlling voice and the dominant actor, he projects, at least through the first half of his Diary, the role of a prophetic American reactionary. Imagining what he would do if he were a president of the United States who had seized dictatorial power, Inman envisioned the necessary salvational course of the nation as follows:

> Restrict voting to land and wealth. Tax all the same percentage, rich and poor alike. Abolish prohibition, the national cancer. Take from the people the election of Senators, and return it to the state legislatures. Ease up on land taxes. Tax

luxuries. Abolish enforced education. Make higher education a privilege rather than a way to keep from going to work for four more years. Tax automobiles and aeroplanes until only the wealthy can afford them. A higher protective tariff. Titles, permanent to Senators, Supreme Court Judges, Presidents, Vice-Presidents, Admirals, Generals, members of Cabinet. Titles to those rich men willing to pay enough. Titles to members of the Order of Cincinnatus. Temporary titles to Congressmen and other Government officials deserving award for merit. Seizure of Canada and Mexico and Cuba. The establishment of an imperial policy, plainly spoken, without hypocrisy. Recognition of colored people and Jews as inferiors, incapable of holding government office. Recognition of the Nordic stock as superior. (I, 343)

One feels that there is a constant equation between Inman's wild dreams of political power and his frustration of the power he truly wanted: literary power, that is to say, the power to influence, perhaps even control, history through the shaping power of words. Basically, he thought of this power as that given to the great poet, and all of his life he kept returning to the idea that in the small body of verse he had composed, most of it in his younger years, he had demonstrated a capacity for greatness in poetry but was ignored in a time when T. S. Eliot was considered to be "next to God." The fact that Inman seldom rose above the level of the romantic magazine versifier lends significance to a passage in the Diary in which the equation between political and literary power virtually becomes overt. The year after Hitler invaded Poland and instigated World War II, Inman, who had just finished a book attacking the elevation of Eliot and Yeats over Stephen Vincent Benet and Carl Sandburg, declared in his Diary:

All very encouraging to me to see such madness put down explicitly in black and white. . . . It's not I who am off the track in this poetry business; it's the elected poets and the hashish-eating critics. The book has encouraged me no end. Reading this book and studying intensively current and classical poetry has encouraged my faith in myself.

Watching Hitler perform has likewise given me one of the largest lifts I have ever received. I wonder if the results of an increased confidence is apparent in what I write? It should be, for I feel less subdued, less mouse-like, insofar as both myself and my work are concerned. If people fail to discern my value as an exceptional person, that is their misfortune. (II, 978–79)

The irony of his rejection of the authoritarian Eliot when he himself was essentially an American fascist altogether escaped Inman, who not only lacked a literary education sufficient for such self-perception but was blinded by his incongruous jealousy of Eliot and his other famous literary contemporaries. Tacitly recognizing that he could not compete with the famous poets of his age, Inman thought of his Diary as an undertaking promising him enduring posthumous fame as the unique voice of his time.

Always maintaining himself as the dominant actor, the controlling voice in his massive story, Inman early on developed an acutely personal anxiety about the fate of his manuscript when inevitably it passed beyond his control. Indeed, the character of his "problematical editor" caused him considerable anxiety. "I am as likely to be given, postmortem, a 'good' editor as a 'bad' one," he wrote hopefully in 1960, but through the years he repeatedly indicated his anxiety, often interrupting his increasingly unwieldy day-to-day record to insert advice to the unknown person who would one day subject it to editorial judgment. Among other things he feared that his Diary might fall into the hands of someone who had not known of his existence until it fell to his lot to edit the Diary. He feared in particular the possibility that editorial censorship of the Diary's indecorous details would impair the relentless honesty that he fancied to be its chief virtue.

Inman's posthumous luck could not have been better. His voluminous life-record passed into the hands of a distinguished Americanist who was willing not simply to undertake the overwhelming task of reducing 155 manuscript volumes to the compass of 2 printed volumes containing something like one million words, but to spend a half-dozen years seeking to understand the quirky, exasperating author and fathom the role he had devised for his editor. One result is that Aaron includes himself in the cast of characters he has provided as a part of his editorial apparatus. The editor, to be sure, not only formally recognizes the integral role Inman had conceived for him in the Diary, but he describes in his introduction to the printed text of the Diary and his editorial headnotes to the six "books" and their various subsections how, being at once "insider" and "outsider," he became conscious during the editorial process that his role was gradually changing from that of "detached observer" to that of "engaged commentator" and finally, in Book VI ("Arthur Doomed: The Chronicler Assessed"), to that of a "one-man chorus." In Book VI the editor becomes fully a character in his own right, exercising a rigid selectivity in the choice of entries and being calculatedly precise in the ordering of those selected. In his extensive interpretive commentary in Book VI, Aaron even invests himself with a certain fictive quality through the device of a series of "letter-essays" to Edna Coffin Mercer, a member of the Garrison Hall "family" in the 1930s. In these letters (presumably never mailed), which are interlarded with passages from the Diary, Aaron uses Edna Mercer, who had proven during his labor on the huge document to be "obliging and perceptive," as "a sounding board for his concluding speculations about Arthur and his ways" (see II, 1529–99).

As we can readily see, the dual problem implied in any kind of editor-author connection—that of the influence of the editor on the author and inversely of the author on the editor—is acutely present in the case of the Inman Diary, for Inman wanted to control his future editor as much as or more than he desired to mold the life of each person who came to him in the intimacy of his dark kingdom in Garrison Hall. To fulfill his obligation to Inman—to be true to him—Aaron ironically had little choice save to seek to enact the role the diarist had written for his future editor. Yet, although it is not a judgment that could be confirmed empirically, even if one undertook an extensive comparison of the Inman manuscript and the printed version, any careful reader of the Aaron edition is likely to feel confident that an honest editor has transcended Inman's desire to manipulate him and at the same time has been scrupulously faithful to the Inman mandate that he be presented to the world as an honest author.

Inman, to be sure, might well object that his editor—who says that after "six years of exposure to the mind and heart of Arthur Inman" may "know him better than I do my closest friends"—has been too honest about the author's professed honesty. In introducing *The Inman Diary,* Aaron sees Inman's motive of "self-discovery" as being largely a strategy of "self-defense" on the part of a "fearful and self-extenuating fellow" whose character "does not change," who— a "self-styled southern aristocrat, the last of the Nordics, the Genghis Khan of Garrison Hall"—remains "incongruous, sublimely asinine, alternately apologetic and arrogant." Inman might have been more satisfied with another facet of his portrayal by Aaron: his depiction as a Don Quixote, a "classic 'sick' soul"—who, an "intrepid Adventure-Entertainer," puts "the reader in a front-row seat to watch the human comedy," in which as the protagonist he "both unashamedly connives, cavorts, and weeps and relives the terrors of his hag-ridden subconscious life" and presents in its abundant vitality "the promiscuous crowd passing in and out of Garrison Hall." But even though in his analysis of Inman, Aaron seems to allow for a dramatic tension between the neo-Confederate aristocrat, or pseudoaristocrat, and the intrepid Adventurer-Entertainer, he considers Inman's character to be fundamentally static. Aaron refers to the abridged Diary, moreover, as a large fragment from the original monolithic whole, "a big chip off the old block" that "will serve well enough for Inman's monument" (I, 12–13).

It almost seems as though, when the editorial labor was done and it came time for Aaron to comment in definitive summation on Inman and the process of editing the Diary, Aaron the outsider, the detached scholarly editor, tended to replace Aaron the insider, or the character Inman had created. In any event, one may question whether Aaron's reduction of Inman's outsized diary is fairly represented in the homely metaphor he employs, "a chip off the old block." Aaron represents Inman's "monument" and his own complex accomplishment in editing it more adequately when, discussing the thematic structure of the Diary, he observes that it may be taken as 1) the case history or "autobiography of a warped and deeply troubled man whose aberrations call for psychiatric probing"; 2) the story of a "son of the South," a "transplanted and self-conscious southerner obsessed with his ancestors . . . his parents, relations, and friends"; 3) an "overview of Boston from the 1920's to the 1960's";

4) a "social history of America" during (if we include Inman's frequent retrospective passages) the first half of the twentieth century; 5) a "gigantic non-fiction novel," in which Arthur Inman "becomes in effect his own literary creation, the hero or antihero of a novel-autobiography." Although no one of these structural elements dominates the rambling dimensions of Inman's work, its overall character, Aaron says, is most adequately discovered when we regard it as combining elements of American social history and the nonfiction novel (I, 4–9). Such a perspective on the Diary finds a sanction in Inman's early notion that he was composing an "American saga."

Does the Diary reveal something like a novelistic—or, in the broad sense of the term, poetic—development, even something close to an episodic kind of plot, or possibly even a "plot line"? As finely attuned as he is to Inman, whether as "engaged commentator" or as "one-man chorus," has Aaron, it seems fair to ask, been sufficiently sensitive to the novelistic aspect of the Diary, particularly to the underlying "plot motive"?

In one of his many reflections on the question of what he is actually doing in his compulsive day-by-day account, Inman says that he is recording "both a history of my times and the story of my self-discovery." He adds: "Nothing (or at least very little) has been held back. My selfishness, cruelty, deception—all are there; but when you come to know the *real* me you will realize that my actions made possible my survival. To be sure it has given me pleasure to improve those near and dear to me, but had I lived for others, I could never have mustered the stamina and courage to surmount my handicaps and complete my grand objective" (I, 11). On the face of it we might assume that in speaking of surviving in spite of his handicaps Inman refers to his survival of multiple physical and psychic ailments. His major physical problem, the chief cause of his invalidism, was the "anatomical anomaly" of "loose joints," or a "disorder of the connective tissues." To treat this condition Inman employed Dr. Cyrus Rumford Pike, an osteopathic physician and a leading character in the Diary, who as an intimate of the Garrison Hall ménage eventually became the lover of Inman's wife Evelyn when she finally decided to take revenge on her faithless spouse. The diarist's second most important malady was photophobia, or an extraordinary sensitivity to light. This phobia, which forced him to spend most of his life in a darkened room, was accompanied by a third, if less severe, affliction, an abnormal sensitivity to sound. Inman's less exotic physical complaints were numerous; he lists them as headaches, constipation, diarrhea, abdominal distention, hemorrhoids, prostatitis, and gallbladder disease. The psychic handicaps he struggled with included depression and nightmares, and, although he himself did not recognize these afflictions as problems, bromide addiction and alcoholism. The need to survive the conditions imposed by his physical and mental liabilities, Inman clearly felt, justified his using his family's wealth (augmented by investments he made) to create a private kingdom, where he could make excessive demands on everyone associated with him and, in short, lead a singularly selfish existence.

In his own eyes, as he points out, Inman justified his way of life partly by his self-enhancing efforts to "improve" the character and well-being of the persons he came to know. Yet, for all the space he devotes in his Diary to maladies of mind and body, Inman would seem never to have thought of them as a spiritual discipline, never to have found the long-lasting sustaining satisfaction some invalids take either in the determination to overcome their afflictions or, knowing them to be beyond remedy, in enduring them. If the real Arthur Inman, the inmost *me* of Arthur, was a survivor, what was he a survivor of? Perhaps it may be said that in the deepest sense he was a survivor of the destructive potential of his own absolute self-awareness. He generalized his condition philosophically as "the predominating consciousness of personal identity which is the joy and curse and the particular trademark of a man" (I, 297); but Inman himself experienced a consciousness of personal identity so intense that more than once he was a near-suicide before he finally used the Colt revolver he had kept against the moment when he would no longer gamble with a drug overdose that he knew would likely be countered by medical attention.

The inmost, the *real,* Arthur Inman is the character in the Diary who wrote its seventeen million words. When this character had fulfilled his primary mission, to discover who he was, the fundamental animating tension in the Diary—the stress between self and history embodied in Inman's figuration of the writer—disappeared. He signaled the arrival of the moment of truth a few days before he pulled the trigger when he confessed to himself: "I have lived too long. I have written too much" (II, 1598). Inman could not live long beyond that admission, for the act of writing the Diary was the only life-defining action he ever took, and he had finished it. The inner drama of the Diary reveals itself in various ways, the most prominent being in Inman's description of his relationship to New England; in his remembrance of his childhood years in post-Reconstruction, turn-of-the-century Atlanta; and, most significantly, in his increasing sense, at times obsessive, of his connection with the Civil War.

Inman's decision to reside permanently in Boston instead of his native city of Atlanta had a good deal to do with the fact that Boston still bore some resemblance to Henry James's "little interesting city" of "character and genius," where Emerson, Hawthorne, Longfellow, Holmes, Ticknor, Prescott, Motley, and Parkman had once walked and conversed—and which in its connection with Cambridge and Concord across the Charles River constituted a community of literary aspiration that was a finely honed expression of the older New England pietas.[3] Inman's affinity for this pietas was strong. He says early in the Diary that Boston "has placed itself in my heart"; he even says that he has the "Boston fever" (I, 177). Studying a photograph of Parkman, "the historian, Boston blue-blood, invalid, aristocrat," Inman traced his own "outstanding features": the "same outthrust chin; the same mouth with close-pressed lips, the upper somewhat weak, a mouth slightly cynical, slightly hard and betokening above all self-discipline and self-repression." Forty years later Inman still found in Parkman a model image: an invalid with "nervous and ocular trouble" but obsessed with producing "a major literary and historical work" and always overtaxing his "quantum of strength" (I, 177–78; II, 1575–76).

Inman was no stranger to New England, his family having long maintained a summer home in Southwest Port, Maine. But this was only incidental to his compulsive attraction to a figure like Parkman. The context of his regard for the author of *The Oregon Trail* was the existence of a bond—spiritual, literary, cultural—between the South and New England. Indissoluble even by the terrors of fratricidal war, a major irony of American history, this relationship between the two regions was perhaps experienced more consciously by the south-

3. Henry James, *The American Scene*, ed. Leon Edel (Bloomington, Ind., 1968), 245.

erner, who regularly sent his sons to Harvard and Yale, than by the New Englander. But Hawthorne, Emerson, and Henry Adams had a profound sense of the connection. That it in fact had something like a symbiotic quality is evident in Inman's expression of his feeling for the heroic cultural life of the old Boston. More than a mere nostalgic gesture, it bears the aspect of a faded symbol of a once powerful cultural situation. This is evident in Inman's agonized but helpless reaction to the demolition of buildings belonging to nineteenth-century Boston and the erection of monuments to a new Boston. Watching the tower of the Prudential Center push upward, Inman observes grimly that it "soon will be goosing God." When the quiet streets immediately surrounding his Garrison Hall bastion began to be made into thoroughfares, and the shattering sounds of wrecking machines and air hammers invaded his neighborhood, Inman entered upon a long period of crisis. Suffering not only from noise but from the fear that new sources of light would be introduced in the reconstructed Boston, he said, "I think I'll get my pistol out of the bathroom" where it was kept, "wrap it in plastic, put it under the bed in a cubby there where, too desperate, I can grasp and use it" (II, 1592, 1590).

But the noisy alteration of the Boston skyline was not the only cause of Inman's feeling that his existence was becoming "less and less propitious by the week with the next japes of fate closer." He was haunted by the sense that his reason for being was disappearing. "What I write," he complained, "is constantly more personal and less worthwhile, the former intensity of curiosity no longer uncontainable and artisanship flagging." In sum, Inman said, he found himself "terribly tired, my allotted historical task all but completed" (II, 1590). The problem—we may speculate with considerable certainty—was not that Inman's writing had become more personal, for, inspired by the vital tension the diarist felt between himself and history, it had always been personal. The problem was that, experiencing a weakening of this tension, Inman knew, if not quite articulately, that the fundamental task he had assumed in his Diary—the search for his inmost being—had effectively concluded six years earlier, when he finally recognized that the central motive of his life had been the "annealment" to the defeated South he says he first experi-

enced when, at the age of twenty, he stood at the grave of his grandfather Samuel Martin Inman (1843–1915).[4] A wealthy Atlanta cotton
broker and philanthropist, who at the time of his death was known
as the "First Citizen" of the preeminent city of the New South, Samuel Inman had been a Confederate cavalryman during the Civil War.
But if his grandfather's life was hardly a symbol of the defeated
South, in the grandson's desperate search for the rationale of his own
life it became so. Defying mundane historical logic, Arthur Inman
identified both his grandfather and himself with the history of the
defeated South and assigned both a place in the mystical Confederacy
of the Soul.

There was an inescapable, transcendent logic in this. Cared for in
his earliest years by "an old black mammy as black as the ace of
spades," Arthur was a child with "Titian red hair, big brown eyes,
extraordinarily dark lashes, dark eyebrows," who had "all the appearance of an angelic cherub." He remembered relatives and servants, even strangers on the Atlanta streets, exclaiming over him, but
his mother, he recalled, was less loving, saying over and over that
she would not "spoil" him "if it kills you" (I, 20–21). An only child,
forced to cope with a "disapproving" father and, it would seem, a
somewhat hostile, "dominating" mother, Inman was more obser-
vant than most children. His fund of memory, stimulated by a certain amount of research, makes his account of the Atlanta of the
wealthy and powerful Inman clan a valuable social document, in no
instance more so than in the rich description of the home of his maternal grandparents, the Benjamin B. Crews, at 33 West Harris

4. The tempering moment at his grandfather's grave seems to have given shape to the
memorial ambience in which Inman spent his years as a child. Witness the following entry in
the Diary formulated in the tense of the historical present:

> What happened during the War between the States seems very real to everyone.
> We are told by schoolbooks that it took place forty and more years ago, but it does
> not seem that way to us. It is more as though it happened yesterday. If anyone calls
> you a goddamn Yankee, you have to fight, just as if in Maine anyone calls you a son
> of a bitch. All the boys have mementoes in the form of Minié balls and old canteens
> and buttons. You can never tell when you are walking in the woods at certain places
> when you will come across old breastworks or step into a soldier's grave. And are
> there not the bullet marks on the brick of the old church that is our school building?
> (I, 75)

Street. The years he lived here, with both his parents and his grand-parents in residence, he knew as much of a stable and rooted life as he was ever to know.

> At the long tablecloth-covered table in the dining room we sat in regular places, Grandfather at one end, Namma at the other end with her back to the coal fire. I know that I sat with my back to the huge black sideboard, for day after day I gazed at a still-life painting of several dead ducks hung upside down by their legs. There was a little handbell to summon the colored maid, and it was never replaced. I grew to know the patterns of the china. Grandfather always said the same blessing, and we always bowed our heads in the same man-ner. The butler's pantry was never altered, nor the latticed way to the kitchen, nor the kitchen with its shelves, its built-in table for the servants to eat at, its big black coal stove, its skeleton-like black gas stove, its table with the marble tomb-stone set in it and the squeezer to make beaten biscuits, the worn wooden floor, the coal scuttle, the two west windows and the open door to the back veranda. (I, 52)

But the nostalgic memory of Benjamin Crew's home did not bind Arthur Inman to the South as forcefully as the less fulsome memory of the mansion occupied by his paternal grandfather and his step-grandmother, Mildred McPheeters Inman. Samuel Inman was a quiet man who had a certain literary bent. He "knew 'Paradise Lost' almost from end to end," his grandson recalls in his Diary, and always kept a copy of the "Life and Works of Milton" on his table. He also loved the theatre, and attended the opera on occasion. In addition, he was a student of military history. Arthur Inman recalls his grandfather "sitting in his black leather chair in the library, velvet smoking jacket on, puffing eternally on big cigars, not saying much, not (to me then) exuding warmth or charm but composure," or he remembers him "at the end of the handsome dinner table, patriarch-ical, telling stories in a quiet, soft voice, chuckling (never laughing)." Samuel Inman "never imposed himself on anyone to my knowl-edge," the grandson says, but "people, by his composure and repu-tation, were drawn to him quietly, gave him their confidence, received him" (I, 45). By the time his grandfather Inman died in 1915, Arthur had spent about seven years in the North. Having been placed in Haverford School in Haverford, Pennsylvania, in 1908, a place he came to detest as no other, he later attended Haverford College, where he had a much better time. His summers were spent in Maine. Meanwhile, he became more or less alienated both from his parents, especially his father, and from his home in Atlanta. In one of several remarkable passages interpreting the motives of his life that he wrote near its end, Inman captures the pathos of his sense of alienation as, at the age of eighteen, he came into a resentful yet dependent young manhood.

I must have told my parents how I felt about Haverford School, how the boys treated me there, though I don't recall actually doing so. However that was, I found myself in the brougham on the last day of my visit alone with my Father driving to the train. I was filled with the dread of returning to the Junior House, hence was receptive to any admonitions which might hold out to me hope of better adjusting to my circumstances in the North. Father's advice was just about the worst advice ever doled out by a parent to his son. A human life, in those few minutes it took to pass the Century Building, Nunnally's, Chamberlin, Johnson, Dubose, and turn up Mitchell Street to the Terminal Station, was—and I do not exaggerate—as much as ruined. I was not, my Father advised me, not to fight back when I was being bullied, whatever the provocation. I was not on any account to "practice self-abuse," for masturbation had, he assured me solemnly, landed more men in the insane asylum than all other causes put together. I was not on any account to go with women, for only dishonorable boys did that, and, furthermore, there were certain diseases I might catch which would ruin my life. I listened. I put the words deep in my inmost self. And all the while, outside the clear glass of the brougham window, I saw people walking back and forth along the sidewalk, saw familiar stores pass by, saw over a low roof, sky. Then the station. Down the long black stairs to the dark train. Smoke and steam rising to the high roof overhead, thundering down and back. People hurrying along the platform. Into the Pullman and into the green plush seat allotted me. It was a long and lonely ride. (I, 90)

But when he was called back from Haverford two years later to attend the funeral of his grandfather, Arthur, in the glow of the recognition accorded him as Samuel Inman's grandson, experienced a transforming sense of importance.

> Mother saw to it that I spent much time in Grandfather's library where relatives of the deceased forgathered. I was heir-apparent of the Shadrach Walker Inman line. I liked the muted bustle of relations coming and going, the fuss made over me, the sort of fustioned [*sic*] greatcoat of acceptance cast over me as an individual by sudden family concentration. I know now that S. M. Inman in his time and region was a superior man, a rich man, a man of notable probity in an era of business ruthlessness, an important man. His reflection for a handful of days shone on me. Never had the Inman and the Crew relations been so anxious to please, and they had always been good to me. It was not beyond concept that Arthur Inman might settle in Atlanta and become a power, so why not curry favor? No one yet knew what wealth had been left to the family-line grandson. At any rate, butter wouldn't have melted in any relation's mouth. . . .
>
> I must say I was stirred by the burial of Grandfather Inman, smoking Atlanta in the background, the colorful Confederate flag over the coffin, relatives in black beside the grave. It impressed me. Also, the headlines in the newspapers. My nature was annealed to the South. For the very first time I hated to leave Atlanta. I was, my diary says, carsick on the ride north. (I, 129)

Inspired by a heightened awareness of his southernism, Inman later became involved in a reprint volume of George E. Pickett's letters to his wife. Engaging his enthusiasm for some time, *Soldier of the South: General Pickett's War Letters to His Wife* was brought out by Houghton Mifflin in 1928. The letters of the leader of the fateful

Confederate charge at Gettysburg are notable, but the introduction to the volume by Inman is an ornate tribute to Pickett that, save as an example of the survival of the grandiloquent memorial style in the South, is of no interest. Inman's self-conscious southernism also inspired another early project, a book-length volume of poems in the form of a diary. To be called "The Book of Randolph Cocke," this work would "trace . . . the life of a Virginia poet and gallant from somewhat before the outbreak of the [Civil] War until its close, or maybe even to 1917." The young poet, a dreamer who believes in "his country and his God," would be put into "the crucible of War," and "after much fighting, unreal to him because subjectively comprehended," he would be "wounded almost to death," lose his faith in God, and be nursed back to health by a woman who had been a childhood playmate. After the fall of the Confederacy, the poet would appear to regain his ambition to be a great poet. Becoming famous, he would laugh at the world because he realized he worked only to gain "forgetfulness and illusory peace." Falling ill, Randolph would die "laughing" (I, 184–85).

Inman's interest both in Pickett's letters and in his never-to-be-realized scheme for "The Book of Randolph Cocke" was largely a self-conscious rhetorical gesture. At this time (1923), although Inman says that his nature was well annealed to the myth of the lost South, he was actually more convincing in asserting his love for Boston and his reverence for Parkman, in recording the experience of the annealment of his nature to the myth of a lost New England. It was only in the later years of his life that Inman's struggle for identity began to turn almost wholly on his sense of being a southerner. Six years before his death he wrote:

> Want it or not—and perhaps this is a key to my nature without which it is meaningless—I am an offspring, as it were, of the Civil War and of the legend it left behind it. I bear the estamp psychically and physically of the War, of what came after: the Donald Fraser companies standing at salute while a Civil War monument was undraped [the Donald Fraser school Inman attended as a boy was in Decatur, Georgia, then a town several miles from Atlanta, now a part of the city]; the Confederate flag on my Grandfather's coffin; pick-

ing up Minié balls where was fought the Battle of Peachtree Creek; Old Lady Marmon in the firelight telling stories of Sherman's march; the little room where people hid in the "old dormitory" at Donald Fraser; the books, so many of them, absorbed before I was 13, read then, read later, read now; a really deep pride at having sprung from "Southern" blood. I bear, as well as the antique dream which has only certain jointures with reality as it was, the stigmata of those four dire years of rebellion and failure and what came appallingly to a conquered land during the Reconstruction. (II, 1563)

A complementary passage from the Diary a year later should also be quoted.

I imagine it sounds silly to sound off over a civil war which happened almost a century ago. I suppose I am a by-product, an extension, a growth of that war in many respects. It was only forty mere years away [actually thirty] when I was born and less than thirty years away from Reconstruction [Inman was born eighteen years after the end of Reconstruction]. I am what I am in large measure, I at least realize, due to the extending ripples of that great and violent war. Wherefore, I feel the war, the aftermath, the legend, the propulsive subsequent attitudes. I wish it were not so, but it is. So if I recur in fascinated fashion to the War, treat it as me myself. I shall not avoid it. World War I was but a cynical interlude. World War II, while touching me closer, still is not so intimate as our Civil War, not so real, not so pertinent. The Spanish War and the Korean War leave me untouched, they being not personalized. (II, 1564–65)

It was not that Inman did not envision himself as existing in a tension toward the nation as a whole instead of simply, on the one hand, toward the South and, on the other, toward New England. "I have sought to understand America," he wrote in 1935, his declaration indicating an awareness of the nation that may bear a certain sense of guilt about his parochialism (I, 631). We may wonder if guilt about the narrowness of his historical and geographical sense of

America did not frustrate Inman's effort simply to dismiss Walt Whitman as a "personality . . . somehow lewd" (II, 966). Instead the great seeker of the American self haunted him. Once Inman—who took great stock in his vivid and constant dream life and seemed to believe it to be essentially a dimension of reality—dreamed that he had a desperate physical encounter with Whitman, who, armed with "an edged tree-saw," cut Inman's "arms and torso . . . to bloody ribbons" (II, 988). But while his involvement with the poet–prophet of American democracy reflects the fact that a conflict between self and nation is a significant dimension of the Diary, the heart of Inman's work lies in the self-portrayal of the vexed identity of the southerner as poet and storyteller. Bearing, it has been remarked, a distinct resemblance to portraits of the southern literary artist as in some sense a victim of the Civil War, this figure, whose shadowy forebear is Roderick Usher (shall we call Roderick a "previctim" of the Civil War?) is personized by writers of the second generation after the war in Quentin Compson in Faulkner's *The Sound and the Fury* and *Absalom, Absalom!* and in Lacy Buchan in Tate's *The Fathers*. His representation by third-generation writers includes Jack Burden in Warren's *All the King's Men* and Lancelot Lamar in Percy's *Lancelot*. Inman's massive effort in autobiographical portraiture— fictive to an indeterminable extent—emerges as a significant symbol of the southern writer's feeling of intimacy with history. To an even more indeterminable but equally significant extent Inman's Diary emerges as a symbol of the literary and cultural—let us say the spiritual—connection between New England and the South.[5] Is not the symbiosis that Aaron points to between Inman and his Diary a uniquely intense expression of the darkly necessary relationship between New England and the South?

Had Inman, like Faulkner, through self-education, or like Tate or Warren, through formal education, acquired a sophisticated acquaintance with modern history and literature, we can imagine that he might have become a unique novelist. I refer to the novelist we have never had, and now will never have: a gifted talent deeply, experientially empathetic with both the South and New

5. See Lewis P. Simpson, *Mind and the American Civil War: A Meditation on Lost Causes* (Baton Rouge, 1989), esp. 70–105.

England. Although he was not by accreditation of birth a New Englander and had never been in the South at the time of its writing, Henry James gives us a hint in *The Bostonians* of what such a novelist might have been. He gives us a more profound hint in the moving, indirectly autobiographical "nonfiction" novel of his later years, *The American Scene*. Here, notably in the chapters recording his revisitation of New England and his first journey into the South, we get a distinct impression of the possibilities of vision on the part of a novelist capable of fully imagining the mystery of the ironic relationship between two nations that, having committed themselves to the idea that in transcendent historical reality they were one republic, ironically fought a tragic war to prove the truth of the commitment.

We have had other novelists besides James who have glimpsed the possibilities of the New England–South mystery, but only in Owen Wister and Faulkner (specifically in *The Virginian: A Horseman of the Plains* and *Absalom, Absalom!*) do we find writers who have more than superficially incarnated it in fictional characters. So far as the abridged version of the Diary shows, Inman never read Wister. Nor, save for *Pylon* (which apparently he read to confirm the common opinion that its author wrote only when he was drunk), did he ever read Faulkner. So Inman never encountered the doomed young Mississippian who, several months before drowning himself in the Charles River on June 2, 1910, sat in a Harvard dormitory room pervaded by the "iron dark" of a New England winter and unfolded to a responsive Canadian friend the story that must be regarded as the supreme embodiment of the great southern novelistic theme— memory and the remembrance of memory. But the dark dormitory room at Harvard in which, at the end of the first decade of the twentieth century, the storyteller from Mississippi tells the story of the House of Sutpen to the young man from Canada provides more than the setting in which the telling occurs. The room is an intrinsic part of the story, and the act of its telling is a necessary one performed by Quentin in the execution of his destiny: to live the death of the myth of the defeated South. Faulkner's imagination of American history required that both Quentin's storytelling session and his suicide occur in New England. His destiny—foreshadowed in the lives of all the young southerners, before and after the Civil War, who had sat in

Harvard dormitories—would incarnate the symbiotic relationship of New England and the South.[6]

Had Inman known the Quentin Compson story, his vision of himself as the doomed southerner might embody an instance of life self-consciously tracking fiction. The evidence being contrary to such a conclusion, we must assume that, although Faulkner's imagination and Inman's imagination are strikingly parallel in some respects, Inman actually lived the self-created fiction of his identity and destiny. A year before he finally killed himself, reflecting on his recollection of a childhood drive with his grandfather Inman in his "big square limousine," Inman posed to himself questions that were always present in Faulkner's imagination: "Was the memory I knew thirty years ago the same memory I own now? Has it altered as if new clothes were on it? How reliable was the past memory set against the present one? What has been left out? What has been added? What governs the remembrance of memories?" (I, 43). By the time Inman framed these questions in 1962, he, or the authorial fictive self he had created to portray the self that was his inmost self, had long known that the key to his being was his governance of the memory of memory. Established in his Garrison Hall quarters—in his New England "cocoon," in his dark domain in the heart of Boston, not far from the Common, the Park Street Church (where abolitionism was first openly espoused), the Massachusetts State House, and the Saint-Gaudens monument to Colonel Shaw and his black regiment—Inman had depended heavily on his procession of talkers to tell him the stories he would, like a psychic vampire, transfuse into parts of the one story he was truly engaged in telling in his gigantic narrative: his own story.

But Inman also depended on moments when he was possessed by his virtually total recall of a childhood lived in a culture in which time was marked in two ways, *before the war* and *after the war*. A visionary distillation of his inherence in a culture of memory, the Diary entries quoted above involving Inman's relation to the Civil War have the character of a definitive self-revelation: the realization by Inman that the whole meaning of his quest for identity was entangled in his identity with the Civil War.

6. See *ibid.*

In asserting such an identity—although, as he says, still bearing the "antique dream" of the South—Inman posted himself outside either the sentimental and nostalgic legend of the South invoked by the Winnie Davis generation or the legend of the South forged by the Ransom generation, at once ironic and pious. We may suppose that when he envisioned the stigmata of the Civil War South that he bore, Inman conceived of all his physical ailments, from loose joints to hemorrhoids and migraine headaches. But he must have referred primarily to the psychic pain resulting from his narcissistic isolation; from tortuous personal relationships, familial and otherwise; and from amazingly detailed, horrendous nightmares that, even if we grant embellishment in the telling, are unequaled by Poe's stories.

Parkman, whose virtues Inman had admired and ascribed to himself, was by the definition of the Boston-Cambridge literary community the New England literary pietas incarnate, a literary saint. Inman was by self-definition the southern pietas incarnate and by self-elevation a literary saint. But although he had conferred on himself citizenship in the southern City of the Soul invented by the Winnie Davis generation, he could not pleasure himself in its transcendent precincts; nor even like some members of the Ransom generation (including Ransom himself) occasionally visit them. Although he had attempted in his search for self-identity to mark himself as a survivor of the Civil War, he had at last conceived himself to be a total casualty.

One of the last passages that Aaron has included in his edition of the Inman Diary records a "scarifying nightmare" Inman had during the final year of his life. (By this time Inman's life had been irrevocably disrupted; he had fled from the noise and light that had by this time completely invaded Garrison Hall to an apartment hotel in Brookline, which, however, proved to be no haven.) In this dream—what Inman sometimes called a "daymare" since it occurred in the middle of the day—the diarist describes the precincts of the city of his imagining in which he held involuntary but irrevocable citizenship.

Was underneath a huge city. Had with me unaccountable score of people, tremblingly old, dependently young. No way up to surface. My responsibility. Miles upon miles of reasonable-appearing yet delusive tunnels, not lighted by any specific lights, rather by bright, disconcerting effulgence. Down steps. Up steps. Through drains. In arched-over back alleys. Up, pulled by cables, flumes of crowded air. Down chutes. Never, ever arriving anywhere. On and on, weariness, disappointment, disgruntlement, an iterated theme never resolving, the very endlessness of the action stultifying to heart, spirit, esprit. Where, the mind asked, will this ever end? People left behind. Stone walls. Hard inimical surfaces. But always, always effulgence of light, stark clear. And no terminus anywhere. (I, 1597)

In such an image of his consciousness—defined by the "extended ripples" of the unredeemable consequences of "that great and violent war" (the Civil War)—Inman wrote an end to the fable of the southern writer as survivor. If the literature of the South affords a preceding example of this act, it is not to be located so precisely in the story of Quentin Compson as in that of Roderick Usher. The narrator of "The Fall of the House of Usher" describes a picture Usher has painted of "an immensely long rectangular tunnel," without openings of any kind, through which rolls a flood of ghastly white light rays. In Usher's strange painting did Poe image the chilling portent of an inescapable, catastrophic civil conflict in America? Taken as a metaphor not only of Usher's hypersensitivity to sound and light but of the central situation in "The Fall of the House of Usher"—the relation between Roderick and his twin sister, Madeline—is the painting by extension a metaphor of what would become overt in 1861, an incestuous preying of Americans on Americans, which may be said to have been most intensely and fatefully expressed in the violation of southerners by New Englanders and of New Englanders by southerners? Are Usher and Madeline the prophetic symbols of the great domestic conflict soon to come that would involve not only brother against brother but brother against sister and sister against sister? After a conflict of such unprecedented civil ferocity, such a perversion of the sacred integrity of the individual as proclaimed by the idealism of the American Revolution and the Republic it had established, could there be any redemption? Quentin has no perverse desire to possess his sister's body; his fatal attachment to Caddy is the symbol of his need—of, in a terrifying way, his duty—to redeem the honor of the Compson family, and the honor of the South, by consigning himself and Caddy to the purifying flames of hell. Loving Caddy himself—finding in her the sister he had never had but had longed for, finding in her brother a persona, and sharing in Quentin's desperate sense of honor—Faulkner conceived of the South as yet possessing the sensibility, if attenuated and grotesque, of the traditional community. His South still had the capacity to understand what Robert E. Lee meant when he said, "Duty is the sublimest word in the English language." But it could only hold this capacity in a tension with the growing insensibility of a society that at once idealized and isolated the anxious democratic, capitalistic self.

Arthur Inman never had a sister either, save the one he imagines in a diary entry in 1945.

> It is strange to be possessed of one's own thoughts and to know many of them to be so antisocial that they are wiser left unexpressed—even to one's diary. It isn't, either, that I am ashamed of my thought. It is in the case of the diary that I have no wish to incense readers needlessly. If you are a reader and I say earnestly that I should have loved to have had an attractive incestuous sister, for it seems to me that no relationship if mutually enjoyed could be closer or more desirable, you are fairly certain to be outraged. I have no inclination, be it understood, to be a libertine; I hold a disgust for those who overindulge in any fashion. I am—or would like to be—arrogant and dictatorial, untrammeled and above social pressure, subject strongly to my own individualistic moral code, a code for friends and loved ones, not for those multitudes of men and women who pass their aggregate existences beyond my immediate ken and interest. (II, 1264–65)

The symbolic import of the Quentin-Caddy relationship in Faulkner—its representation of a tension in Quentin's mind between honor and duty on the one hand and the inexorable force of historical circumstance on the other—is lacking in the relationship Inman envisions with his dream sister. This is more akin to Roderick Usher's relationship with his twin sister, whom he entombs alive, and who then returns in terrifying survival from her tomb. In the symbolic moment toward which the "The Fall of the House of Usher" moves, she appears "trembling and reeling to and from upon the threshold" before, "with a low moaning cry," falling heavily inward upon the person of her brother. In her "violent and final death agonies," she bears "him to the floor a corpse, and a victim to the terrors he had anticipated." The terrors derive from the psychological fact that the perversity of the Lady Madeline's vampirish will has been willed by the perversity of Roderick's narcissistic compulsion. In contemplating the character of "Our Cousin, Mr. Poe," Allen Tate said that Roderick and Madeline lived "in each other's insides, in the hollows of which burns the fire of will and intellect." The "great subject" of modern literature, Tate said, is the "atrophy of feeling by will and intellect," or, as this may be put in another way, the "disintegration of personality." The subject was "discovered" by the southerner Edgar Allan Poe, the effective sign of this discovery being, in Tate's interpretation, Poe's negation of the "sensibility," which "keeps us in the world," by his obsessive emphasis on "sensation," which, locking us into the self, feeds "upon the disintegration of its objects . . . absorbing them into the void of the ego."[7] Inman's "attractive incestuous sister" is his own self-image.

Lacking a sophisticated literary education that would have informed him about the context of his Diary in Poe and others, including the Symbolists, Inman discovered for himself the great modern subject. Scattered throughout his voluminous diary are many passages that mark stages in the drama of discovery. An observation Inman made in 1934, some ten or twelve years after he began his Diary, is darkly hopeful: "Now that I have grown in years I understand the possibility, nay, the probability of such a man as Pym, or Poe himself for that matter, writing against death. It was the thread through the labyrinth to be followed until it broke, or, perchance, having maintained sanity along dark stressful passages, led to safety." A later remark is darkly conclusive: "I possess a vast sense of insecurity and no sense of duty. I find life vastly exciting, yet would rather far not be living in it" (I, 81–90; II, 1556). Inman made the last

---

7. Allen Tate, "The Angelic Imagination," in *Essays of Four Decades* (Chicago, 1969), 407–408, and "Our Cousin, Mr. Poe," *ibid.,* 390–94.

remark in 1956. By then he was no longer thinking about writing against death. In some strange way, living his reclusive life in a dark room in Back Bay Boston in the company of his talkers and readers and lovers, he was at once living the death of New England and the death of the South, being a self-conscious victim of their incestuous violation of each other in a great civil conflict.

IX

From Thoreau to Walker Percy
Home by Way of California;
or, The End of the Southern Renascence

Taking his stand as a "reconstructed but unregenerate" southerner, John Crowe Ransom said in the Agrarian declaration of 1930 that in order to survive as a definitive region the South must "reënter the American political field with a determination and an address quite beyond anything she has exhibited during her half-hearted national life of the last half a century." He saw the hope for such a possibility tied in part to the "community of interest" between the South and the West. Predominantly rural, both regions, Ransom said, "desire to defend home, stability of life, the practice of leisure" against their "natural enemy," the "insidious industrial system" of the North and the East. United as natural allies, they could do much to exalt the rural life in America and make the world safe for farmers.[1]

The historical context of Ransom's assumption in *I'll Take My Stand* that the West is a natural extension of the South is Thomas Jefferson's hope that the westward expansion of the nation born of the American Revolution would result in the creation of a great pastoral republic. Distant from the evils of the Old World, especially the factories and great cities associated with a manufacturing economy, possessing enough land to ensure room for all its citizens and their descendants "to the thousandth & thousandth generation," the new nation would forever be the homeland of "those who labour in the earth." They are, Jefferson said, "the chosen people of God, if ever he had a chosen people." In their "breasts he has made his peculiar deposit for substantial and genuine virtue."

1. John Crowe Ransom, "Reconstructed But Unregenerate," in *I'll Take My Stand: The South and the Agrarian Tradition* (Baton Rouge, 1977), by Twelve Southerners, 24–25.

When he expressed these sentiments in the *Notes on the State of Virginia* (1787) and in his "First Inaugural Address" (1801), Jefferson was dreaming of a more limited Canaan than the prospect that was in view by the time he began his second term as president in 1804. By then he had negotiated one of the major real estate deals in history and added half a continent to the territory possessed by the fledgling American Republic. Interestingly enough, Jefferson did not immediately accommodate the sudden expansion of the nation across a continental vastness to his pastoral dream. The dream had been motivated by the desire to remove the new nation from its implication in European history, and insofar as the Louisiana Purchase was made to secure America against the imperial designs of European rulers like Napoleon, his action was entirely consistent with the dream. But at the same time—engineered as it had been in the Old World courts of intrigue and, moreover, at the expense of Jefferson's regard for the strict interpretation of the Constitution—the acquisition of the Louisiana Territory had compromised the policy, announced by George Washington and subscribed to by Jefferson, against entangling the new nation in the nightmare of European history. Five years before Jefferson died, another consequence of the Louisiana Purchase began to emerge when, in the crucial struggle over whether Missouri should be admitted to the new nation as a free or slave state, it became obvious that the deal with Napoleon represented the entanglement of the new nation in a historical nightmare of its own making as well as in the European nightmare.

The crisis of 1820 over the admission of Missouri to statehood was owing, however, not only to an irrepressible issue in the American politics of morality but to a novel and irreversible historical force, the application of technology to nature. Represented by the steamboat and the railroad, and soon by repeating firearms, this new force made nonsense of Jefferson's projection in 1801 that it would take two thousand generations (or something like 60,000 years) simply for the full expansion onto the land between the Alleghenies and the Mississippi. Indeed, if he had come back to life at the beginning of the twentieth century, Jefferson would have learned that all the usable free land from the Alleghenies to the Pacific Ocean had been preempted. This would hardly have been good news to him. He would no doubt have been disheartened to learn that a good part of the land space had been converted into holdings far larger than a respectable freehold. He would have been still more disheartened to find that, while Americans still subscribed to the poetry of his dream of the West as an escape from history, they had made the hero of the western settlement not the yeoman farmer but a landless frontier wanderer called the cowboy, who utterly disdained farming.

Of Mexican origin and associated with the sixteenth-century Spanish imperial conquest, the cowboy, after his heyday in the brief moment of the Cattle Kingdom, was removed altogether from the realm of historical reality and, as Leatherstocking had been made the mythic hero of the great woodland frontier east of the Mississippi, was made the mythic hero of the western plains. His James Fenimore Cooper was Owen Wister, who in 1902 wrote the central story in the American mythology of the cowboy, *The Virginian: A Horseman of the Plains.*

Wister, a Pennsylvanian with a strong southern connection, tells the story of a veteran of the Army of the Confederacy who leaves his native state when the war ends and goes to the Wyoming cattle country, where he is known only as "the Virginian." Even though he was imbued with the Rousseauistic sensibility, Jefferson would not easily have comprehended the association of natural virtue with a Virginian who does nothing but ride across a sublime landscape, who never touches a plow handle but only lariat, branding iron, and six-shooter; who spends his time chasing unfenced cattle, lynching cattle thieves, and killing unfriendly Indians, save for the necessary moments when he must duel with peers who cheat at poker or speak dishonorably of respectable women (although his own taste is for saloon girls who require no defending). Jefferson, of course, would have understood the part about defending feminine honor. But yoking violence and nature in the production of virtue would have puzzled one reared in a culture in which the tendency—revealed in a succession of gentleman storytellers from William Byrd II to George Washington Harris—was to associate violence in the natural landscape with low-life people who lack any capacity for virtue.

Jefferson's redoubtable New England co-conspirator in the American Revolution, John Adams, might have understood Owen Wister's concept of the Virginian better than Jefferson, for he perhaps would have sensed in the cowboy as Wister represents him a reincarnation of the fatal motive of the New England character: the zealous and relentless desire to purify history in the name of the autonomy of the individual soul. And in recognizing this motive in the Virginian, Adams, if we may envisage him as a ghostly revisitant, would surely have connected the cowboy not so much with Increase and Cotton Mather as with their heretical yet direct inheritors, the transcendental Emerson and his disciple Thoreau. Indeed, our ghostly Adams, aware of the chapter entitled "Higher Laws" in *Walden,* might well have seen the connection to be more precisely with the disciple.

In "Higher Laws," Thoreau records that shockingly vivid moment on the twilight path from Walden Pond when, glimpsing a woodchuck, he experienced "a strange thrill of savage delight, and . . . was strongly tempted to seize and devour him raw." It was not, Thoreau says, "that I was hungry then, except for that wildness which he represented." He further records that "once or twice" while living at the pond he found himself "ranging the woods, like a half-starved hound, with a strange abandonment, seeking some kind of venison which I might devour, and no morsel could have been too savage for me." We readily suppose, as Thoreau did, that his bloodlust is metaphorical rather than actual. But it is a metaphor for a dark aspect of the transcendental motive, being evidence that entrance into "a higher, or as it is named, spiritual life" is only through the recognition of the instinctive, the "primitive rank and savage," life in us. One enters into the higher life through a life lived in intimacy with nature akin to that known by hunter and trapper. At an earlier stage of his life, Thoreau says, he carried a gun; now he carries a fishing pole, but he still knows the necessary experience of killing. The "original part" of ourselves, the hunter and fisher, is necessary to the later and higher part. "When some of my friends have asked me anxiously about their boys, whether they should let them hunt," Thoreau remarks, "I have answered, yes—remembering that it was one of the best parts of my education,—*make* them hunters, though sportsmen only at first, if possible, mighty hunters at last, so that they shall not find game large enough for them in this or any vegetable wilderness,—hunters as well as fishers of men."[2]

2. Henry David Thoreau, *Walden,* in *The Writings of Henry David Thoreau,* ed. J. Lyndon Shanley (Princeton, N.J., 1971), 210–11.

The Thoreauvian advice to parents is chilling in its implied expression of a dark awareness of the human cost of seeking the realm of transcendence. Cryptically amending the charge by Jesus to the Galilean fishermen that they be fishers of men to include the idea that they be hunters of men as well, Thoreau suggests that the transcendental aesthetic and ethic is a sublimation of the killer instinct. Had D. H. Lawrence included Emerson and Thoreau in his vision of American types in *Studies in Classic American Literature,* he might well have perceived in the austere thrust of the Emersonian-Thoreauvian imperative to assert the self's dominion and power a remarkable intensification of what he finds in Cooper's Leatherstocking: the "essential American soul . . . hard, isolate, stoic, and a killer." He might have discovered in Walden Woods the mightiest of American hunters, the self pursuing all that is "not self."

> If the red slayer think he slays
> Or if the slain think he is slain,
> They know not well the subtle ways
> I keep, and pass, and turn again.[3]

Of these familiar Emersonian lines, Perry Miller grimly observes, "Those who shoot and those who are shot prove to be identical . . . in the realm of the transcendental there is nothing to choose between eating and being eaten."[4] On the path to the realm of the Over Soul, in other words, a decision has been made: this to murder the self that is the creature of history and society. Even though the path to the Over Soul traversed the woods adjacent to Concord village, a place that is in the best Emersonian sense a natural fact corresponding to a spiritual fact, Thoreau recognized, even as he celebrated Walden, that it was a confinement. "Our sympathies in Massachusetts are not confined to New England," Thoreau says in "Walking" (written in 1852 but not published until 1862); "we may be estranged from the South, we sympathize with the West." Following a "subtle magnetism in Nature," he always found himself

---

3. D. H. Lawrence, in *The Shock of Recognition,* ed. Edmund Wilson (New York, 1943), 965; Ralph Waldo Emerson, "Brahma," quoted in Perry Miller, *Errand into the Wilderness* (New York, 1964), 186.

4. Miller, *Errand into the Wilderness,* 186.

heading "between west and south-west." The "future," he said, "lies that way. I must walk toward Oregon, not toward Europe."

But Oregon was not enough for Thoreau. He dreamed of getting utterly away from any semblance of the self of history, of taking a pure and undefiled path to the westward—of discovering "absolute freedom and wildness, as contrasted with freedom and culture merely civil"; of becoming "an inhabitant, or a part and parcel of Nature." Getting to the farthest continental point would be only the culmination of crossing the Lethe of the Atlantic. Beyond lay the "lethe of the Pacific." In *Walden* (1854) the westward journey reaches its ultimate formulation in Thoreau, becoming the symbol of a journey out of history into the absolute freedom of the transcendent inner territory of self: "Explore thyself. Herein are demanded the eye and the nerve. Only the defeated and the deserters go to the wars, cowards that run away and enlist. Start now on the farthest western way, which does not pause at the Mississippi or the Pacific, nor conduct toward a worn-out China or Japan, but leads on direct a tangent to this sphere, summer and winter, day, and night, sun down, moon down, and at last east down too."[5] In *Walden* the westward passage becomes a metaphor of a triumphant transfiguration of the New England culture.

To multiply examples of the image of New England with reference to the image of the West is beyond my present scope. Let me refer only to the most prominent among several pertinent sources of documentation, the work I alluded to earlier, Wister's *The Virginian*. The specific symbol of transfiguration in this story is the description of the idyllic month the ideal cowboy, the Virginian, spends in the high country with his ideal bride, Molly Woods, the New England schoolmarm, who has presumably been conquered at last by the code of the West as it is embodied in a former Confederate soldier who has transformed himself into a cowboy.

They made their camps in many places, delaying several days here, and one night there, exploring the high solitudes together, and sinking deep in their romance. Sometimes when

---

5. *The Writings of Henry David Thoreau* (Boston, 1893), 266–67; Thoreau, *Walden,* in *The Writings of Henry David Thoreau,* ed. Shanley, 322.

he was at work with their horses, or intent on casting his brown hackle for a fish, she would watch him with eyes that were fuller of love than of understanding. Perhaps she never came wholly to understand him; but in her complete love for him she found enough. He loved her with his whole man's power. She had listened to him tell her in words of transport, "I could enjoy dying"; yet she loved him more than that. He had come to her from a smoking pistol, able to bid her farewell—and she would not let him go. At the last white-hot edge of ordeal, it was she who renounced, and he who had his way.[6]

Yet we may doubt if the white-hot moment of truth is to be identified as the moment when Molly yields to the embrace of the Virginian after his deadly encounter with Trampas. This moment, and Molly knows it, had occurred earlier, when she discovered the Virginian out on the range, lying unconscious by a spring, critically wounded, the victim of an Indian ambush. When the Virginian had regained consciousness and urged her to leave him and flee, she had "glanced at him with a sort of fierceness, then reached for his pistol, in which was nothing but blackened empty cartridges," and throwing these away had drawn six fresh cartridges "from his belt, loaded the weapon, and snapped shut its hinge."[7] One need not explicate the sexual symbolism in this scene. In the moment she takes possession of the pistol and resolves to use it, the New England girl becomes the bride of her cowboy lover; after the Virginian kills Trampas, her physical surrender to him simply confirms the mystical surrender she has already made to the Higher Law of the West (or the law of nature). In the act of surrendering to this law, the young New England schoolmarm, in a delightfully ironic sense, has fulfilled Thoreau's transcendental quest westward, as incarnated in a southerner whose name, the Virginian (he is given no other name in the novel), has become synonymous with the image of the western hero. In effect Molly's action has assimilated the Higher Law of the West to the Higher Law of the New England transcendentalists. The

6. Owen Wister, *The Virginian* (New York, 1951), 431.
7. *Ibid.*, 288.

wedding journey of Molly and the Virginian—who are bonded to each other through their deeper bond to the West, to nature—confirms the entrance of the bride and groom into an intrinsic union that exists beyond history. In the last pages of *The Virginian,* published some thirty-five years after the bloodiest civil war in history, the South, New England, and the West are brought into indissoluble unity: the nation that had been divided against itself is made whole. The wedding journey through the pure mountain air—its pristine quality enhanced, sanctified, by the aromatic incense of gunsmoke—confirms the American nation, the Second American Republic, as a perfect union of the slayer and the slain.

Perhaps the rise of the vogue of multiculturalism in the later years of the twentieth century will render the Wisterian metaphor obsolete. But testimony to the effectiveness of the metaphor of the nation as restored and solidified through the transfiguring assimilation of New England (or more broadly, the North) and the South to the image of the West continues to be writ large in the ongoing history of American popular culture. Its power is also attested to by the response the metaphor has evoked in writers less well known but of a more serious and sophisticated turn than Wister. We think in particular of Robinson Jeffers, a highly self-conscious voice from the farthermost point of the western coast. Jeffers' primary significance is that his poems react bitterly and with cogent irony to the obvious failure of the nation (and Jeffers would have regarded Wister's novel as illustrative of this failure) to achieve its incarnation in an image of the western self. Standing against the involvement of America in Europe, yet feeling that America was being overwhelmed by history, Jeffers offered a final, desperate poetic resistance to history. In his murky yet compelling advocacy of what he called "inhumanism" (which envisions the transformation of man into something "notman"), Jeffers sought to murder both the historical self and the transcendental self, leaving only nature purified of man, whose consciousness is at once the source of history and the source of the desire to transcend it. Seeming to mark the end of the Thoreauvian dream of the westward movement as a transcendence of history, poems like "Tamar" and "The Women at Point Sur"—which dramatize the agony of Jeffers' effort to transcend history through nature cleansed of man—suggest a striking inverse vision of the underlying motive of the transcendental ethos, a vision of the self willing the self to become a nonself. But is not this struggle to imagine nonbeing a paradoxical strategy of the modern self to survive history? In the end Jeffers comes to an acceptance—reluctant, desperate—of Americans as creatures of history, destined to bear its burden and to survive it. Seeing the "corrupting burden and curse of victory" that would be placed on America at the end of World War II, Jeffers in 1943 wrote in "Historical Choice":

> Here is a burden
> We are not fit for. We are not like Romans and
>   Britons—natural world rulers,
> Bullies by instinct—but we have to bear it. Who has
>   kissed fate on the mouth,
> And blown out the lamp—must lie with her.[8]

It is notable that in one way or another in all his work, Jeffers, like Wister a Pennsylvanian, though with no southern connection, displays a feeling commensurate with a distinguishing mark of the literary sensibility of, as Harold Bloom might say, the "stronger," poets and novelists of the American South: their imaginative involvement in the drama of the modern endeavor to cope with man as a self-conscious historical being, a self doomed to live altogether in the nontranscendent mode of existence termed secular history. This imagination of the condition of the southern writer was early anticipated in the way in which the southern colonies became attuned to the radical secularity of the thought of the European seventeenth and eighteenth centuries, as opposed to the attunement of the New England theocrats to their essential continuity with the older European sense of religiosity.

Elsewhere in these pages I have remarked on how the tendency toward secularity in the South would seem to account for the optimistic and decisive world-historical vision of man advanced by Thomas Jefferson.[9] But the southern secularity also accounts for the pes-

---

8. Robinson Jeffers, "Historical Choice," in *The Collected Poetry of Robinson Jeffers,* ed. Tim Hunt (4 vols.; Stanford, Ca., 1988), IV, 122.

9. See Lewis P. Simpson, "The Act of Thought in Virginia," *Early American Literature,* XIV (Winter, 1979–80), 253–68.

simistic vision of the arrival of democratic man on the stage of world history, as this is set forth not only by an anti-democratic member of Jefferson's own class like John Randolph of Roanoke but by a succession of popular southern writers known as humorists. I refer to writers such as Augustus Baldwin Longstreet, Johnson Jones Hooper, and George Washington Harris, in whose tales of the frontier South— of the southern West, the Old Southwest (Georgia, Alabama, Mississippi, Louisiana, Tennessee, and Arkansas)—the virtuous Jeffersonian yeoman is replaced by Ransy Snaffles, Simon Suggs, and Sut Lovingood.

Such inversions of the yeoman ideal—all of them offered by their authors as exemplifications of the historical degradation of civic virtue under democratic circumstances—are followed by Huckleberry Finn. Although Huck has often been regarded as representing the transcendence of democratic virtue, it takes a determined Rousseauistic idealist to see him in this light. "Lighting out for the Territory," defeated by history, the Huck of the *Adventures* anticipates his later appearance as Niklaus in *The Mysterious Stranger*. In this fragmentary work of his later years, Mark Twain transforms the nineteenth-century frontier South (Missouri and Arkansas) into the Austria of the Middle Ages. Here Niklaus and Theodore (Tom Sawyer) encounter a transhuman agency in the mysterious stranger, a nephew of Satan, who reveals not only that the consciousness of history is a grotesque and foolish dream but that the very consciousness of being is an illusion. Yet the most interesting aspect of *The Mysterious Stranger* is not Mark Twain's unconvincing attempt to negate the human consciousness but his translation of the historical setting of the Missouri-Arkansas extension of the South into the depths of medieval Europe. In his tortured effort to write *The Mysterious Stranger,* Mark Twain was involved in the same endeavor James Joyce was shortly to be engaged in as he imagined the Stephen Dedalus of *Ulysses* struggling "to awake from the nightmare of history." For all his association with the American West, we may conclude, Mark Twain remained an untransfigured southerner, who in relocating Huck and Tom in medieval Austria presented a symbol of a profound truth of American history, a truth he feared and resisted yet must recognize: the unwilling but deep American complicity in the long nightmare of European history.

Expressing a fundamental tension in the American historical situation—markedly visible at the present moment of ardent denunciations of "Eurocentrism"—Mark Twain suggests a way of looking at American literary history: whereas a self-conscious motive of New England transcendentalists was the desire to fulfill the literary destiny of their region through the assimilation of the West and the South to their vision of the nation as New England writ large, a motive—less self-conscious, perhaps involuntary—of twentieth-century southern writers has been the desire to assimilate the West to its historical vision of America as an inescapable, indeed an integral, part of the historic European culture—and thus an integral part of the evils of history.

Among the twentieth-century southern novels that may be taken as specific symbols of the southern vision of history are Faulkner's novel-play, *Requiem for a Nun,* Robert Penn Warren's *All the King's Men,* and Walker Percy's *Lancelot.* Faulkner's novel-play may be read as both one of the most provocative histories of the South and one of the most appropriate symbols of the southern literary imagination. A sequel to *Sanctuary,* this work takes up the further adventures of Temple Drake at the point of a singularly horrible murder. Motivated by the hope of saving Temple's soul, Nancy Mannigoe, Temple's black maid, has killed Temple's baby. Exploring this odd and shocking situation, Faulkner entangles us in the history not only of Jefferson and Yoknapatawpha County, the state of Mississippi, and the American Republic but of Western culture, even to the remote ranges of its prehistory. In the prologue to the last act of *Requiem for a Nun,* Faulkner subtly juxtaposes the crucial decision Temple makes to return from California—where, like so many Americans, she has fled to escape her history—with the story of the daughter of the jailor in Jefferson at the time of the Civil War.

A girl of "invincible inviolable ineptitude," Cecilia Farmer has used her grandmother's wedding ring to scratch her name on a windowpane in the family living quarters of the jail: *Cecilia Farmer April 16, 1861.* During Sherman's invasion of Mississippi, a lieutenant in a Confederate cavalry unit fighting a desperate rearguard action in the streets of Jefferson rushes past the jail and sees "the frail and useless girl musing in the blonde mist of her hair beside a windowpane." The eyes of the girl and the "gaunt and tattered, battle-grimed and fleeing and undefeated" soldier meet for an instant "across the fury and pell mell of battle." Then the soldier is gone. But after Appomattox he comes back all the way from Virginia. Astride a mule instead of a battle steed, and carrying a sack of corn acquired in Pennsylvania, he finds the girl still musing at the windowpane on which she has inscribed her "significantless name." He marries her at once, puts her on the mule behind him, and the "gaunt and undefeated paroled cavalry subaltern" and the "fragile and workless girl" ride off. But not to some "simple frontier"—to "Texas, the West, New Mexico: a new land," where they would be "engaged only with wilderness and shoeless savages and the tender hand of God." To begin their life together they hurry toward the soldier's farm in Alabama, a place that "had been rendered into a desert (assuming that it was still there at all to be returned to) by the iron and fire of civilization."[10]

The narrator of the prologue to the third act of *Requiem for a Nun,* an "outland" visitor to the old jail in Jefferson, gets the romantic notion that Cecilia Farmer is an avatar of Lilith—the demonic first wife of Adam, destroyer of men and murderer of children. How this idea bears on the story of Nancy and Temple is by no means explicit, but its most powerful effect is to suggest that the vision of the American West as the future is an illusion. History is never transcended. "The past is never dead," the philosophical lawyer and moral historian of Yoknapatawpha, Gavin Stevens, says to Temple, "It's not even past."[11] Gavin tries to lead Temple to a moral recovery of her past: to (to employ a favorite word play by Faulkner) transform Was into Is, or to make the Is that exists in Was luminous with meaning. He is at least partially successful. At the end of her story Temple has become a self-conscious survivor of history, aware of the intricate complicity of the self in Is and Was.

Four or five years before Faulkner published *Requiem for a Nun,* he was the publisher's reader for a manuscript by Robert Penn Warren entitled "All the King's Men." Although he did not like the novel very much, we may wonder if Faulkner was possibly influenced by one incident in it, Jack Burden's flight to California. At any rate, this incident in the career of the student of history who tells the story of

10. William Faulkner, *Requiem for a Nun* (New York, 1951), 232, 257–59.
11. *Ibid.,* 92.

All the King's Men—whose story, as a matter of fact, it essentially is—may be compared to *Requiem for a Nun* in at least one significant respect. Unlike Temple, Jack does discover God in California, the Great God Twitch being revealed to him after he has made a journey to the West Coast that in his imagination ironically replicates the American conquest of the continent.

> For that is where you come, after you have crossed oceans and eaten stale biscuits while prisoned forty days and nights in a storm-tossed rat-trap, after you have sweated in the greenery and heard the savage whoop, after you have built cabins and cities and bridged rivers, after you have lain with women and scattered children like millet seed in a high wind, after you have composed resonant documents, made noble speeches, and bathed your arms in blood to the elbows, after you have shaken with malaria in the marshes and in the icy wind across the high plains. That is where you come, to lie alone on a bed in a hotel room in Long Beach, California. Where I lay, while outside my window a neon sign flickered on and off to the time of my heart, systole and diastole, flushing and flushing again the gray sea mist with a tint like blood.[12]

Having "drowned in the West," his body "having drifted down to lie there in the comforting, subliminal ooze on the sea floor of History," Jack dreams the "dream of our age": that "all life is but the dark heave of blood and the twitch of the nerve." In the West, the psychic homeland not only of America but of the modern age, it is revealed to Jack that his life is entirely innocent of crime and sin. In Twitch's dominion, moral categories do not exist. Relieved of all sense of collusion in history, Jack returns to the southern state (nameless in the novel) from which he has fled after discovering that the girl he loves, Anne Stanton, has become the mistress of Willie Stark, the populist governor who has become a dictator. But after the assassination of Willie, Jack (who has been his hatchet man) comes to see that Twitch is an illusion. He interprets his flight from history as

---

12. Robert Penn Warren, *All the King's Men* (New York, 1955), 309–11.

an attempt to escape from the truth that we live "in the agony of will." This truth—the truth that "history is blind, but man is not"—gives the "past back" to Jack. Like the speaker in Warren's poem "Rattlesnake Country," having followed his compulsion "to try to convert what now is *was* / Back into what *is,*" Jack recognizes, in his well-known last words in *All the King's Men,* that he is a moral participant in history. He will "go out of history into history and the awful responsibility of Time."[13]

Yet in his very affirmation of the individual's capacity to influence history—to make history—Jack Burden implies the terror of history. Out of history into history: Is the survivor of history, we may ask, never to be unburdened of history? How much self-conscious complicity in history can the self stand? So far as Warren's imagination responds to the question in subsequent novels—and each represents a strenuous effort to respond—the answer is simply, not too much. Warren's formulation of the response to self and history tends toward the attitude expressed by the soldier in the Vietnam poem:

> History is what you can't
> resign from, but
> There is always refuge in the practice
> Of private virtue,
> Or at least in heroism.[14]

Warren's clear implication, it has frequently been said, is that Jack has assumed a constructive responsibility for what he will do in the future. Speaking of Jack, Warren himself seemed to confirm this interpretation. But one may question whether it is entirely convincing. Warren's story of Jack Burden carries another implication. Has not Jack imposed a monstrous burden on himself? Will the pressure of his acceptance of his moral responsibility for history force him to take refuge again in the automatism of the Great God Twitch? Or worse, will Jack discover that self-will is a god far more compelling than Twitch? That history is blind but man is not is a dangerous

13. Robert Penn Warren, "Rattlesnake Country," in *Selected Poems, 1923–1975* (New York, 1976), 50; Warren, *All the King's Men,* 311, 438.

14. Robert Penn Warren, "Shoes in the Rain Jungle," in *Selected Poems,* 159.

revelation, prompting as it does the tempting idea that the self may transcend all gods save the self and, having become God, may manipulate history according to its own dreams and desires.

That he did not imagine another character who takes such an affirmative view toward history indicates that Warren became wary of Jack's resolution to be responsible for history. Willie Proudfit, the rustic Kentuckian in Warren's first novel, *Night Rider,* goes west to become a buffalo hunter. Experiencing a kind of apocalyptic moment of self-identity when he returns to his home valley and drinks from the spring near New Bethany Church, he is in a sense a precursor of Jack Burden. Jeremiah Beaumont in *World Enough and Time,* Brad Tolliver in *Flood,* and Jed Tewksbury in *A Place to Come To* are distinct successors to Jack. But although his novels continue to focus on the relationship of self and history, after *All the King's Men* the protagonists in Warren's fiction express an irresolute knowledge of the self's condition in history. Yet if Warren did not again imagine a character who takes such a potentially apocalyptic view toward his own involvement in history as Jack does, all of his writings—novels, poems, and essays—bear a relation to *All the King's Men* as a fable about the moral meaning of the history of the American Republic.

Of the writers associated with the Agrarian movement, Walker Percy felt closer to Allen Tate than to Warren, but he did not seek to cultivate an affinity with either. As a matter of fact, Percy asserted his distinction from all the writers associated with the flowering of southern letters in the 1920s and 1930s. Their concern with the agrarian life versus the industrial, with family history, the Civil War, etc., was, he said, not his. It "interests me as a backdrop to something more important," he said. "What happens when you find yourself in the second half of the twentieth century with all this history behind you? And then you have to figure out how to live in the here and now." But in entertaining the question of how to live in the existential moment, Percy's profoundly satirical imagination, as he himself well knew, embraced the southern "backdrop," which was not to be separated from his troubled experience of life as a member of the southern patriciate.

Both Percy's fiction and his nonfiction may be viewed as constituting a loosely autobiographical narrative about what happened to a young physician (M.D., Columbia College of Physicians and Surgeons, 1941) during the course of his life (1916–1990). A member of a distinguished Mississippi family, Percy had his childhood shattered by the suicide of his father and the early death of his mother. The most important person in his life became his second cousin, William Alexander Percy of Greenville, Mississippi ("Uncle Will"), who adopted Walker and his two brothers upon the death of their mother. Poet and man of letters—who is remembered for his autobiography, *Lanterns on the Levee*—William Alexander Percy made his home into something of a literary salon.

Having chosen a medical career not because he was keen on being a doctor but because familial obligation seemed to dictate that he have a career in a proper patrician profession—planting, law, or medicine—Walker Percy made another career choice after tuberculosis, contracted during an internship in pathology at Bellevue, suddenly arrested the progress of his career in medicine. Having, as one did in those days if one became tubercular and had enough money, gone into forced exile in "an old-fashioned sanitorium" at Saranac Lake in upper New York State (a sanitorium, he said, "like the one in Thomas Mann's *The Magic Mountain*"), the young doctor, already disposed to an interest in psychology, philosophy, and theology, began deeply to question his commitment to the scientific exploration of the "physiological and pathological processes within man's body." A far more significant problem presented itself: "the problem of man himself . . . specifically . . . the predicament of man in a modern technological society." Abandoning his medical career, and at about the same time becoming a convert to Roman Catholicism, Percy gambled that he could give up the comfort of the structured personal and social identity offered by the medical profession and discover for himself a different way of being in the world, this to be defined by the relationship between what he was yet to write and a responsive audience he was yet to have. Seeking to locate the point "where philosophy and art come together," Percy sought the model of himself as a philosopher-artist in the "so-called European existentialist novelists," Sartre and Camus in particular, while at the same time "keeping hold of hard-headed Anglo-American empiricism." The intensity of his complex effort to fashion a coherent image of his vocation reveals itself clearly at one of its most critical points in the bizarre, oblique portrait of the alienated philosopher-artist as he is mirrored in the violent, murderous, latter-day southern Calvinist of Percy's fourth novel, *Lancelot* (1977).

What is the consequence of the gnostic moment when one goes out of history into history and assumes responsibility for time? In the mad master of Belle Isle, a showplace antebellum plantation house on River Road near New Orleans, we witness a return of Warren's scion of the Louisiana patriciate and survivor of history, Jack Burden. But Lancelot, we note, is far worse off than Jack. He is a southerner who, in spirit if not in body, has made his pilgrimage to California—precisely to the California of the "nowhere people" of the world of Raymond Chandler's hard-boiled detective Philip Marlowe—and has taken up his spiritual residence in the "crummy lonesome Los Angeles of 1933." Merely his body, Lancelot believes (or wants to believe), resides at Belle Isle.

> The reason I was happy was that I was reading for perhaps the fourth or fifth time a Raymond Chandler novel. It gave me pleasure (no, I'll put it more strongly: it didn't give me pleasure, it was the only way I could stand my life) to sit there in goldgreen Louisiana under the levee and read, not about General Beauregard, but about Philip Marlowe taking a bottle out of his desk drawer in his crummy office in seedy Los Angeles in 1933 and drinking alone and all those nowhere people living in stucco bungalows perched in Laurel Canyon. The only way I could stand my life in Louisiana, where I had everything, was to read about crummy Los Angeles in the 1930s. Maybe that should have told me something. If I was happy, it was an odd sort of happiness.
> But it was odder, even than that. Things were split. I was physically in Louisiana but spiritually in Los Angeles.[15]

After he has blown up Belle Isle, together with his faithless wife and her lover, and been committed to a New Orleans asylum for a time, Lancelot is ready to return from Los Angeles and make a shattering response to the question he has propounded during his incarceration: "What do survivors do?"[16] He will, he announces, become

---

15. Walker Percy, *Lancelot* (New York, 1977), 24–25.
16. *Ibid.*, 37.

the redeemer of America, inaugurating his redemptive mission not in California but in the true ideological and spiritual homeland of America, where both the First American Revolution, the revolt against the British Empire, and the Second American Revolution, the South's rebellion against the Union, had their effective beginnings. As the seat of a third revolution, Virginia will oppose and destroy the Sodom and Gomorrah that America has become.

In a confused statement Lancelot speaks of Virginia, "where it started," as a transcendent entity, somehow "neither North nor South but both and neither," yet in the same breath speaks of Jefferson as the archetypal southerner.

> Betwixt and between. An island between two disasters. Facing both: both the defunct befouled and collapsing North and the corrupt thriving and Jesus-hollering South. The Northerner is at heart a pornographer. He is an abstract mind with a genital attached. His soul is at Harvard, a large abstract locked-in sterile university whose motto is truth but which has not discovered an important truth in a hundred years. His body lives on Forty-Second Street. One is the backside of the other. The Southerner? The Southerner started out a skeptical Jeffersonian and became a crooked Christian. That is to say, he is approaching and has almost reached his essence, which is to be more crooked and Christian than ever before. Do you want a portrait of the New Southerner? He is Billy Graham on Sunday and Richard Nixon the rest of the week. He calls on Jesus and steals, he's in business, he's in politics. Everybody in Louisiana steals from everybody else. That is why the Mafia moved South: because the Mafia is happier with stealing than with pornography. The Mafia and the Teamsters will end up owning the South, the pornographers will own the North, movies, books, plays, the works, and everybody will live happily ever after.
>
> California? The West? That's where the two intersect: Billy Graham, Richard Nixon, Las Vegas, drugs, pornography, and every abstract, discarnate idea ever hit upon by man roaming the wilderness in search of habitation.[17]

17. *Ibid.*, 219–20.

Although I assume this is not intended by Percy, Lancelot's version of what has happened to the West of the New England imperative, the West of the transcendental cowhand and his six-shooter, is strangely connected with the possibility that while Lancelot may be said to suggest the return of Jack Burden, in a shadowy and disquieting way he intimates the return of Wister's Virginian. Having come back to his true spiritual homeland from a false spiritual homeland, Percy's Louisianian, in his transformation into a Virginian, reveals himself as he really is: a gone-to-seed version of the southerner as, to use Allen Tate's identification, "the last European." Removed from his origin in (according to Wister) the Virginia yeomanry, the Virginian incarnated in Lancelot Lamar ironically bears a relation to Lancelot du lac, knight of the Round Table. But a fuller dimension of the ironic significance of Lancelot emerges when we seek his association with the image of the southern aristocrat as Greco-Roman Stoic than as Arthurian knight. Percy first portrayed the southerner as Stoic in Binx Bolling's remarkable Aunt Emily in *The Moviegoer;* then, still more poignantly, in Will Barrett's father in *The Last Gentleman*. In the novelistic delineation both of Aunt Emily and of Will's father he re-creates his cousin William Alexander Percy. "Uncle Will" was well enough known as a poet in the 1920s to be selected as the first editor of the Yale Series of Younger Poets. But since he seemed to represent to the Fugitive poets what they said they were bent on "fleeing from," the Brahmin style of southern poetry, he was never an intimate of the Nashville circle. Yet if the Fugitives were generally unreceptive to him, William Alexander Percy embodied to a marked degree, it may be argued, the very essence of the spirit of one of the mandates Allen Tate proclaimed in 1929 in his "tactical program" for the Agrarian movement. We must base this, Tate declared, "less upon the actual old South than upon its prototype, the traditional European social and religious" society. "We must be the last Europeans—there being no Europeans in Europe at present."[18]

18. Allen Tate to Donald Davidson, August 10, 1929, in *The Literary Correspondence of Donald Davidson and Allen Tate*, ed. John Tyree Fain and Thomas Daniel Young (Athens, Ga., 1974), 230. See Robert Buffington's accounts of the life and thought of the young Tate in "Young Hawk Circling," *Sewanee Review* LXXXVII (Fall, 1979), 541–56. Also see Philip Castille, "East Toward Home: Will Percy's Old World Vision," in Philip Castille and William Osborne, *Southern Literature in Transition: Heritage and Promise* (Memphis, 1984), 101–109.

The Fable of the Southern Writer

The first European to experience the solitude of the individual in history, the Greco-Roman Stoic has returned in modern times in many philosophical and literary guises. In Walker Percy's treatment of him, he is the southern last gentleman. The first of the last southern gentlemen had been John Randolph of Roanoke, although the prototype is discernible even in the later Jefferson. Descending in various guises, the last gentleman was distinctively reincarnated in William Alexander Percy in his eminently self-conscious opposition of the moral authority of honor to the corruption of a disintegrating society. In parodic guise the last gentleman appears in Lancelot's appeal to the wisdom of those who compose an elite society of like minds. Thus Lancelot speaks to Percival (the boyhood friend and priest to whom he addresses the monologue that is the structure of Percy's novel) about the "new order of things" he and those like him will create:

> We? Who are we? We will not even be a secret society as you know such things. Its members will know each other without signs or passwords. No speeches, rallies, political parties. There will be no need of such things. One man will act. Another will act. We will know each other as gentlemen used to know each other—no, not gentlemen in the old sense—I'm not talking about social classes. I'm talking about something held in common by men, Gentile, Jew, Greek, Roman, slave, freeman, black, white, and so recognized between them: a stern code, a gentleness toward women and an intolerance of swinishness, a counsel kept, and above all a readiness to act, and act alone if necessary—there's the essential ingredient—because as of this moment not one in 200 million Americans is ready to act from perfect sobriety and freedom. If one man is free to act alone, you don't need a society. How will we know each other? The same way General Lee and General Forrest would know each other at a convention of used car salesmen on Bourbon Street: Lee a gentleman in the old sense. Forrest not, but in this generation of vipers they would recognize each other instantly.[19]

19. Percy, *Lancelot*, 156–57.

But, although he dreams of the campaigns of the noble Stoic emperor Marcus Aurelius Antoninus, Lancelot is a vividly degraded Stoic who mocks the Stoic sensibility of order. Essentially he knows only the godhead of Twitch. Having undergone no spiritual metamorphosis like Jack Burden, he has in his imagination of himself left his spiritual home in the West and returned eastward bearing the .44 of the Los Angeles private dick instead of the six-shooter of the cowboy. He is a disincarnate will wandering the Sun Belt, which, embracing a new political and economic concept of the South and West, stretches from the Carolinas to California: the newest of the New Souths, the newest of the New Wests, the newest of the New Americas, the newest of the New Worlds, destined, according to demographic forecast, to become the new population center of the nation.

Having survived his act of blowing up one small part of Sodom and Gomorrah, having discovered through this act that there is "nothing at the heart of evil . . . no secret . . . no flickering of interest . . . nothing at all, not even evil," Lancelot, the Virginian as Louisiana hedonist, is truly "hard, isolate, stoic, and a killer." So incidentally, or not so incidentally, is Anna, the victim of a gang rape whom Lancelot has met in the madhouse. Once she has killed enough men to prove to herself that she has not been victimized, Lancelot says, she will join him in the Shenandoah Valley and help him make a new world.[20]

The law, Wister's Virginian says, is the one honest man in five hundred miles. Affirming what Jack Burden rejects—that the "dark heave of blood and twitch of nerve" is truth; stripping the motive of the Emersonian honest man of all moral idealism; revealing that the real motive of life is "violence and rape," Lancelot stands as a purely honest man, honest enough to be the only law in three thousand miles.

A student of the Agrarian movement cannot fail to note that, whether or not Percy knew at first hand Allen Tate's *I'll Take My Stand* essay called "Remarks on the Southern Religion," it is clearly a part of the southern backdrop in *Lancelot*. But it is more than backdrop. Lancelot's vision of a violent reaffirmation of the southern code—the southern religion of honor—is, in fact, a highly ironic

20. *Ibid.*, 252–53.

reflection of the mandate Tate asserted in his essay. Concerned with the question of how the twentieth-century southerner can "take hold of his tradition," Tate bears "witness" in his essay to "a fact of great significance" in the "cultural sense": whereas New England was "one of those abstract-minded, sharp-witted," culturally parasitic "trading societies" spawned by "capitalistic enterprise," the South in its deepest being "*was* Europe," and though southerners had been misled by a scientific rationalist like Thomas Jefferson into the temptation of believing that "the ends of man are sufficiently contained in his political destiny," they had remained fundamentally "religious," "contemplative," and "qualitative" in their way of life. How shall the southerner take back his spiritual inheritance when "it was never articulated and organized for him"? "The answer," Tate says, is "by violence"—that is, by using the only method he has available, the Jeffersonian method of political action, "violent and revolutionary": "The Southerner is faced with the paradox: He must use an instrument, which is political, and so unrealistic and pretentious that he cannot believe in it, to re-establish a private, self-contained, and essentially spiritual life. I say that he must do this; but that remains to be seen."[21]

It did remain to be seen. Written in 1930—some twenty years before his quest for an "essentially spiritual life" led Tate (as Percy already had five years earlier) to become a Catholic—Tate's words anticipate the creation of Percy's tortured avenger and prophet almost fifty years later. Not long after *Lancelot* appeared, Percy published his outrageous self-interview called "Questions They Never Asked Me, So He Asked Them Himself," which is essentially a comment on the "knack" of being a novelist in the situation in which Percy finds himself: that of holding a general citizenship in the "here-and-now" of the second half of the twentieth century and a particular citizenship in the American South. A novelist in this situation, Percy says (adapting Camus), has a relation to the world that is like that of an "ex-suicide." He "realizes that all is lost, the jig is up, that after all nothing is dumber than a grown man sitting down and making up a story to entertain somebody or working in a 'tradition' or

21. Allen Tate, "Remarks on the Southern Religion," in *I'll Take My Stand,* by Twelve Southerners, 170, 171, 173, 174, 175.

'school' to maintain a reputation as a practitioner of the *nouveau ro-man* or whatever." When "one sees that this is a dumb way to live, that all is vanity sure enough, there are two possibilities: either commit suicide or not commit suicide." If the choice is against suicide, the here and now of the present century opens to the novelist, and he comes into a sense of creative freedom. Not the freedom of God on the first day of creation, but a freedom like that known to a man who has undergone the disaster of shipwreck and been cast up on a remote beach. If the castaway is a writer, his freedom is the realization that dead writers may be famous, but they are also "dead ducks" who can't write anymore. "As for me," the survivor says, "I might try a little something here in the wet sand, a word, a form . . ."

Percy then asks what the novelist's metaphorical identity as an ex-suicide has to do with "being southern." The answer, he says, is both negative and positive, for the southern writer, with all his "special miseries . . . isolation, madness, tics, amnesia, alcoholism, lust and loss of ordinary powers of speech," is "as marooned as Crusoe" and can be as individual as he wants to be. Or could. In today's "Sun Belt South" the writer is in danger of losing his greatest asset, his sense of eccentricity. If he is deprived of his psychic distance from nonsouthern writers, what will the southern writer do? Start writing like Saul Bellow? The deprivation entailed in the modification and disappearance of southern eccentricity affects the southern writer's strongest resource, the resource that made the French "go nuts over Poe and Faulkner," the feeling of being "somewhat extraterrestrial . . . different enough from the main body of writers to give the reader a triangulation point for getting a fix on things."

In comments he made after the fact of the novel, the author of *Lancelot* held that his intention in writing it was to "get a fix on things." He indicated that, in spite of Lancelot's Puritanical zeal to have his own way and conform the world to his own apocalyptic desiring, the perverse knight of Belle Isle would at last yield to the redemptive way symbolized by Percival, the priest who listens in silence to his story. Even so, viewed in his actual novelistic context Lancelot may well appear to the reader to be an incarnation of the unredeemable alienating force of malevolent evil. One is led to wonder if in *Lancelot* Percy does not reflect a crisis in the very motive of his search, at least to the extent of implying an anxious concern about its obsessive intensity on the one hand and its terrifying ambiguity on the other. Perhaps Lancelot indicates that Percy even had a deep fear—suppressed through the gift of faith though it was—of the wayfarer becoming alienated from his search by the unspeakable loneliness of history.

In any event, in his ironic vision of the southerner as the last European, Walker Percy extends the southern prophetic imagination of the moral complicity of the individual in history. He continues, we may say, in the vein of the southern literary difference, yet even as he does so he suggests a vital relationship between the South, the West, and New England. Simultaneously he brings to the relationship between Is and Was the sense—intimated in Warren and Tate, yet more strongly intimated in Percy than in either—not only that this relationship is losing its meaning in the South but that this loss symbolizes its general loss in Western civilization. A student of Kierkegaard, at times a quasi disciple, Percy intimates in the drama of his stories something that Kierkegaard himself never seems quite to have grasped: in its motive to be passionately inward, the self both resists and effects a radical, unprecedented subjectification of history. This act on the part of the modern self distinguishes it from the self in any other age. In its knowledge of the Kierkegaardian duality—of, on the one hand, its freedom and, on the other, its historical finitude—the modern secular self knows the difficult encumbrance of history. The self also knows—intuits, at any rate—that it has the will to transcend this encumbrance, even if it must abrogate history and become God. In Percy's conception of Lancelot there seems to be an allowance for the possibility that Lancelot may forbear the assumption of the godhead. As a southerner—as a self fully conscious of the intricate impositions of history—he may, Percy hints, still have the capacity to experience God's saving grace. Lancelot informs Percival, who in a way is his confessor, that he will wait for a time to give Percival's God a chance. Maybe Lancelot means this; maybe he is awakening to the need to distinguish between God and self; maybe his need to be God will be alleviated. Maybe he has truly come home from California. Percy would seem to leave to the reader the task of working out the final outcome of Lancelot Lamar's story. But it is intriguing to think that, although he fancied he was isolated by the distance he carefully maintained between himself and the major figures of the Southern Renascence, Percy, without deliberate, or even conscious, intention, suggested a remarkable similarity between two scions of the southern patriciate, Lancelot Lamar and Jack Burden, the one a football player at LSU and the other a graduate student in history at a state university that, though nameless, is LSU. Both are oblique portraits of the writer; both are indeed portraits of their author-creators. Is Lancelot's lurid story a symbol of the fate of Jack's conception of redeeming himself by assuming moral responsibility for history? Does the fable of the southern writer as embodied in Jack Burden reach its conclusion in his declaration of responsibility for history? Or does the fable of the southern writer as embodied in Jack Burden reach its conclusion in its terrifying embodiment in Lancelot Lamar? Does Lancelot's crazed effort to be the moral agent of the redemption of history represent the abortive fulfillment of Jack's vision of assuming the awful burden of responsibility for time? In creating Lancelot Lamar, did Walker Percy signal the failure of what he so wanted to do, introduce a new age, a new language? In creating Lancelot, did he put a final, brilliant period to the mid-twentieth century renascence in southern literary expression? The answers to such questions lie with the existing, or the surviving, reader.

Epilogue
A Personal Fable: Living with Indians

Historical sense and poetic sense should not, in the end, be contradictory, for if poetry is the little myth we make, history is the big myth we live, and in our living, constantly remake.
— Robert Penn Warren

An old-fashioned Hollywood Indian would say that I speak with a forked tongue. My actual personal experience with Indians, at least with plainly identifiable ones, has been mostly incidental to travels in the western states, Alaska, and the Yukon. I recall a conversation one night on an airplane between Kansas City and Omaha with a darkly handsome, well-dressed young insurance salesman from Oklahoma (I took him to be a Comanche) who had plainly made a successful entrance into the mainstream. I recollect more vividly a brief talk in the fabled seat of the Yukon gold strike, Dawson City, with a middle-aged Indian (I did not learn his tribal identity) who, after being hospitalized with a stomach ulcer, was returning to the wilderness to work a promising claim he had staked out before his illness. I recall more vividly still a frozen moment on the main street of a small Wyoming town when a young brave (Cheyenne, I think), a complete stranger, fixed his deep black eyes on me in a stare of utter contempt, if not sheer hatred. At least I think I interpreted his glance correctly. If my reaction to the chance meeting of our eyes was overly sensitive, this may be owing to the fact that in my imagination I have lived a good deal with Indians and, in my imagination at least, know something about how in spite of defeat, dispossession, and poverty they have tried to hold onto a sense of a determinate past; and in doing so, being the only native Americans—the only

Americans who ever truly belonged to the land, possessed by it but never its possessors—have been a constant reproach to the alien presence of their imperial conquerors. I have also, for a reason that will become apparent, lived a good deal in my imagination with Indians who lost their identity through mixing their blood with that of the conquerors.

I think I first had a certain awareness of the deeply ironic cultural situation of the native Americans when as a kid I attended the county fairs held in my hometown, a small community in northwest Texas named Jacksboro. The seat of Jack County, Jacksboro is located west of Fort Worth on the route that leads northward for a hundred miles or so to the Red River and Oklahoma and westward to Wichita Falls and Breckenridge and on out to the high plains of far west Texas. When I was born in 1916, the town was more than sixty years old, but it was not yet quite beyond the frontier stage. Self-conscious celebrations of the movement from pioneer primitivism to civilization, the fairs were held yearly on the old parade ground of Fort Richardson. Situated on the southern edge of town, this abandoned federal military post had for a few years after its establishment in 1868 been the largest army installation in post–Civil War America. Garrisoned by units of the army that had recently been the enemy of the citizens of Jack County—at first by the Sixth Cavalry, U.S.A., later by various other units, including the Tenth Cavalry, which was composed predominantly of black troopers and white officers—"the sentinel of the southern plains" (as its best historian, Allen Lee Hamilton, calls Fort Richardson) was decommissioned at the end of the Red River War in 1876.

By then the sentinel of the southern plains had fulfilled the purpose for which it had been built. This was to put a stop to the Kiowa, Comanche, and Kiowa-Apache warriors, who, violating their confinement to the reservation lands in Oklahoma, nearly every "Comanche moon" (as the settlers fearfully called the period of the full moon) crossed the Red River and made bloody incursions into the sparsely settled northwestern areas of Texas. The refusal of these dispossessed "Overlords of the Southern Plains" to stay complaisantly on the land assigned to them was of considerable concern not only to Texas but to Washington, D.C. The effective termination of the "Indian depredations," however, was not the result of military action but the consequence of a decisive civil action. On July 1, 1871, a Jack County grand jury indicted two leading Kiowa chiefs, named Big Tree and Satanta (White Bear), for the massacre of seven members of a wagon train on its way from Fort Griffin to Fort Richardson. Shortly before the massacre occurred, General William Tecumseh Sherman, general-in-chief of the United States army, who was on a three-week inspection tour of federal military posts on the Texas frontier, had passed the same way, but, according to the story, the Kiowas, already waiting in ambush, followed the advice of their medicine man and waited for the more profitable prey he had seen in his vision.

After the massacre Satanta talked too much—in fact, openly boasted of the raid—and he and Big Tree, together with an older accomplice, Satank, were arrested on the order of General Sherman. But at this point the army decided on an innovative move in the effort to establish peace on the Texas frontier and ordered that the three warriors be transported to Jacksboro, the intention being not to bring them before a military court at Fort Richardson, which would have conferred on them at least the quasi status of prisoners of war, but to have them tried as common felons by the Court of the Thirteenth Judicial District of Texas. Not far from the starting point of the journey to Jacksboro, Satank in effect committed a dramatic suicide by a hopeless escape attempt. The subsequent trial of Big Tree and Satanta for their part in the Warren Wagontrain Massacre (or, as it was also known, the Salt Creek Massacre) marked not only the first time Indians had appeared in the white man's court in Texas but the end of the desperate dream of the southern plains tribes that they could somehow resist the remorseless destruction of their ancient buffalo culture by the greedy slaughter of millions of buffalo to provide hides for the New England leather manufacturers.

Thus in one of the towns that had figured prominently in the "hide" trade (among the most brutal American folk ballads, "The Ballad of the Buffalo Skinners" tells the story of a slaughtering expedition that set out from Jacksboro in 1873 for the "plains of the buffalo"), Big Tree and Satanta, for acting "with force and malice[,] not having the fear of God before their eyes, but being moved by and seduced by the instigation of the devil," were indicted for committing the murder of seven teamsters. Promptly but duly convicted, they were sentenced to be hanged, but they were deprived of their final chance for dignity, tribal martyrdom, when Ulysses S. Grant, the president of the United States, decided that a wiser course than execution would be the commutation of their sentence to life imprisonment and so advised the Reconstruction governor of Texas, Edmund J. Davis. Incarcerated in the Texas State Penitentiary at Huntsville by the authority of the civil polity of the white man, Big Tree and Satanta—most notably Satanta, who had been a speaker at the great Medicine Lodge conference in 1867 and was one of the most prominent leaders of the plains tribes—were convincing symbols of the defeat of their ancient warrior society. The Kiowas, Comanches, Kiowa-Apaches, and Cheyennes were clearly facing the time when they would recognize that they were condemned to internal exile on the lands "reserved" for their forcible relocation; or to assimilation in the general society; or to a worse fate: an indeterminate existence in some dismal urban ghetto. But there was still the possibility of suicidal acts of defiance by the defeated warriors. Big Tree and Satanta had a chance to seize such an opportunity when Texas authorities released them on parole from the Huntsville penitentiary in late 1873. In spite of general protest, the officials were following the advice of the Secretary of the Interior, who was so anxious to secure peace on the frontier that he accepted a pledge by the Kiowas and Comanches that upon the release of the two chiefs, they would henceforth follow that path of peace.

Hostilities continued nonetheless, and a year after their release Big Tree and Satanta were arrested for parole violation. After an investigation Big Tree's parole was reinstated, but Satanta was returned to Huntsville for his involvement in the Red River War. By 1878 Satanta had had enough. The details of the story of his suicide vary, but it is clear that he managed to crawl through a high window of the Huntsville facility and leap headfirst to his death on the bricks of the prison yard. The warrior chief Big Tree, returning to the reservation and accepting pacification, lived on in the pathos of exile. He later became a Christian and eventually a deacon in the Baptist church. At times the old ways would come back to him and he would proudly recount his merciless acts against the white man, though always remembering to conclude with the comfortable observation that God had forgiven him for these "hideous" things.

Surviving his comrade Satanta by fifty years, Big Tree died in 1929. It is possible, I suppose, that he might have at some time been among the Indians who pitched their tepees on the Jack County fairgrounds, peddled the products of their craftsmanship, performed tribal dances, and in general entertained the enemies they had once scalped—and who had not infrequently scalped them. It is a fact that a great-grandson of Satanta participated in a reenactment of the trial of Big Tree and Satanta I saw at Fort Richardson in 1940.

I sometimes fancy that as a child I might have had an unusual empathy with Indians. Not that in emulation of the cowboy heroes of Hollywood I did not kill my share of these barbaric enemies of civilization. I remember the excitement of finding the appropriate uniform for an Indian fighter, a complete cowboy outfit, six-shooter, holster, caps, and all, under the Christmas tree one year. Yet I recall more graphically one Christmas when I received a Montgomery Ward "Indian suit." I remember the strange excitement of quickly putting it on over my pajamas and, wearing a bonnet of varicolored feathers and carrying bow, arrows, and hatchet, walking out of the front door into an alien world.

My sense of Indians was no doubt owing in part to the haunting presence of the old fort in our feeling of community identity; it owed still more to the presence in our household of my paternal grandmother, a living embodiment of local history, whose stories of Satanta, Big Tree, and Satank and other Indian chiefs, like Quanah Parker, were a feature of daily life. Perhaps in some metaphysical way my sense of Indians was fundamentally owing to the fact that, like my grandmother, to a degree I belonged to both the conquerors and the conquered.

But oddly I didn't know this fact until it emerged one evening some twenty years ago, when, during the course of a dinner conversation in a mid-Manhattan restaurant, my sister Betty referred to our paternal great-grandmother as having been at least a half-blooded Cherokee. Assuming I had long known this exotic aspect of the family history, Betty was surprised at my ignorance of it. I thought it surprising, too, and even—in a poetic or dramatic sense at any rate—a little shocking to discover that my grandmother had told many stories about Indians without intimating in so much as a word that she was one-fourth Cherokee; and for that matter that neither my father nor my mother had ever said anything about the Cherokee blood. The most intriguing aspect of the surprise was the realization that I had for all these years, and this in the very bosom of my family, in a shadowy kind of way lived with Indians.

Yet in itself my belated exposure to the fact that my great-grandmother had been the product of marriage between a white man and a Cherokee woman was no more than an intriguing surprise. Although marriages between white men and Cherokee squaws had not been conventional on the southern frontier, men in a world where they might have little opportunity to seek wives among women of their own race not uncommonly found wives among the women of the most civilized of American Indian tribes. Furthermore, although the children of such unions might be stigmatized as half-breeds, they were more commonly simply accepted by white society. This was true in the case of Dorcas Matilda Bowen Ham, who—although she was not (as family legend, in obedience to romantic convention, would have it) a descendant of a displaced tribal princess—was evidently a person of some education and considerable refinement. These qualities are reflected in the impassive yet quietly defiant regard of the dark eyes that look out at you in the only likeness of her known to exist. A photographic portrait made in later life, it does not reveal a physiognomy of grandmotherly serenity. Dominated by the severe features so characteristically Indian, including prominently high cheekbones, the portrait almost makes one believe Matilda was wholly the child of her mother. In a private memoir entitled "Berry Lewis Ham and his descendants so far as I knew them," committed to the pages of an old ledger in 1964, my mother says that the portrait of Matilda Ham is of "a strong, intellectual face."

The face we see in the portrait also suggests a life lived amid difficulties, never with resignation, but with endurance engendered by pride and courage and, one must think, not less by love than by hate. There was something more surprising than her unorthodox ancestry in the relation of Matilda Bowen to my life I discovered in my encounter with her that night in Manhattan. It was something that had not been entirely unknown to me. I had intimations of it in childhood in the looks on faces and in the intonations of voices, or in the sudden fall of voices when one entered a room. Most of all, I think, I had intimations of it in what was never spoken. But I had ignored the intimations of a past preserved in silence. Looking back to childhood, I think my unawareness of what had gone on—and what was still going on, the past, as Faulkner said, never being past—had something to do with my being not only the firstborn son but the firstborn child in a large family. In the kind of world in which I was brought up, I can now see, this privileged position implied a sense of identity that simply assumed the unity of the personal and the familial and thus tended to confer on me a stronger sense of the inviolability of the family relationships than my three brothers and, especially, my four sisters could quite assume. In any event, Betty (like me a person with a literary bent; now deceased but at that time an editor associated with a New York publisher) from her childhood, I found out, had been curious about the family history. This had led her to the discovery of some of its intricacies, including a record of Faulknerian intensity about relationships that had been less than inviolable, these centering specifically in extended divorcement proceedings in the early 1860s between my half-Cherokee great-grandmother and my Scottish great-grandfather, Berry Lewis Ham. This bitter contest, prolonged for two years, had resulted in my great-grandfather's winning custody of my grandmother and her five sisters and two brothers. It had also resulted in a legacy of enmities within the family and the community that were never to be resolved. Some measure of the passionate sensitivity that perpetuated this legacy is indicated by the fact that in 1900 or thereabouts—thirty-five years after the trial—the transcript of the courtroom testimony in the case of Dorcas Matilda Ham and Berry Ham mysteriously disappeared from the courthouse records.

For me the most intimate, and the most disturbing, aspect of the legacy was, as I have indicated, a haunting silence. If my great-grandfather was only an occasional presence in my grandmother's stories, my great-grandmother was never present, so far as I can recollect, even in indirect reference. An austere, unbreakable silence had fallen between a nine-year-old girl and her mother with the end of her parents' marriage in the early 1860s. (According to the records, the divorce decree was handed down in 1863.) The silence had evidently also fallen between my great-grandmother—who remarried in 1871—and my grandmother's brothers and sisters. In the memoir I mentioned earlier, my mother recalled that "in all her association" with my grandmother and her brothers and sisters, she "never heard" the name of my great-grandmother "mentioned." Reflecting on the unhappy drama she had unfolded in her memoir of the Hams and Simpsons, my mother became doubtful of her motive in doing so. "Maybe I shouldn't ever have dug up this ancient history," she wrote, but the compelling interest that had prompted her is revealed in the question she adds: "Have all those who lived in such vital relationships here now met in another life?"

At the burial service for my mother in Oakwood Cemetery in Jacksboro on a beautiful May afternoon in 1981, I was aware of the close proximity of the Simpson and Ham family plots. I wondered where the gravesite of Dorcas Matilda (Ham) Williams might be, and I have since found out that it is located at a considerable distance beyond the Simpson and Ham graves. Driving back across the courthouse square after the interment service, we passed the marble courthouse that my father, in his capacity as the county judge, had dedicated the last year or two of his life to securing for the county. The new building was incomplete when he suddenly died in 1939. I thought about how this structure of imported marble had replaced the native-limestone courthouse built in 1886 when my father was a boy; about how this building had replaced the crude 1872 sandstone structure where Satanta and Big Tree had been convicted; about how this had replaced the still ruder building erected in the early 1860s where the divorce trial had been held; about how this primitive structure had replaced the still more primitive structure—with a buffalo robe for a door—that my great-grandfather, as a member of Jack County's first commissioners' court, had assisted in building when the county was organized in 1857. I thought, with appalled incredulity, about how the life that had been "lived in such vital relationships" belonged to the intricate history of a frontier people who had simultaneously fought the Indians, engaged in the American Civil War, and struggled, often passionately, at times violently, among themselves, yet had consistently kept the courthouse and the courthouse square at the center of their history.

Sometimes in quiet moments, with no Proustian sign, it is 1925 or 1926 and there comes to me a detailed image of the courthouse square in Jacksboro and of the surrounding community as I knew this world when I was nine or ten years old. On the west side, altogether the most substantial side, there is the continuous block of two-story native-limestone buildings, housing on the south end the First National Bank of Jacksboro and on the north end Walters Drug Store and in between the Timberlake dry goods store, Spears Drug Store, Shabay Brothers dry goods, the Opera House Picture Show, Wells Hardware, Breech's Barber Shop (with hot baths for gentlemen), and R. H. Austin, Jeweler and Optometrist. On the south side there is at the west end the Fort Richardson Hotel and on the east end Cope's Grocery Store and in between Hensley's Meat Market, Eakman's Cafe, Brown's Barber Shop (with a dry-cleaning establishment in the rear), and the Jacksboro National Bank. On the east side there is S. O. Hess's undertaking establishment and furniture store and the Jacksboro *Gazette* and printing shop; in between, Bynum's bakery and, adjacent to each other, in incongruous juxtaposition, Morgan's blacksmith shop and Patton's automotive garage. On the north side there is Price's photography studio and a Chevrolet agency, and in between S. O. Callahan's plumbing business (also an agency for the sale of windmills), the Jacksboro Volunteer Fire Department, and the Farmer's Union Grocery Store (now privately owned but a relic of the Populist era in Jack County).

Right off the square to the northwest is Spivey's grocery store, Gwaltney hardware, the St. Frances Hotel, Johnny Hines's plumbing shop, and a hide-and-fur agency; off the square to the south there is Stewart's Grocery, Fain's Confectionery, the post office, Sewell's lumberyard, a big cotton warehouse, and a wagonyard (with rude accommodations for the wagoners who haul freight destined for the railroads or who haul independently from one place to another in a world that has as yet no hard-surface roads). Off the square to the southeast there is the limestone jail. Well removed from the square to the south is the station of the Gulf, Texas, and Western Railroad and beyond that, across a rattling iron bridge over Los Creek, the Rock Island railroad station. Several blocks to the west of the square on what is known as College Hill (where in the 1890s North Texas Baptist College had been located) is the red brick structure that houses both the grammar school and the high school, while to the south, near the creek, is the small wooden one-room schoolhouse for black children, some of them descendants of the approximately fifty slaves in the county in 1860. In the same vicinity is the small wooden structure known as Mount Pisgah Methodist Church, a congregation of blacks and the oldest church in the town. At close remove from the square are the First Christian Church (the Disciples of Christ), which we attend, the Baptist church, the Presbyterian church, and Methodist Church South. The "Holy Rollers" (Assembly of God) hold their lively services in an unpainted wooden structure down below the jail. The Episcopal faith is unrepresented, but near the town cemetery, Oakwood, several blocks from the square to the north, is an abandoned Roman Catholic chapel that has been repeatedly vandalized, the relic of an effort to bring a Catholic presence into a world so thoroughly White Anglo-Saxon Protestant that a Catholic is regarded as an exotic and may even be regarded with dark suspicion.

Also adjacent to the cemetery is a barren expanse that is used as a playing field not only for the town baseball team but for the high school baseball and football teams, there being no adequate area on the school grounds. This space is also used by the circus when it comes to town. Another, smaller expanse of ground located near the jail is used for carnivals, tent shows, medicine shows, and the annual Chautauqua. Regardless of whether there are any special attractions in town, each Saturday is a crowded day in the Jacksboro square, where everybody in the county who can get there gathers for a day of selling, shopping, and visiting. A series of hitching chains supported by wooden posts (rather than by hitching rails) entirely surrounds the courthouse, for although a good many farmers own Model T's, the wagon is still the chief means of getting into town with a full load of family plus products to sell or exchange. In the afternoon the Opera House Picture Show is sold out to a mixed audience of cowhands, farmers, country kids, and town kids for the showing of a western, possibly one featuring William S. Hart, Tom Mix, or Hoot Gibson. Pete Shabay and the patrons of Shabay Bros. store, which is directly underneath the second-story theater, glance apprehensively at the ceiling as the excitement of the chase begins to mount and, moving to a player-piano rendition of the William Tell overture, shoes and boots begin to stomp more and more violently.

The image of Jacksboro that comes to me is of a place that no longer exists save in remote semblance. It returns because this town, however imaginary, is still the center of the world for me.

At the center of my vision stands one building, the native-limestone courthouse that was torn down fifty years ago and replaced with the functional modern structure. A semi-Gothic structure, the old courthouse—our "Temple of Justice," the Jacksboro *Gazette* called it when it was dedicated in 1886—had four turrets trimmed with galvanized iron and boasted as its crowning glory a tower surmounted by a serene nine-foot blindfolded lady trimmed in gold leaf, who held aloft in her right hand the scale of justice and in her left hand, the blade pointed downward, the sword of justice. What the completion and dedication of the courthouse meant to the town and the county is indicated in an account in the Jacksboro *Gazette* of the laying of the cornerstone a year earlier in a "solemn and impressive" ceremony conducted by the "grand order of Free Masonry" and the attendant ceremonial by the "glorious old United Friends of Temperance," four of whose members united in a quartet to render the "beautiful" song "Brave Temperance Boys." The dedication was further graced by a long oration by the most distinguished jurist in the area, Judge T. D. Sporer, who spoke on "the history of Jack County from the time it was first settled to the present day."

The span of time he covered was only forty years, but it was burdened with meaning; and Judge Sporer was aware of the symbolic import of his words. The epoch of the settlement was ending. There were still saloons on the square, and there were still cowboys who came into town every Saturday and drank too much and who occasionally shot holes in the nine-foot lady poised a hundred and fifty feet above them atop the Temple of Justice. But not for long; the day of the Temperance Boys had come. The open range in that part of the world was disappearing, as was the cowboy as he had been known. The Jack County that had been organized in 1857 out of homesteading territory now belonged to an immemorial past and the county seat that in the Reconstruction period had been a garrison town and one of the roughest towns of the southern plains (where Doc Holliday had gambled and such establishments as Mollie McCabe's Palace of Beautiful Sin had done a thriving business) had become a memory. Like the Comanches and the Kiowas—now effectively penned up on reservations in the Oklahoma Territory a hundred or so miles to the north—vanquished too were the old southerners who, like my paternal great-grandfather, had come out onto the southern plains dreaming of land and wealth, and perhaps too of the South's expansion into a mighty slave empire extending southward across the Caribbean and westward over the far reaches of the continent to the Pacific.

I know somewhat more about Berry Lewis Ham than about Dorcas Matilda Ham. Although the most interesting history of Jacksboro and Jack County, Ida Lasater Huckabay's *Ninety-Four Years in Jack County, 1854–1948* (published in 1948), never mentions my great-grandmother, it celebrates my great-grandfather as a hero of the progressive spirit and a precursor of the New South progressivism my father would represent later on: "B. L. Ham was among our first commissioners who bargained for Jack County's first courthouse; a crude building with a buffalo hide for a door. No doubt as he urged his pony homeward towards the setting sun after an eventful day with court affairs, he dreamed of the future—the better things to come. Perhaps in a mirage he caught glimpses, saw the imprint of Jack County's courthouse in 1948; in the construction of which figured so triumphantly, the efforts of his grandson, Judge John P. Simpson."

But the portrait of Berry Ham we derive from the known facts of his life is at once far more complex and less comfortable than this cliche portrayal of the noble pioneer. My great-grandfather was something like the kind of figure Faulkner might have found prototypical if he had been writing about Texas instead of Mississippi, which is not to imply that Berry Ham was a Thomas Sutpen, save in that he had the same kind of drive. Born in 1813 in Tennessee, he was, according to one story, a classic runaway who, having effected a stereotypical escape from a cruel stepmother, made his way to Texas. At some point, either before he left Tennessee or after he arrived in Texas, he is said to have formed an attachment with a family of emigrants who were part of the Moses Austin Colony. But this story is unsupported by any facts, and Berry Ham may have gotten to Texas in some more conventional way. In any event, it is known that in his teens he found employment as an agent of Lorenzo, one of the Mexican impresarios engaged in bringing settlers to Texas. Later he was to pay tribute to Lorenzo by naming one of his two sons James Lorenzo. In 1835, when Texas settlers, mostly Anglo-Americans, rebelled against the Mexican government, he joined the

Army of the Texas Republic and was very likely, at the age of seventeen, in the decisive battle of Jacinto on April 21, 1836.

What Berry did between 1838 and 1854, when he took up land in what was to become Jack County, is more or less a blank. Although it is doubtful that he had any kind of formal education, he obviously had enhanced his innate ability to make his way in the world that was before him by acquiring the basic skills of reading, writing, and figuring. By the time he came to the northwest Texas frontier with Dorcas Matilda and six children, he had acquired land in four counties, and it would seem several slaves. Since gang slavery was not economically feasible beyond the plantation country of East Texas, these would have been mostly household servants and hands to work cattle. But Berry Ham was as militantly proslavery as a planting master, accepting the institution of slavery as a necessary part of his world. I still experience a chill when I read the following document:

> The State of Texas
> County of Collin
>   Know all men by these Presents that we Charlotte J. Robinson and James S. Robinson of the County and State aforesaid for and in consideration of the sum of one thousand dollars we have this day sold to B. L. Ham of the County of Jack in the State aforesaid one Negro woman by the name of Lucy about twenty-five years old and we hereby warrant her sound in body and mind and a slave for life.
>   Given under our hands this the 13th day of December A.D. 1858.
>
> Charlotte J. Robinson
James S. Robinson
>
> Attesting Witnesses:
> B. W. Bell
> Samuel B. Reder

I have found no trace of what Lucy did or what happened to her. I don't recall that my grandmother ever mentioned her. At times she mentioned a slave child of about her own age who waited on her and was her companion for a time, but she seldom mentioned slavery, save to say, always defensively, that she was "glad that Mr. Lincoln freed the slaves." Conceivably Lucy's descendants were represented in the small black community that provided servants for my family and others when I was a child. Maybe one of her kin was the very black woman, known as "Nigger Ad," who came once a week to boil the family wash in a large iron pot on a wood fire she made in the backyard. The image of Ad's visits focuses on my recollection of her laughter once when I asked her if the white on the inside of her hands was from washing clothes all of the time.

Berry Ham's reputation was that of a frontier baron. According to family legend, he decked himself out in a coonskin cap and "walked the earth like a king." He kept the best coon dogs, raced fine horses, and frequently gambled at cards. He had a passion for winning. One story is that when he and his companions raced their slaves against each other, a sport that apparently filled in when horse races could not be arranged, Berry Ham always situated himself at the end of the course and held aloft a gold coin as an incentive for his entries. When he established his household at a place eight or nine miles west of Jacksboro—this would become known as Ham Springs—he enclosed his dominion in a stockade for protection against Indian attacks, and it became a regular stop on the famous Butterfield Overland Stage route. The often-repeated story that Berry managed through trickery to obstruct the designated route, thus forcing the stage to pass through Jacksboro and Ham Springs, is apocryphal but true to his character as a ruthless frontier opportunist who kept on acquiring more and more land. When the war came, however, his increasing affluence was arrested by his loyalty to the South. Pledging himself wholly to the War for Southern Independence, he converted all his money into Confederate currency. (Perhaps some of Berry's useless money made up the stack of Confederate bills that my grandmother got out of her trunk one day and gave to us to play with.) But if my great-grandfather lost his money, he held on to much of his land and after the war continued to enjoy a state of relative affluence until he died in 1879.

By this time everything seemed to point toward the postfrontier future. The new courthouse, as the Jacksboro *Gazette* indicates, was accepted by most people as a symbol of progress earned by a difficult and heroic past. But in fact the celebration of the new Temple of

Justice in 1886 was premature. The building was not completed in one major respect for another twenty-five years, for it was not until then that the county commissioners found the money to utilize the space in the tower immediately below the figure of Justice for its intended purpose, the housing of a large, four-faced clock. Robert H. Austin, the town jeweler and optometrist, was awarded the contract for the installation of the clock. But Mr. Austin, who seems to have had little engineering skill, misfigured in his calculations and found that the clock was so large that it could not be accommodated by the opening provided in the original design. It had to be hoisted up over the roof and installed in a special way by a crew of several men instead of two or three, and took several days' work instead of one or two. Mr. Austin, who was our next-door neighbor for a number of years, easily reconciled his position as an elder of the Presbyterian church and his affiliation with the American Socialist Party. (His politics seem to have been regarded as no more than a mere eccentricity; he was the only Socialist in town.) But neither Christian charity nor economic idealism softened the fact that he came out of the clock episode with only forty dollars' profit. Possibly he came to see his installation of the clock as a labor of love; at any rate, he took a proprietary attitude toward the clock, and for nearly the span of its life he fixed it when it didn't work. Nobody else knew how.

Thus in 1910 to the symbol of the implacable judgment of Justice—the lady with the scales and the sword who had presided over the community since 1886—was added the awesome symbol of the judgment of time. Meanwhile, the introduction of electricity to Jacksboro in 1891 made possible a further enhancement of the symbolic meaning of the courthouse—this when its four turrets were surmounted with electric bulbs. These not only served the practical purpose of illuminating the square but, visible from a distance to returning travelers, became the ineffable, never-to-be-forgotten beacons of home.

I knew the courthouse intimately. My father, one of the two or three attorneys in the town, was one of its most prominent citizens; moreover, he was twice in the office of county judge, and for several years in the 1920s—this was the time I was most often in the courthouse—he was the prosecuting attorney for the county. I knew all the rooms and offices of the county courtroom and the larger district courtroom upstairs, where the circuit judge of the district presided and where my father, as defending or prosecuting attorney, was involved in many trials, including several sensational murder cases. I knew the county clerk's office, the district clerk's office (where you always found Mr. Nelms, who held the office for countless terms, always signed himself as "your humble servant," and walked fourteen miles a day round trip from a small home in the country to keep an eight-hour day, six days a week). I knew the office of the superintendent of the county schools, the sheriff's office, and the county surveyor's office, and besides Mr. Nelms I knew most of the other courthouse officials.

But there was a place in the courthouse I did not know, although I longed to know it. This was the place of the big clock. I almost crawled into it one summer afternoon after climbing a forbidden staircase. But when I stood beneath the awesome sound of the clock's implacable movement, I realized I didn't know the hour. I panicked when I thought it might almost be the moment of the mighty hammer on the bell, and fled in terror.

There was nothing more lonely than the experience of being awake at two or three o'clock in the morning and hearing the clock speak its message to the dark town. The quality of loneliness was enhanced by the striking, usually I think a minute or two later, of the modestly baroque Seth Thomas clock that sat on one of the two bookcases dividing the living room from the dining room in our high-ceilinged, wood-frame, story-and-a-half house. (These bookcases, a prime source of my literary education, held about half the library my father had accumulated, including complete sets of Mark Twain and Bret Harte, Robert Louis Stevenson, and Bulwer Lytton. They also held various volumes of Charles Dickens, Robert Browning, Ralph Waldo Emerson, Henry Wadsworth Longfellow *et al.*)

Located about four or five blocks east of the square, our house was on a street that had a name, but since nobody ever used it, and most people didn't know the name anyway, it was essentially a nameless street. Most of the streets in the town—a few were graveled, most were dirt—were unknown by name, names being unnecessary in a town that had a population of no more than two thousand. One simply referred to "the street the Simpsons lived on," etc. Actually, I wasn't born in the house of my childhood, but in a house only two blocks southwest of the courthouse. A pleasant cottage, it no doubt had some claim to elegance in its time—certainly it was more elegant than the house I first consciously remember—but for several years before my mother came there as a bride in 1915 it had not been a happy house. Nine years before, my father's first wife, together with a first-born child, had died there. For a long time my father endured a grief so inconsolable that his family feared for his sanity. But the darkness eventually lifted; and by the time my mother, supported by a freshly granted temporary teaching certificate, came to Jacksboro High School in 1910, he was fulfilling the profession of law to which he had pledged himself in 1904 when he entered the University of Texas Law School.

Earlier my father had been provided with the best education circumstance could afford. He had been sent as a boy to a small private academy in a little town called Whitt, and he had attended the Jacksboro public school, and North Texas Baptist College, where he learned enough Greek and Latin to be qualified to teach there himself for a time before the school was closed. He had had some small-town newspaper experience, having served as a correspondent for the Jacksboro *Gazette* before he and a friend named Frank Groner somehow managed to inaugurate and conduct a weekly county newspaper called the Jacksboro *News* for about six months in 1901 and 1902. Whether my father and Groner went broke or not I don't know, but the paper was successful enough to attract a buyer, Tom Marks, who was later to found the 4-H Club movement in Jack County and see it spread across the country. Marks kept the *News* going for a number of years. While my father was editing the paper, he published several of his own stories and poems in its pages, some of these under his own name, others under the satirical pseudonym "Don Delmugado." His most extensive and serious literary ventures were in fiction. Three of these efforts were several chapters in length; I guess you might call them novellas. Entitled *Love amid the Shadows of War: A Story of Southern Life, The Sentinel Boy of the Maine,* and *For God and Liberty: A Tale of the Texas Revolution,* they were each ascribed to his own name. My father also served a year or so as the principal of the high school in this early period. During this time he was postponing his plan to go to law school in order to support his beloved younger brother's attendance at Texas A&M.

A Personal Fable

I don't know precisely when my father met "Miss Grace"—as she was known by many and was still known by some when she died at the age of ninety-three. It must have been soon after her arrival that the two were introduced. This was perhaps at some kind of school event, since it was proper for my mother to come unescorted, and proper for my father to ask if he might walk her home. She accepted the invitation but was struck by the fearful thought as they strolled to her boarding place that her companion might be someone of doubtful reputation. After he left her at her door, she rushed to her landlady for information about her escort and was both relieved and intrigued to find she had been in the company of an eminently respectable widower. Indeed he was a well-known lawyer, who was also well known for his oratory, and who was, moreover, a member of the school board that had employed her.

The courtship relationship was lengthy. In fact, my mother and father were not married until 1915, when he was thirty-seven years old and she was twenty-seven. I would judge that in the beginning of the friendship my father was more interested in my mother than she was in him. She was determined to further her education, at least to the extent of fulfilling the requirement for a permanent teaching certificate. Thus she spent a year or two—with, I take it, the approval of the local school authorities—at the University of Texas. It was not easy. She had to make her way by teaching for her board and room at small and rather impoverished Texas Wesleyan College in south Austin (where breakfast, she recalled, was invariably soggy milk toast and coffee). But she was a proud, beautiful young woman who was used to hardship, having been reared as the eldest in a large farming family that had moved from Kentucky in the 1880s to the cotton belt in Texas. She was no stranger to farm labor, including that of picking cotton. Somehow, although her family's intellectual interests centered almost exclusively on questions of biblical interpretation and related matters, she managed to acquire something approximating a serious, if limited, education in secular literature before she went to the university. Here in 1913 and 1914 she was the president of the Pierian Literary Society, the motto of which was Pope's noted admonition: "A little learning is a dangerous thing, / Drink deep or taste not the Pierian spring."

At some point during the courtship my father received, in his words, "one certain cruel letter." I think at issue may well have been my mother's aspiration to a degree of feminine—I don't think it was "feminist," but feminine—independence. I deduce this from reading the fragmentary correspondence that is to be found in the miscellany of things my mother stored through the years in a big, old-fashioned trunk. The letters seem to show a long period of silence between the two in 1913. In early 1914 my father, who was by then serving two consecutive terms as the county judge of Jack County, saw my mother once again. Evidently it was a restrained reunion, but immediately afterwards he appealed to her with flowers and a note that, in terms of the sensibility of an age in which the language of love was still carefully cultivated, is masterly:

> For the sake of Auld Lang Syne, I have employed these flowers to speak for me. May they be eloquent and convincing: During the past I have wondered if I would ever see you again, and after the "reproof" I knew I would not—and then—as truth is stranger than fiction—out of the many months you appeared and spoke to me, and I found the same splendid, charming girl as ever. It is a rare pleasure to know you and an honor to be admitted to the circle of your friends. I will not say more—because of one certain cruel letter of ages ago—than to add that among your many friends—you have no better.

The chill was broken, but my mother left a little frost in the air when she replied on February 27, 1914, in a formal note of thanks for the flowers that begins "Dear Mr. Simpson" and ends, "I am sincerely yours." Yet she managed to convey a receptivity to a further stage in the renewal of the relationship. She first threw her suitor off balance by accusing him of having forgotten (though my father had not referred to forgetfulness as an issue). "Surely," she wrote, "one who 'forgot' deserves forgiveness when he remembers so beautifully." If a certain letter seemed cruel, she meant it only to express "the utmost kindness toward a man for whom I have only sincere regard." She would, she told my father, "be happy to count you as a friend," and it would give her "pleasure" to prove herself to be a friend. "There is a certain stimulation in making and being friends with people who are trying to 'do things' in the world that is ever an inspiration to me," she declared. "And while the silence of many months has lasted, I have not been indifferent to the success that has been coming your way. And it is with the greatest sincerity that I wish for you an increasing continuance of it."

Of what took place during the rest of 1914 I find no record, save that on November 13 my mother, now back at her post in the Jacksboro school, wrote a note to acknowledge another gift of flowers (chrysanthemums were specifically mentioned in this one) and once again called to my father's attention something he had forgotten: "Once when you had forgotten, you remembered most beautifully. But today you remembered more beautifully than ever." This note began "Dear Mr. Simpson" and ended even more formally than the one back in February, "Very truly yours"; but the formal dance of courtship was nearing its end. My mother's decision to marry my father is recorded in a letter of surrender (undated but I would conjecture written in the early part of 1915). It begins "My dearest Friend and More" and not only concludes "Lovingly" but is signed only with "Grace," my mother's first name. "How I want to be good to you and make you happy all your life," my mother wrote, adding significantly, "And I'm not independent as you have guessed me. I'm depending on you, and have been more than you know all this year." She also said, "And I never was more sure of anything in my life as I am of my confidence in you."

In the light of the remark about "confidence," one may wonder if her reference to a forgetfulness on my father's part may not have been to the fact that at some point in their relationship my mother had become jealous of her suitor for seeming to forget her in his attentiveness to someone else. If so, my father's diverted attention may have been a response to my mother's independence. But if her independence of spirit had been an impediment to the courtship, and had inspired my father to whatever action provoked my mother's jealousy, now all was right, and in June of 1915, the two were married in my mother's parental home and went off to Colorado on an idyllic wedding journey. They brought back as one memento a few small gold nuggets from the famous Cripple Creek mine, which my mother used to show us. What finally happened to them I don't know. As prophetic tokens of a union "blessed with the treasure of children," they were accurate enough. When I was born a little over a year after the marriage, I was to be the first of nine children. As prophetic emblems of material wealth, the little nuggets were hardly accurate. My father's economic fortunes were good for ten years or so after World War I, but were to be cruelly reversed as the Great Depression deepened in the 1930s. More out of desperation than desire for the office, he would stand for county judge again, suffer the humiliation of defeat, then two years later stand again to be elected, to die in office at the age of sixty-two.

A battered idealist and, I think, a shaken Christian, my father said to me in the last year or two of his life that he had always been too much "the opportunist," never able to fix a goal and pursue it unrelentingly—with "everlasting stick-to-itness," as he put it—until victory was won. He told me too that he was thinking of running for governor. When he saw that I knew what he knew too, that the idea was incredible, he smiled and said, "Well, just run to get acquainted." But he had long ago become acquainted: when he died, newspapers throughout the state noted the event. I have often thought since about the pathos of his situation. Back when he first held political office before his second marriage—in those years when my mother had told him that she was "not indifferent" to his success—he must have aspired to higher political station. Maybe he had even dreamed of occupying the governor's mansion in Austin. Now—though he could not have known that before long, shortly after getting up at four o'clock in the morning as usual, he was to die—he ironically blamed himself for not having stuck to the fulfillment of his dream. The family physician pronounced him dead with the observation, "Another victim of the Depression."

But his failure to achieve a greater measure of fame, I suspect, was not entirely owing to hard times and his inordinate family obligations. Having irrevocably committed himself to the ideal of history as a fulfillment of the ethic of progress, he lacked any real capacity for power politics. In spite of the personal injury that political machinations inflicted on him, he lacked, I think, even a conceptual grasp of power politics. To compound the irony, at my youthful age I had acquired some notion of how big-time politics operates, for in 1935 my father, in an act that was rare for him, took advantage of his longtime personal acquaintance with one of the members of the

Texas Railroad Commission and secured for me an essentially political patronage position as a part-time clerk in the office of the Oil and Gas Division of the commission, an agency that after the opening of the great East Texas Field in the early 1930s was one of the most economically powerful and politically sensitive agencies in the state. I wasn't any Jack Burden, but I did not remain a political innocent. I came to know a Sadie Burke or two; and—as I somewhat uncertainly fulfilled the real purpose of my job at the state capitol, which was to enable me to attend the University of Texas—I learned something about the inner practicalities of "practical politics." To compound the irony further, I had already done what my father would never do. I had in my last year in high school (I was sixteen as I recall) spent a night in the governor's mansion, where I had slept in the great bed of Sam Houston and had breakfast (served by trusties of the state prison system) with Governor and Mrs. Ross Sterling. Although my father had supported Sterling and would support him again in a race he lost to Pappy Lee O'Daniel, patronage was not the reason for my invitation to the mansion. I had won first prize in an essay contest sponsored by the Texas Federation of Women's Clubs, and a night in the mansion was part of the prize package. The contest called for an essay on the requirements of good citizenship, which I had down pat, having seen them incarnated in word and deed in the lives of my father and mother. I don't remember much about what I said in the composition I submitted, except for the ending: a dramatic pronouncement to the effect that when I died I wanted only the words "He was a Good Citizen" inscribed on my tombstone. I could envision the monument erected in Oakwood Cemetery and the admiration my piety of community evoked on behalf of my memory.

But I think I knew—though I don't suppose I consciously said this to myself or maybe even consciously thought it—that I could never share with my father and mother their seemingly invincible belief in progress. My increasing doubts about living one's life on behalf of this faith tended to be conclusive by the end of my first year in Austin. This could not, however, be attributed solely, or even primarily, to the experience of working at the capitol. The experience of coming of age in the 1930s did not have a uniformly corrosive effect on the souls of my peers, for even though it was the *great* depression, it did not uniformly reduce middle-class families to a state of genteel poverty. And if you had to live in that state, you felt that you could not admit it but had to keep up appearances. Living in this kind of tension produced feelings of anxiety and guilt, and in one of a sufficient sensitivity, doubts about the purpose of existence. Symptomatic of this was that somewhere in my second year in college I ceased to attend church. At the same time, of course, I not only began to read more widely on my own but was exposed to some of the more penetrating minds on the University of Texas campus.

Still and all, looking back from the perspective of fifty years, I conceive that an underlying, perhaps crucial, influence on my deeper penetration of things was the experience of living with my grandmother Simpson. After my grandfather Simpson died in 1910, she had lived with my father, now a widower, and was evidently considered to be a part of the household when he married for a second time. So until I graduated from high school there was no point when I was not with her almost daily, save when on infrequent occasions she would spend a week or so visiting relatives elsewhere. The relationship among my father, my mother, and my grandmother was, I grasp more now than ever before, a difficult one that might have intrigued a D. H. Lawrence, and is I think well beyond my powers of analysis. This is not to say that it was altogether an unhappy relationship, merely that it was always a complex one and was at times unhappy, especially so, I think, when my grandmother, as she invariably did, sided with the children against any punishment my mother—never undertaken in the first place until she was reduced to desperation—might try to impose on us.

But while siding with the child might have been prompted by the desire to make an antagonistic gesture toward my mother, such a motive I would think was secondary to an acute sympathy my grandmother felt for anyone on whom pain or suffering was inflicted. This sensitivity did not derive, I take it, from an altruistic view of human nature. Nor did it arise from a view of compassionate revulsion against the evil in human nature, at least not from a revulsion against evil as defined in theological doctrine. Her sympathetic reaction to the pain of others had its source more nearly in her inarticulate but appalling recognition—Hebraic or Old Testament in its intensity—of the expense of history for the individual life. In her later eighties, when the Germans invaded Poland, she said to me,

"I've lived through four wars; I don't want to live through another one." I could only think of three wars before the one just beginning—the Civil War, the Spanish-American War, and World War I—then I realized the fourth was the conflict she knew most intimately, the Indian Wars. She was not to live through her fifth war, though it did spark her interest. Shortly after the invasion of Russia by the Germans, I recall, as she started to move one day from our front porch over to her nephew's porch next door (where there was shade in the afternoon), she said in what had become a very old and weary voice, "If the Russians [she pronounced the word with a long *u*] whip the Germans, let me know. Don't bother to come over. Just yell across." But it was becoming impossible for my mother, who, forced to find a source of income for the family, had by now been elected to the office of county clerk, to take care of my grandmother as she became progressively more enfeebled. For a time she was in a nursing home in Fort Worth, but that was a terrible place for her; eventually her other daughter-in-law, also a widow, took her into her home, a block off the square in Jacksboro. But by this time the darkness had closed in completely, and she had become quite irrational. In 1943, when death finally released her, the Fort Worth and Wichita Falls papers, as well as the Jacksboro *Gazette,* reported that "Jack County's oldest citizen" had died, and duly recorded some of the details of her life in what had become for most readers of the obituary a distant, romantic never-never time of the brave and hardy pioneers.

By then the somber notes of the courthouse clock had ceased. The limestone courthouse, the figure of Justice, and the clock were in truth all gone. The new courthouse my father had succeeded in getting under construction before his death had been made absolutely necessary by a deterioration of the old courthouse so marked that for several years the walls had been bolted together by steel rods. Some thought the building had not been constructed to hold the weight of the big clock.

My grandfather Simpson died in 1910, the same year the clock was installed; and no doubt, as my grandmother began thirty-three years of widowhood, it spoke to her more of time past than time future. Although she was only sixty-two years of age in 1910, she was entering into the experience of outliving one's self. The experience in itself was not unusual; in fact, each generation of Americans, belonging to a nation that came into self-conscious national existence at the very moment of the invention of the cotton gin, the steamboat, and interchangeable parts—of an unprecedented application of the powers of nature to nature, or against nature—has had the experience of outliving itself. Living long enough, each American has had the generational experience of being displaced in time—of becoming at first one of the "old ones," then, if life extends long enough, one of the "ancient ones."[1] The experience of being a survivor of the world that was an outermost extension of the frontier South was one of the more extreme versions of the American experience of displacement. And if the survivor of the northwest frontier of Texas in 1910 could not take refuge in the faith in justification by progress, as most of my grandmother's peers did, of course, justification was hard to come by.

My grandmother never so far as I know attempted to make any kind of written record of her life, but she did engage herself in the composition of a kind of oral autobiography. I think, in fact, the narrative of her life was almost constantly running through her mind. As her eyesight became impaired and her freedom of movement impeded by arthritic pain (to some extent relieved by small amounts of phenobarbital, and perhaps by the habit of using snuff, for which she reproached herself every day for seventy-five years or more), she would enjoin any grandchild who came near: "Sit down, let me tell you something." It was like the command of the Ancient Mariner. And if you sat down, you were in for it; you had heard it all before, though sometimes the details varied enough to give a fresh spark of interest to the story.

The story began with my grandmother's marriage and in its main line of development followed three removals. The first was from Ellis County, where my grandmother and grandfather started their married life in 1877 under decent circumstances and had their first child, my father, but were soon cruelly reduced in fortune as a result of my grandfather's liability for a heavy debt incurred when he guar-

---

1. At least it used to be this way. Now the old, becoming more numerous all of the time, are segregated in retirement communities or warehoused in "rest" homes. Ironically, however, they have by becoming organized acquired a special status and a notable political potency.

anteed a loan of an ostensible friend who defaulted and fled. Now penniless save for a rather large parcel of wilderness land her father had given her, my grandmother, with her husband and their first-born, went to this land to establish a new home. Living first in a tent, then in a cabin, my grandmother—a woman who had been brought up in an affluent home—faced a hard situation. After a year or so "down on the Keechi" (as she always put it), she and my grandfather decided to sell the Keechi holding and buy the land about seven miles west of Jacksboro that was to become known as the Simpson place and remain in the family for seventy-five years. Once again they set up a tent. In one of the lighter episodes in her narrative, my grandmother told about how she burned down the tent one day when she tried to flush a skunk out of a nearby log by setting the stump on fire. For several days the family lived under a tree. Eventually my grandfather brought hand-hewn lumber back from East Texas and built a roomy house (one I remember vividly) with two fireplaces. A good well and a windmill provided a convenient water supply. A large orchard my grandfather planted was still bearing apples, pears, peaches, apricots, and grapes when I was a child. But my grandmother didn't, as I remember, dwell on the amenities of life on the Simpson place, nor did she say anything about the beauty of the location of the house at the bottom of a wooded hill, the largest of three hills that ranged along the western side of the Simpson place. We called them "Mountains." Once blue and serene in the distance as seen from the highway leading west, the range of hills has all but disappeared, graded down by bulldozers when they became the site of oil wells in the 1950s.

My grandmother's narrative of life on the Simpson place was chiefly one of dark moments, one of the darkest, rendered in a restrained, succinct account, being her own delivery of her third son in 1888 when she suddenly went into labor with my grandfather gone and any assistance miles away. The child was named Edward and called Teddy; within three months he was dead. There were numerous other dark moments: one was the time my grandfather was again bilked out of most of his money by a crooked banker. (With some restraint my father once said of his father, "One of his greatest faults, as far as financial success goes, was too much confidence in his fellow man.") Another tough time my grandmother dwelled on was the great drought of 1886–87. Then, too, there was the story of how, as the result of his effort to save his cattle during a fierce blizzard in the nineties, my grandfather developed a severe rheumatic condition from which he would never recover. As a consequence, the Simpsons moved into town and used what money my grandfather could command to open a general merchandise store. Maybe he did fairly well with this store, for the record shows that he was a member of the board of directors of the Jacksboro Mill and Elevator Company when it was founded in 1898. But at this point my grandmother's narrative tended to become diffuse. She avoided going into the story of the mental depression my grandfather suffered from in his last years, a condition that made it necessary to put him in a private hospital in Fort Worth.

I have referred to Ida Huckabay's work as historian of Jack County. Descended from the Lasaters, a family on the ground in Jack County as long as mine, she is the most appealing of the local historians. Although she had all the faults of the amateur historian, she had a quality of mind and spirit that makes the book I referred to above, *Ninety-Four Years in Jack County, 1854–1948,* a remarkable work. Attempting to do more than her limitations either as a researcher or as a writer allowed, Mrs. Huckabay had a vision that transcended the merely antiquarian and genealogical and that—if we translate it in terms of its implications—suggests that the history of Jack County, Texas, is a microcosmic expression of the way in which for Americans history has meant living the ironic, tragic implications of the myth of America as the redemption of the world—of living in the tension between the demand of the myth that it be affirmed in one's life and the actuality of existence in the awful caldron of societal and personal relationships, in the terrifying mysteries of greed and generosity, honor and deceit, pride and humility, jealousy, love, and hate. Although she does not consciously recognize it, the tension is constant in Ida Huckabay's attitudes. The epic subtitle of her history—*A History of the Coming of the Settlers, Indian Depredations, Government Protection, Days of Old Jacksboro and Fort Richardson, the Trial of Satanta and Big Tree, Cattle industry and Trail Drivers, Educational, Religious and Agricultural Progress, Building of Railways and Highways, Oil Development and Disappearance of the Frontier*—is a large, celebratory expression of an assured concept of progress as the meaning of history. Yet the last event in the procession of great local events that Mrs. Huckabay delineates is a terminal one, the disappearance of the frontier. In her implied recognition of this historical event she is quietly eloquent of the loss of the promise that had driven the settlers to confront the terror of the frontier experience.

What happens when the chief motive of the frontier is gone forever? Walter Prescott Webb, the greatest historian of the phenomenon of the frontier in modern history, was obsessed with this problem, but he could suggest no solution. In explaining her approach in the introduction to her history of Jack County, Mrs. Huckabay says: "The author has weighed each subject with care. Remember the construction of this volume has been like unto gathering the fragments of a broken vase." The metaphor, echoing the passage in Ecclesiastes about the breaking of the golden bowl, reflects what this committed and passionate historian of Jack County, which for Mrs. Huckabay was truly the center of the world, possessed as a hidden knowledge—a tragic knowledge she hid carefully from herself—namely, that in working to reconstruct out of memories and documents the wholeness of the past, one must come to suspect that the motive is illusory.

It is interesting to reflect on how in actuality and in memory one has been involved in the intricate, indeterminate American story of dispossessors becoming possessors only to be themselves dispossessed. Specifically, one finds oneself involved in a story about the slow dispossession of the blood of the Cherokee nation that began with the union of an Indian great-great-grandmother and an Englishman and continued in the union of a great-grandmother and a Scottish great-grandfather. Supported by his half-Indian wife in his role as ruthless dispossessor of the Kiowas and Comanches from their ancient homeland, the great-grandfather voluntarily dispossessed himself from his citizenship in the Republic of Texas, which at the risk of his life he had helped to found through the violent dispossession of the Mexican government that had supported him in Texas in the first place. He had done this in order to establish citizenship in the Republic of the United States, but only a few years later he pledged his unmitigated allegiance to the Confederate States of America; forcibly dispossessed of his Confederate citizenship, he had again pledged himself to the American Union. One finds oneself involved, too, in the story about one's grandmother and her sisters and brothers, one's great-aunts and great-uncles, all bearing Cherokee blood, who survived not only the Civil War and the Indian Wars but the everyday physical and psychic perils of a frontier existence. One also finds oneself involved in the story of one's father and his brother who bore the trace of Cherokee blood; and one finds oneself involved in the story of one's own brothers and sisters and of oneself, all bearing some tincture of the same Indian blood, of an original act of dispossession that occurred one night—may one suppose?—in a cabin a great-great-grandfather had built for an Indian bride. Altogether it is the indeterminate story of five generations of dispossessors and possessors, and of dispossessors dispossessed—the story that, though it takes many forms, is the underlying history of America. It is a complexly ironic story, often a somber one, but it is exciting and romantic, for the participants assumed—and still assume, if less confidently—that even if they can never quite define the place they seek, they will finally come into possession of it, no matter how dark the drama of the quest becomes. In an interview discussion touching on the question of the meaning of American history, Robert Penn Warren said: "There is a kind of extraordinary romance about American history. That's the only word for it—a kind of self-sufficiency. You know the grandpas and the great grandpas carried the assumption that somehow their decisions were important; that as they went up, down, here and there, such a life was important and that it was man's responsibility to live it."

Recently I was back in Jacksboro briefly for a reunion with some of my brothers and sisters. I stayed in the place we now call the homeplace; it is not the old house but one that my mother built after I left Jacksboro and where my youngest brother still lives. Although it is located on the other side of the square—up on the hill, as we say—the "new" house is not much farther away from the square than the old place.

One night during my visit, after we had been telling stories all day and into the evening, I went to bed, only to awaken after a few hours and find my mind still occupied with our tales. I switched on the light and looked at my wristwatch. It was nearly three o'clock in the morning. I turned off the light and looked into the dark and listened to the silence. Broken sporadically by the barking of a dog down the street, the night silence had once, I remembered, been occasionally penetrated by the yelping of coyotes somewhere off in the dark pastures and woods, and once in a while by the faraway, austere, frightening loneliness of a wolf's howl. Remembering the lost sounds of night, I almost expected to hear the old courthouse clock speak again, and tell me the real time.

Writing these words down now—remembering the clock and the memory of remembering—I suddenly recall a moment in the life of a ten- or eleven-year-old boy. It is not a story I told that night, and may never have told.

One Sunday morning after church, all dressed up in my Sunday suit and shoes, I am walking home with my father. As we come into the square we pass the steps leading up to an iron-gated side entrance to the First National Bank, a favored haunt of hard-luck cases and ne'er-do-wells. Four or five men are seated on the steps smoking and talking. One or two of them wear relics of better days: a soiled Stetson hat, cowboy boots with run-down heels. As we pass by, they greet my father with grave respect. One or two even rise. The return greeting is equally grave and formal. We start to walk past the stores on the west side of the square. Everything is closed except Spears Drug Store. The courthouse clock has already struck the noon hour, and the square is entirely cloaked in Sunday quiet. Suddenly, moved by a nasty, childish sense of self-righteous superiority, I say that I wonder if those loafers back there actually have souls. My father stops. I look up at him as he fixes his gray eyes on me and says with quiet, judicial intensity: "Son, everybody has a soul." Ashamed, feeling penitent, I make no reply. We walk home in a silence that I still hear.

Acknowledgments

Grateful acknowledgment is made for permission to reprint or adapt for republication the various essays in this volume.

"Prologue: John Randolph and the Inwardness of History" is adapted from "The Inwardness of History," *Virginia Quarterly Review*, LVII (1981), 158–67.

"The Fable of the Agrarians and the Failure of the American Republic" is adapted from "Southern Criticism and the Failure of the Republic," *Mississippi Quarterly*, XLIII (Fall, 1990), 465–73.

"History and the Will of the Artist: Elizabeth Madox Roberts" first appeared as "The Sexuality of History" in the *Southern Review*, n.s., XX (1984), 785–802. I am grateful to the heirs of the estate of Elizabeth Madox Roberts, especially their representative, Ann Wood Roberts, for permission to quote various passages from the Elizabeth Madox Roberts papers deposited in the Library of Congress.

"A Fable of White and Black: Jefferson, Madison, Tate" first appeared as "The Autobiographical Impulse in the South" in *Home Ground: Southern Autobiography*, ed. J. Bill Berry (Columbia, Mo.: University of Missouri Press, 1991), 63–84.

"War and Memory: Quentin Compson's Civil War" first appeared as "On William Faulkner's *Absalom, Absalom!*" in *Classic Civil War Novels*, ed. David Madden and Peggy Bach (Jackson, Miss.: University Press of Mississippi, 1991), 151–73.

"The Tenses of History: Faulkner" first appeared as "William Faulkner of Yoknapatawpha" in *The American South: Portrait of a Culture*, ed. Louis D. Rubin, Jr. (Baton Rouge: Louisiana State University Press, 1979), 227–44.

"The Poetry of Criticism: Allen Tate," under the title "The Critics Who Made Us: Allen Tate"; "The Last Casualty of the Civil War: Arthur Crew Inman"; and "The Loneliness Artist: Robert Penn Warren" first appeared in the *Sewanee Review,* XCIV (1986), 471–85; XCV (1987), 149–62; XCIX (1991), 337–61. Copyright 1986, 1987, 1991 by Lewis P. Simpson. Reprinted by permission of the editor.

"From Thoreau to Walker Percy: Home by Way of California; or, The End of the Southern Renascence" first appeared as "Home by Way of California: The Southerner as the Last European" in *Southern Literature in Transition: Heritage and Promise,* ed. Philip Castille and William Osborne (Memphis, Tenn.: Memphis State University Press, 1983), 55–70.

"Epilogue: A Personal Fable: Living with Indians" first appeared as "Living with Indians: Memoirs of a West Texas Southerner" in the *Southern Review,* n.s., XXVI (Fall, 1990), 741–45.

Grateful acknowledgment on my part for various kinds of assistance should properly be made to many individuals. Since in the past, however, I have made many specific acknowledgments of the kind help I have received in connection with my projects, I trust that I may simply add to these a general recognition of all the invaluable assistance I have had in writing this book. Let me be content to mention directly only three people who have been of special help to me: the editor and author Charles East, William H. Slavick, the biographer of Elizabeth Madox Roberts, and Thomas Underwood, the biographer of Allen Tate.

Index

Index